"Few people at the beginning of the nineteenth century needed an adman to tell them what they wanted."

THE HISTORY OF MATERIAL OPULENCE FOR THE MASSES IS RELATIVELY SHORT IN THE HISTORY OF MANKIND. JOHN KENNETH GALBRAITH BELIEVES THAT ECONOMIC PRECEPTS BASED UPON AN ECONOMY OF POVERTY NO LONGER APPLY IN AN AFFLUENT SOCIETY. HIS FAMOUS WORK SETTING FORTH AN ARGUMENT FOR A NEW ECONOMIC STRUCTURE HAS AROUSED ENTHUSIASM AND CONTROVERSY THE WORLD OVER . . .

"I put it in the same category as Tawney's *The Acquisitive Society* and Keynes's *Economic Consequences of the Peace.* It is unique, witty and inescapable."
—MALCOLM MUGGERIDGE

"The most brilliant essay in politico-economic criticism in a decade."
—KERMIT GORDON

"Lo, what a man of wit has arisen to do biopsy on what Carlyle called 'the dismal science' of economics."
—*Chicago Sunday Tribune*

"Galbraith has done an enormous service to the cause of intelligent economic and social debate. In the end, he may have done as substantial a service to the prestige of economics itself."
—*New Republic*

MENTOR Books of Related Interest

THE
AFFLUENT
SOCIETY
John Kenneth Galbraith

A MENTOR BOOK

PUBLISHED BY
THE NEW AMERICAN LIBRARY, NEW YORK AND TORONTO

MENTOR TRADEMARK REG. U.S. PAT. OFF. AND FOREIGN COUNTRIES
REGISTERED TRADEMARK—MARCA REGISTRADA
HECHO EN CHICAGO, U.S.A.

MENTOR BOOKS are published *in the United States* by
The New American Library, Inc.,
1301 Avenue of the Americas, New York, New York 10019,
in Canada by The New American Library of Canada, Limited,
295 King Street East, Toronto 2, Ontario

PRINTED IN THE UNITED STATES OF AMERICA

To Emily,
Peter and Jamie

The economist, like everyone else,
must concern himself
with the ultimate aims of man.

ALFRED MARSHALL

FOREWORD

SINCE I sailed for Switzerland in the early summer of 1955 to begin work on this book I have accumulated a large and cosmopolitan set of obligations. Thus a Guggenheim fellowship facilitated that movement as did my wife, Catherine A. Galbraith. She also typed copy, checked references, and revised proof and had a corrective influence when my skill in identifying problems too grossly exceeded my facility in solving them. I am grateful to the librarians at the Palais des Nations, as also at Harvard, for their help, and to the university students in Geneva on whom I first tried out the core of these ideas. I also used many of these ideas in a series of lectures given under the auspices of the Haynes Foundation at the California Institute of Technology in January 1957. I would like to thank the Foundation, the Institute, and my longtime friend Alan Sweezy for arranging this trial run and for allowing publication in this form. The chapter on poverty toward the end draws heavily on research financed by a grant from the Carnegie Corporation. My good friend and assistant, Ruth M. Parks, took responsibility for the whole tedious task of manuscript preparation, for which I am also most grateful.

I have never quite understood why publishers, who are said to be human, do not get tired of authors. Probably they do, but those with whom I have been so happily associated conceal it with a rare and kindly skill.

Two of my colleagues, Arthur M. Schlesinger, Jr., and Carl Kaysen, read the manuscript or proof, and I accepted nearly all of their suggestions. I owe debt to the much larger group of people who, by suggestion or persuasion, led me to problems or solutions I had not previously seen. Thus my colleague Seymour E. Harris, the most diligent and useful of all economists, began several years ago to question the current stereotypes on public finance. Had it not been for him, liberals would have been spared the present proposals for a greatly expanded use of the sales tax. To go farther afield, Governor Luis Muñoz-Marin first persuaded me to question the wisdom of our pre-occupation with more and more consumer goods as a goal. And any number of other points, large and small, were suggested to me by colleagues, friends and students. Authorship of any sort is a fantastic indulgence of the ego. It is well, no doubt, to reflect on how much one owes to others.

J. K. Galbraith

Cambridge, Massachusetts
March 1958

CONTENTS

CHAPTER I
The Affluent Society   13

CHAPTER II
The Concept of the Conventional Wisdom   17

CHAPTER III
Economics and the Tradition of Despair   27

CHAPTER IV
The Uncertain Reassurance   37

CHAPTER V
The American Mood   47

CHAPTER VI
The Marxian Pall   59

CHAPTER VII
Inequality   69

CHAPTER VIII
Economic Security   84

CHAPTER IX
The Paramount Position of Production   101

CHAPTER X
The Imperatives of Consumer Demand   114

CHAPTER XI
The Dependence Effect   124

CHAPTER XII
The Illusion of National Security   131

CHAPTER XIII
The Vested Interest in Output   146

CHAPTER XIV
The Bill Collector Cometh   157

CHAPTER XV
Inflation   167

CHAPTER XVI
The Monetary Illusion   179

CHAPTER XVII
Production versus Price Stability   189

CHAPTER XVIII
The Theory of Social Balance   198

CHAPTER XIX
The Investment Balance   212

CHAPTER XX
The Transition   220

CHAPTER XXI
The Divorce of Production from Security   228

CHAPTER XXII
The Redress of Balance   240

CHAPTER XXIII
The New Position of Poverty   250

CHAPTER XXIV
Labor, Leisure, and the New Class   259

CHAPTER XXV
On Security and Survival   270

Index   277

CHAPTER I

The Affluent Society

WEALTH IS NOT without its advantages and the case to the contrary, although it has often been made, has never proved widely persuasive. But, beyond doubt, wealth is the relentless enemy of understanding. The poor man has always a precise view of his problem and its remedy: he hasn't enough and he needs more. The rich man can assume or imagine a much greater variety of ills and he will be correspondingly less certain of their remedy. Also, until he learns to live with his wealth, he will have a well-observed tendency to put it to the wrong purposes or otherwise to make himself foolish.

As with individuals so with nations. And the experience of nations with well-being is exceedingly brief. Nearly all throughout all history have been very poor. The exception, almost insignificant in the whole span of human existence, has been the last few generations in the comparatively small corner of the world populated by Europeans. Here, and especially in the United States, there has been great and quite unprecedented affluence.

The ideas by which the people of this favored part of the world interpret their existence, and in measure guide their behavior, were not forged in a world of wealth. These ideas were the product of a world in which poverty had always been man's normal lot, and any other state was in degree unimaginable. This poverty was not the elegant torture of the spirit which comes from contemplating another man's more spacious possessions. It was the unedifying mortification of the flesh—from hunger, sickness, and cold. Those who might be freed temporarily from such burden could not know when it would strike again, for at best hunger yielded only perilously to privation. It is improbable that the poverty of the masses of the people was made greatly more bearable by the fact that a very few—those upon whose movements nearly all recorded history centers—were very rich.

No one would wish to argue that the ideas which interpreted this world of grim scarcity would serve equally well for the contemporary United States. Poverty was the all-pervasive fact of that world. Obviously it is not of ours. One would not expect that the preoccupations of a poverty-ridden world would be relevant in one where the ordinary individual has access to amenities—foods, entertainment, personal transportation, and plumbing—in which not even the rich rejoiced a century ago. So great has been the change that many of the desires of the individual are no longer even evident to him. They become so only as they are synthesized, elaborated, and nurtured by advertising and salesmanship, and these, in turn, have become among our most important and talented professions. Few people at the beginning of the nineteenth century needed an adman to tell them what they wanted.

It would be wrong to suggest that the economic ideas which once interpreted the world of mass poverty have made no adjustment to the world of affluence. There have been many adjustments, including some that have gone unrecognized or have been poorly understood. But there has also been a remarkable resistance. And the total alteration in underlying circumstances has not been squarely faced. As a result we are guided, in part, by ideas that are relevant to another world; and as a further result we do many things that are unnecessary, some that are unwise, and a few that are insane. We enhance substantially the risk of depression and thereby the threat to our affluence itself.

II

The foregoing tells the purpose of this book. The first task is to see the way our economic attitudes are rooted in the poverty, inequality, and economic peril of the past. Then the partial and implicit accommodation to affluence is examined. The next task is to consider the devices and arguments, some elaborate, some meretricious, some in a degree dangerous, by which, in vital matters, we have managed to maintain an association with the older ideas which stemmed from a world where nearly all were poor. For no one should suppose that there is anything convenient or agreeable about the assumption of affluence. On the contrary, it threatens the prestige and position of many important people. And it exposes many of us to the even greater horror of new thought. We face here the greatest of vested interests, those of the mind.

Finally, as we escape from the obsolete and contrived preoccupations associated with the assumption of poverty, we are able to see for the first time the new tasks and opportunities that are before us. This is not as reassuring as it sounds. One of the best ways of avoiding necessary and even urgent tasks is to seem to be busily employed on things that are already done.

Such is the purpose. But first there is some preparatory work. For we have not clung to obsolete and impalpable assumptions concerning our society purely as the result of obtuseness and ignorance. Powerful as these influences may be, they are not that strong. On the contrary, in matters of social discussion, there are active and pervasive influences which bind us to the past and which, on occasion, even cause us to try to recover the moribund. We must first be aware of our captivity by these forces if we are later to engineer an escape. That is the task of the next chapter.

III

No one will think this an angry book. Some may think it lacking in that beguiling modesty which is so much in fashion in social comment. The reader will soon discover that I think very little of certain of the central ideas of economics. But I do think a great deal of the men who originated these ideas. The shortcomings of economics are not original error but uncorrected obsolescence. The obsolescence has occurred because what is convenient has become sacrosanct. Anyone who attacks such ideas must seem to be a trifle self-confident and even aggressive. Yet I trust that judgments will not be too hasty. The man who makes his entry by leaning against an infirm door gets an unjustified reputation for violence. Something is to be attributed to the poor state of the door.

Originality is something that is easily exaggerated, especially by authors contemplating their own work. There are few thoughts in this essay, or so I would imagine, which have not occurred to other economists. The reaction of many will be to welcome the elaboration of ideas to which evidence has already brought them. But these are also days in which even the mildly critical individual is likely to seem like a lion in contrast with the general mood. These are the days when men of all social disciplines and all political faiths seek the comfortable and the accepted; when the man of controversy is looked upon as a disturbing influence; when originality is taken to be a mark of instability; and when, in minor modification of the scriptural parable, the bland lead the bland. Those who esteem this world will not enjoy this essay. Perhaps they should return it to the shelf unread. For there are negative thoughts here, and they cannot but strike an uncouth note in the world of positive thinking.

IV

No student of social matters in these days can escape feeling how precarious is the existence of that with which he deals. Western man has escaped for the moment the poverty which was for so long his all-embracing fate. The unearthly light of a handful of nuclear explosions would signal his return to utter deprivation if, indeed, he survived at all. I venture to think that the ideas here offered bear on our chances for escape from this fate. Illusion is a comprehensive ill. The rich man who deludes himself into behaving like a mendicant may conserve his fortune although he will not be very happy. The affluent country which conducts its affairs in accordance with rules of another and poorer age also foregoes opportunities. And in misunderstanding itself it will, in any time of difficulty, implacably prescribe for itself the wrong remedies. This the reader will discover is, to a disturbing degree, our present tendency.

Yet it would be a mistake to be too gravely depressed. The problems of an affluent world, which does not understand itself, may be serious, and they can needlessly threaten the affluence itself. But they are not likely to be as serious as those of a poor world where the simple exigencies of poverty preclude the luxury of misunderstanding but where, also and alas, no solutions are to be had.

CHAPTER II

The Concept of the Conventional Wisdom

THE FIRST REQUIREMENT for an understanding of contemporary economic and social life is a clear view of the relation between events and the ideas which interpret them. For each of these has a life of its own, and much as it may seem a contradiction in terms each is capable for a considerable period of pursuing an independent course.

The reason is not difficult to discover. Economic, like other social life, does not conform to a simple and coherent pattern. On the contrary, it often seems incoherent, inchoate, and intellectually frustrating. But one must have an explanation or interpretation of economic behavior. Neither man's curiosity nor his inherent ego allows him to remain contentedly oblivious to anything that is so close to his life.

Because economic and social phenomena are so forbidding, or at least so seem, and because they yield few hard tests of what exists and what does not, they afford to the individual a luxury not given by physical phenomena. Within a considerable range he is permitted to believe what he pleases. He may hold whatever view of this world he finds most agreeable or otherwise to his taste.

As a consequence in the interpretation of all social life, there is a persistent and never-ending competition between what is relevant and what is merely acceptable. In this competition, while a strategic advantage lies with what exists, all tactical advantage is with the acceptable. Audiences of all kinds most applaud what they like best. And in social comment the test of audience approval, far more than the test of truth, comes to influence comment. The speaker or writer who addresses his audience with the proclaimed intent of telling the hard, shocking facts invariably goes on to expound what the audience most wants to hear.

Just as truth ultimately serves to create a consensus, so in the short run does acceptability. Ideas come to be organized around what the community as a whole or particular audiences find acceptable. And as the laboratory worker devotes himself to discovering scientific verities, so the ghost writer and the public relations man concern themselves with identifying the acceptable. If their clients are rewarded with applause, these artisans are qualified in their craft. If not they have failed. However, by sampling audience reaction in advance, or by pretesting speeches, articles, and other communications, the risk of failure can now be greatly minimized.

Numerous factors contribute to the acceptability of ideas. To a very large extent, of course, we associate truth with convenience—with what most closely accords with self-interest and individual well-being or promises best to avoid awkward effort or unwelcome dislocation of life. We also find highly acceptable what contributes most to self-esteem. Speakers before the United States Chamber of Commerce rarely denigrate the businessman as an economic force. Those who appear before the AFL-CIO are prone to identify social progress with a strong trade union movement. But perhaps most important of all, people approve most of what they best understand. As just noted, economic and social behavior are complex and mentally tiring. Therefore we adhere, as though to a raft, to those ideas which represent our understanding. This is a prime manifestation of vested interest. For a vested interest in understanding is more preciously guarded than any other treasure. It is why men react, not infrequently with something akin to religious passion, to the defense of what they have so laboriously learned. Familiarity may breed contempt in some areas of human behavior, but in the field of social ideas it is the touchstone of acceptability.

Because familiarity is such an important test of acceptability, the acceptable ideas have great stability. They are highly predictable. It will be convenient to have a name for the ideas which are esteemed at any time for their acceptability, and it should be a term that emphasizes this predictability. I shall refer to these ideas henceforth as the conventional wisdom.

II

The conventional wisdom is not the property of any political group. On a great many modern social issues, as we shall see in the course of this essay, the consensus is exceedingly broad. Nothing much divides those who are liberals by common political designation from those who are conservatives. The test of what is acceptable is much the same for both. On some questions, however, ideas must be accommodated to the political preferences of the particular audience. The tendency to make this adjustment, either deliberately or more often unconsciously, is not greatly different for different political groups. The conservative is led by disposition, not unmixed with pecuniary self-interest, to adhere to the familiar and the established. These underly his test of acceptability. But the liberal brings moral fervor and passion, even a sense of righteousness, to the ideas with which he is most familiar. While the ideas he cherishes are different from those of the conservative, he is not likely to be much less emphatic in making familiarity a test of acceptability. Deviation in the form of originality is condemned as faithlessness or backsliding. A "good" liberal or a "tried and true" liberal or a "true blue" liberal is one who is adequately predictable. This means that he forswears any serious striving toward originality. In both the United States and Britain, in recent times, liberals and their British counterparts of the left have proclaimed themselves in search of new ideas. To proclaim the need for new ideas has served, in some measure, as a substitute for them.

Thus we may, as necessary, speak of the conventional wisdom of conservatives or the conventional wisdom of liberals.

The conventional wisdom is also articulated on all levels of sophistication. At the highest levels of social science scholarship some novelty of formulation or statement is not resisted. On the contrary, considerable store is set by the device of putting an old truth in a new form, and minor heresies are much cherished. And the very vigor of minor debate makes it possible to exclude as irrelevant, and without seeming to be unscientific or parochial, any challenge to the framework itself. Moreover, with time and aided by the debate, the accepted ideas become increasingly elaborate. They have a large literature, even a mystique. The defenders are able to say that the challengers of the conventional wisdom have not mastered their intricacies. Indeed these ideas can be appreciated only by a stable, orthodox, and patient man—in brief, by someone who closely resembles the man of conventional wisdom. The conventional wisdom having been made more or less identical with sound scholarship, its position is virtually impregnable. The skeptic is disqualified by his very tendency to go brashly from the old to the new. Were he a sound scholar he would remain with the conventional wisdom.

As the same time in the higher levels of the conventional

wisdom originality remains highly acceptable in the abstract. Here again the conventional wisdom often makes vigorous advocacy of originality a substitute for originality itself.

III

As noted, the hallmark of the conventional wisdom is acceptability. It has the approval of those to whom it is addressed. There are many reasons why people like to hear articulated that which they approve. It serves the ego: the individual has the satisfaction of knowing that other and more famous people share his conclusions. To hear what he believes is also a source of reassurance. The individual knows that he is supported in his thoughts—that he has not been left behind and alone. Further, to hear what one approves serves the evangelizing instinct. It means that others are also hearing and are thereby in process of being persuaded.

In some measure the articulation of the conventional wisdom is a religious rite. It is an act of affirmation like reading aloud from the Scriptures or going to church. The business executive listening to a luncheon address on the virtues of free enterprise and the evils of Washington is already persuaded, and so are his fellow listeners, and all are secure in their convictions. Indeed, although a display of rapt attention is required, the executive may not feel it necessary to listen. But he does placate the gods by participating in the ritual. Having been present, maintained attention, and having applauded, he can depart feeling that the economic system is a little more secure. Scholars gather in scholarly assemblages to hear in elegant statement what all have heard before. Yet it is not a negligible rite, for its purpose is not to convey knowledge but to beatify learning and the learned.

With so extensive a demand, it follows that a very large part of our social comment—and nearly all that is well regarded—is devoted at any time to articulating the conventional wisdom. To some extent this has been professionalized. Individuals, most notably the great television and radio commentators, make a profession of knowing and saying with elegance and unction what their audience will find most acceptable. But in general the articulation of the conventional wisdom is a prerogative of academic, public, or business position. Thus any individual, on being elected president of a college or university, automatically wins the right to enunciate the conventional wisdom should he choose to do so. It is one of the rewards of high academic rank, although such rank is also a reward for expounding the conventional wisdom at a properly sophisticated level.

The high public official is expected, and indeed is to some extent required, to expound the conventional wisdom. His, in many respects, is the purest case. Before assuming office he ordinarily commands little attention. But on taking up his position he is immediately assumed to be gifted with deep insights. He does not, except in the rarest instances, write his own speeches or articles; and these are planned, drafted, and scrupulously examined to insure their acceptability. The application of any other test, e.g., their effectiveness as a simple description of the economic or political reality, would be regarded as eccentric in the extreme.

Finally, the expounding of the conventional wisdom is the prerogative of business success. The head of almost any large corporation—the United States Steel Corporation, General Motors, the Radio Corporation of America—is entitled to do so. And he is privileged to speak not only on business policy and economics but also on the role of government in the society, the foundations of foreign policy, and the nature of a liberal education. In recent years it has been urged that to expound the conventional wisdom is not only the privilege but also the obligation of the businessman. "I am convinced that businessmen must write as well as speak, in order that we may bring to people everywhere the exciting and confident message of our faith in the free enterprise way of life . . . What a change would come in this struggle for men's minds if suddenly there could pour out from the world of American business a torrent of intelligent, forward-looking thinking."[1]

IV

The enemy of the conventional wisdom is not ideas but the march of events. As I have noted, the conventional wisdom accommodates itself not to the world that it is meant to interpret, but to the audience's view of the world. Since the latter remains with the comfortable and the familiar, while the world moves on, the conventional wisdom is always in danger of obsolescence. This is not immediately fatal. The fatal

[1] Clarence B. Randall, *A Creed for Free Enterprise* (Boston: Atlantic-Little, Brown, 1952), pp. 3, 5.

blow to the conventional wisdom comes when the conventional ideas fail signally to deal with some contingency to which obsolescence has made them palpably inapplicable. This, sooner or later, must be the fate of ideas which have lost their relation to the world. At this stage the irrelevance will often be dramatized by some individual. To him will accrue the credit for overthrowing the conventional wisdom and for installing the new ideas. In fact, he will have only crystallized in words what the events have made clear, although this function is not a minor one. Meanwhile, like the Old Guard, the conventional wisdom dies but does not surrender. Society with intransigent cruelty may transfer its exponents from the category of wise man to that of old fogy or even stuffed shirt.

This sequence can be illustrated from scores of examples, ancient and modern. For decades prior to 1776 men had been catching the vision of the liberal state. Traders and merchants in England and in the adjacent Low Countries, and in the American colonies, had already learned that they were served best by a minimum of government restriction rather than, as in the conventional wisdom, by a maximum of government guidance and protection. It had become plain, in turn, that liberal trade and commerce, not the accumulation of bullion, as the conventional wisdom held, was the modern source of national power. Men of irresponsible originality had made the point. Voltaire had observed that "It is only because the English have become merchants and traders that London has surpassed Paris in extent and in the number of its citizens; that the English can place 200 warships on the sea and subsidize allies."[2] These views were finally crystallized by Adam Smith in the year of American independence. *The Wealth of Nations,* however, continued to be viewed with discontent and alarm by the men of the older wisdom. In the funeral elegy for Alexander Hamilton in 1804, James Kent complimented his deceased friend on having resisted the "fuzzy philosophy" of Smith. For another generation or more in all western countries there would be solemn warnings that the notion of a liberal society was a reckless idea.

Through the nineteenth century, liberalism in its classical meaning having become the conventional wisdom, there were solemn warnings of the irreparable damage that would be done by Factory Acts, trade unions, social insurance, and

2 "Tenth Philosophical Letter." Quoted by Henri Sée, *Modern Capitalism* (New York: Adelphi, 1928), p. 87.

other social legislation. Liberalism was a fabric which could not be raveled without being rent. Yet the desire for protection and security and some measure of equality in bargaining power would not down. In the end it became a fact with which the conventional wisdom could not deal. The Webbs, Lloyd George, LaFollette, Roosevelt, Beveridge, and others crystallized the acceptance of the new fact. The result is what we call the welfare state. The conventional wisdom now holds that these measures softened and civilized capitalism and made it tenable. There have never ceased to be warnings that the break with classical liberalism was fatal.

Another interesting instance of the impact of circumstance on the conventional wisdom was that of the balanced budget in times of depression. Almost from the beginning of organized government the balanced budget or its equivalent has been the *sine qua non* of sound and sensible management of the public purse. The spendthrift tendencies of princes and republics alike were curbed by the rule that they must unfailingly take in as much money as they paid out. The consequences of violating this rule had always been unhappy in the long run and not infrequently in the short. Anciently it was the practice of states to cover the deficit by clipping or debasing the coins and spending the metal so saved. The result invariably was to raise prices and lower national self-esteem. In modern times the issue of paper money or the obtaining of soft loans from banks had led to the same results. As a result, the conventional wisdom had never emphasized anything more strongly than the importance of an annually balanced budget.

But meanwhile the underlying reality had gradually changed. The rule requiring a balanced budget was designed for governments that were inherently or recurrently irresponsible on fiscal matters. Until the last century there had been no other. Then in the United States, England and the British Commonwealth, and elsewhere governments began to calculate the fiscal consequences of their actions. Safety no longer depended on confining them within arbitrary rules.

At about the same time, there appeared the phenomenon of the truly devastating depression. In such a depression men, plant, and materials were unemployed *en masse;* the extra demand from the extra spending induced by the deficit—the counterpart of the extra metal made available from the clipped coinage—did not raise prices uniquely. Rather it mostly returned idle men and plant to work. The effect, as it were, was horizontally on production rather than vertically on prices. And such price increases as did occur were far from being an unmitigated misfortune; on the contrary, they retrieved a previous, painful decline.

The conventional wisdom continued to emphasize the balanced budget. Audiences continued to respond to the warnings of the disaster which would befall were this rule not respected. The shattering circumstance was the Great Depression. This led to a severe reduction in the revenues of the federal government; it also brought increased pressure for a variety of relief and welfare expenditures. A balanced budget meant increasing tax rates and reducing public expenditure. Viewed in retrospect, it would be hard to imagine a better design for reducing both the private and the public demand for goods, aggravating deflation, increasing unemployment, and adding to the general suffering. In the conventional wisdom, nonetheless, the balanced budget remained of paramount importance. President Hoover in the early thirties called it an "absolute necessity," "the most essential factor to economic recovery," "the imperative and immediate step," "indispensable," "the first necessity of the Nation," and "the foundation of all public and private financial stability."[3] Economists and professional observers of public affairs agreed almost without exception. Almost everyone called upon for advice in the early years of the depression was impelled by the conventional wisdom to offer proposals designed to make things worse. The consensus embraced both liberals and conservatives. The Roosevelt Administration was also elected in 1932 with a strong commitment to reduced expenditures and a balanced budget. In his acceptance speech in 1932 Roosevelt said, "Revenue must cover expenditures by one means or another. Any government, like any family, can for a year spend a little more than it earns. But you and I know that a continuation of that habit means the poorhouse." One of the early acts of his Administration was an economy drive which included a horizontal slash in public pay. Mr. Lewis W. Douglas, through a distinguished life a notable exemplar of the conventional wisdom, made the quest for a balanced budget into a personal crusade and ultimately broke with the Administration on the issue.

In fact, circumstances had already triumphed over the conventional wisdom. By the second year of the Hoover Administration the budget was irretrievably out of balance.

---

[3] Arthur M. Schlesinger, Jr., *The Crisis of the Old Order* (Boston: Houghton Mifflin, 1956), p. 232.

In the fiscal year ending in 1932, receipts were much less than half of spending. The budget was never balanced during the depression. But not until 1936 did both the necessities and advantages of this course begin to triumph in the field of ideas. In that year, John Maynard Keynes launched his formal assault in *The General Theory of Employment, Interest and Money*. Thereafter the conventional insistence on the balanced budget under all circumstances and at all levels of economic activity was in retreat. Keynes, as we shall see presently, was also on his way to constructing a new body of conventional wisdom, the obsolescence of some parts of which, in its turn, is now well advanced.

V

In the following pages there will be frequent occasion to advert to the conventional wisdom—to the structure of ideas that is based on acceptability—and to those who articulate it. These references must not be thought to have a wholly invidious connotation. (The warning is necessary because, as noted, we set great ostensible store by intellectual innovation though in fact we resist it. Hence, though we value the rigorous adherence to conventional ideas, we never acclaim it.) Few men are unuseful and the man of conventional wisdom is not. Every society must be protected from a too facile flow of thought. In the field of social comment a great stream of intellectual novelties, if all were taken seriously, would be disastrous. Men would be swayed to this action or that; economic and political life would be erratic and rudderless. In the Communist countries stability of ideas and social purpose is achieved by formal adherence to an officially proclaimed doctrine. In our society a similar stability is enforced far more informally by the conventional wisdom. Ideas need to be tested by their ability, in combination with events, to overcome inertia and resistance. This inertia and resistance the conventional wisdom provides.

Nor is it to be supposed that the man of conventional wisdom is an object of pity. Apart from his socially useful role, he has come to good terms with life. He can think of himself with justice as socially elect, for society in fact accords him the applause which his ideas are so arranged as to evoke. Secure in this applause he is well armed against the annoyance of dissent. His bargain is to exchange a strong and even lofty position in the present for a weak one in the future. In the present he is questioned with respect, if not at great length, by Congressional Committees; he walks near the head of the academic processions; he appears on symposia; he is a respected figure at the American Assembly, he is hailed at testimonial banquets. He risks being devastated by hostile events. But by then he may be dead. Only posterity is unkind to the man of conventional wisdom, and all posterity does is bury him in a blanket of neglect. However, somewhat more serious issues are at stake.

VI

No society seems ever to have succumbed to boredom. Man has developed an obvious capacity for surviving the pompous reiteration of the commonplace. The conventional wisdom protects the continuity in social thought and action; in the immediately following chapters we shall see how great this continuity is. But there are also grave drawbacks and even dangers in a system of thought which by its very nature and design avoids accommodation to circumstances until change is dramatically forced upon it. In large areas of economic affairs the march of events—above all, the increase in our wealth and popular well-being—has again left the conventional wisdom sadly obsolete. It may have become inimical to our happiness. It has come to have a bearing on the larger questions of civilized survival. So while it would be much more pleasant (and also vastly more profitable) to articulate the conventional wisdom, this book involves the normally unfruitful effort of an attack upon it. I am not wholly barren of hope, for circumstances have been dealing the conventional wisdom a new series of heavy blows. It is only after such damage has been done, as we have seen, that ideas have their opportunity.

Keynes, in his most famous observation, noted that we are ruled by ideas and by very little else. In the immediate sense this is true. And he was right in attributing importance to ideas as opposed to the simple influence of pecuniary vested interest. But the rule of ideas is only powerful in a world that does not change. Ideas are inherently conservative. They yield not to the attack of other ideas but to the massive onslaught of circumstance with which they cannot contend.

CHAPTER III

Economics and the Tradition of Despair

ECONOMICS, not entirely by accident, became a subject of serious study at an important turning point in the history of western man. This was when the wealth of national communities began, for the first time, to show a steady and persistent improvement. This change, which in advanced countries like England and Holland came some time in the eighteenth century, must be counted one of the momentous events in the history of the world. "From the earliest times of which we have record—back, say, to two thousand years before Christ—down to the beginning of the eighteenth century, there was no very great change in the standard of living of the average man living in the civilized centers of the earth. Ups and downs certainly. Visitations of plague, famine and war. Golden intervals. But no progressive violent change."[1]

Some of the intervals had been extended. For something over a century in medieval England—from perhaps 1380 to 1510—workers or at any rate skilled artisans seem to have enjoyed a period of considerable prosperity. But as always before, the good times came to an end; by the close of the sixteenth century the purchasing power of an artisan's wage had fallen by more than half. It remained low through the disorders of the Civil War, and progress was uncertain for a long time thereafter. Then early in the last century these wages began the rise which, with slight interruption, has since continued.[2]

There were reasons for the age-old stagnation as there were also reasons for the change. The productivity of an economy based on agriculture and household industry had inherent

[1] J. M. Keynes, *Essays in Persuasion*. Economic Possibilities for Our Grandchildren. (London: Macmillan, 1931), p. 360.

[2] E. H. Phelps Brown and Sheila V. Hopkins, "Seven Centuries of the Prices of Consumables, Compared with Builders' Wage Rates." *Economica*, New Series; vol. XXIII, no. 92 (November 1956).

limits. And before the appearance of the national state any
surplus that might be accumulated was subject to the spolia-
tion of diverse armed marauders and might, in fact, attract
their attention.

In the latter part of the eighteenth century the factory
began to replace the household at an accelerating rate as the
center of productive activity. Output per man-hour was no
longer limited by the simple technology and the small capital
of the household and by the need to rely mostly on human or
animal power. The new national states had begun to make
effective the guarantee of internal order. Armies would still
cross national frontiers and with considerable capacity for
doing damage where they fought and trod. But the economic
consequences of national armies in the age of nationalism
have been almost infinitely small as compared with the damage wrought by feudal, marauding, or crusading armies in
the centuries before. Within a few years following the two
World Wars the standard of living of Western European
countries, even those that were defeated and devastated, was
higher than ever before. The economic life of the Middle
East never recovered from the imaginative and highly co-
ordinated destruction, pillage, and massacre of Genghis Khan.
In contrast with recent experience, Germany required a
hundred years to recoup the destruction and disorganization
of the Thirty Years' War. However, a future national war
might well bring destruction abreast of the ancient art.

But it would have been surprising if, as the conditions of
life gradually improved in the eighteenth and nineteenth
centuries, man had quickly forsaken the lessons of all the
preceding ages and supposed this improvement to be permanent. This was all the more improbable for, in the early years
of the Industrial Revolution, the rewards of increased efficiency were distributed very unequally. It was the wealth of
the new entrepreneurs, not that of their workmen, which
was everywhere celebrated. Those who owned the new
factories, or the raw materials or railroads or banks that
served them, lived in mansions by which the century is still
marked. Their workers lived in dark and noisome hovels,
crowded on dirty and unpaved streets along which mission-
aries and social reformers ventured with a considerable sense
of their own courage. And in the factories themselves the old
and the very young worked from early to late and for a
pittance. In England in the first half of the nineteenth century both total production and output per person were rising
rapidly. The number of people of means was increasing. So,

too, as the mid-century approached, were real wages. But the improvement in the position of the masses was far less evident than the increase in industrial and mercantile wealth. If the poor were becoming less poor, this change was slight as compared with the growing contrast between the rich and the poor.

Economic ideas began to take their modern form in the late eighteenth and early nineteenth centuries. It was against this background of centuries-old stagnation relieved now by increasing wealth, but wealth not of the many but the few, that they were first worked out and offered. Economists would indeed have been indifferent to both history and environment had they not taken the privation and economic desolation of the masses for granted. In economics misfortune and failure were normal. Success, at least for more than the favored few, was what had to be explained. Enduring success was at odds with all history and could not be expected. This was the legacy of circumstances to ideas. As we shall see, it has enjoyed a remarkable vitality.

II

In the history of economic thought Adam Smith (1723-1790), the first great figure in the central economic tradition,[3] is counted a hopeful figure. In an important sense he was. His vision was of an advancing national community, not a stagnant or declining one. His title *An Inquiry into the Nature and Causes of the Wealth of Nations* had an obvious overtone of opulence and well-being. He offered an all but certain formula for economic progress. This was the liberal economic society in which regulation was by competition and the market and not by the state, and in which each man, thrown on his own resources, labored effectively for the enrichment of the society.

But it was of aggregate wealth that Smith spoke. He had little hope that the distribution between merchants, manu-

[3] I have used the phrase "central tradition" to denote the main current of ideas in descent from Smith. The more common reference to the "classical tradition" is ruled out by a difference of opinion, in my opinion a rather futile one, as to whether classical economics should or should not be considered to have ended with John Stuart Mill and J. E. Cairnes. Another possible reference is to the orthodox tradition. But this, by implication, excludes those like Keynes who, though working in the same current of ideas, have taken sharp issue with accepted conclusions.

facturers, and landlords on the one hand, and the working masses on the other, would be such as much to benefit the latter. Smith regarded this distribution as depending in the first instance on relative bargaining strength. And he did not believe it difficult "to foresee which of the two parties must upon all ordinary occasions have the advantage in the dispute." In an admirably succinct comment on the balance of eighteenth-century economic power he added: "We have no acts of Parliament against combining to lower the price of work; but many against combining to raise it."[4] So in the normal course of events the income of the working masses would be pressed down and down. There was a floor below which they would not fall. "A man must always live by his work, and his wages must at least be sufficient to maintain him. They must even upon most occasions be somewhat more; otherwise it would be impossible for him to bring up a family, and the race of such workmen could not last beyond the first generation."[5]

But this obviously was not much. On the contrary, although Adam Smith is rarely identified with the idea, this was one of the beginnings of perhaps the most influential and certainly the most despairing dictum in the history of social comment, the notion that the income of the masses of the people—all who in one way or another worked for a living and whether in industry or agriculture—could not for very long rise very far above the minimum level necessary for the survival of the race. It is the immortal iron law which, as stiffened by Ricardo and refashioned by Marx, became the chief weapon in the eventual ideological assault on capitalism.

Smith was not categorical about the iron law—he was categorical about almost nothing, and ever since economists have always been at their best when they adhered to his example. Thus he conceded that a scarcity of workers might keep wages above the subsistence level for an indefinite time. Under conditions of rapid economic growth wages would also rise. Growth was much more important than wealth *per se* in its effect on wages. "It is not the actual greatness of national wealth, but its continual increase, which occasions a rise in the wages of labor. . . . England is certainly, in the present times, a much richer country than any part of

---

[4] *Wealth of Nations,* ch. VIII. (There are so many editions of this famous work that it seems idle to cite the pages of the particular edition one happens to use.)
[5] *Ibid.*

North America. The wages of labor, however, are much higher in North America than in any part of England."[6]

III

Smith's two great successors in the central tradition were David Ricardo (1772-1823) and Thomas Robert Malthus (1766-1834). With Adam Smith they were the founding trinity of economics, at least as the subject is known in the English-speaking countries. As the man who first gave economics its modern structure—who looked at the factors determining prices, rents, wages, and profits with a sense of system that has served economists ever since—Ricardo has a special claim to have bent the twig. Marxians and non-Marxians are equally in his debt.

With Ricardo and Malthus the notion of massive privation and great inequality became a basic premise. These conclusions were never wholly unqualified. But the qualifications were only qualifications. It was to Ricardo and Malthus that Carlyle alluded when he spoke in 1850 of the "Respectable Professors of the Dismal Science" and gave to economics a name that it has never quite escaped because it was never quite undeserved.

Of Malthus it is necessary to say only a word. Through the nineteenth century and to our own day he has been intimately and all but exclusively identified with his *Essay on Population*. Though he had other and important things to say on economics which have been the subject of a latter-day rediscovery, it is for his views on population that he will be always known.

The number of people who can live in the world is obviously limited by the number that can be fed. Any increase in the supply of food would bring, in Malthus' view, an increase in the number of people to consume it. Nothing but stark need limits the numbers who are propagated and who endure. As a result, men will forever live on the verge of starvation. In the latter editions of the *Essay* Malthus hedged somewhat; the increase in response to a surplus over subsistence might be tempered by "moral restraint" and also, somewhat more ambiguously, by "vice." In other words, people might indefinitely protect their standard of living at a

[6] *Ibid.* Smith observes that this was written in 1773 before "the commencement of the late disturbances," meaning the American Revolution.

level above subsistence, and this would become all the more
likely once both restraint and vice were abetted by effective
contraceptive techniques. But as also with Ricardo, Malthus'
qualifications were lost in the sweep of his central proposition.
This was the inevitability of mass poverty. There was also
the considerable fact that for a large part of the world, the
central proposition was valid and the qualifications were
unimportant. So it was and so it remains in much of Asia.
Malthus, it may be noted, was professor of political economy
in Haileybury College, an institution maintained by the East
India Company for training its servants who would serve in
India.

Since most men had always been poor, it is hardly surprising that Malthus was on the whole unperturbed by his
conclusions and that he did not feel called upon to propose
any remedy. (He confined himself to urging the postponement of marriage and to recommending that there be incorporated into the marriage service a warning that the
husband and not the state would be responsible for the children of the union so that if these were excessive the parents
could expect to be punished by want.) "The note of gloom
and pessimism which distinguished so much of the economic
doctrine of the nineteenth century is in no small measure the
legacy of Malthus."[7]

IV

Both Adam Smith and Malthus had an instinct for national
aggregates—for the forces which acted to enrich the nation.
While Malthus was concerned with showing how increased
national wealth might be used up in the explosive impulse to
procreate, neither was centrally concerned with how different
individuals and classes might share in what the economy
produced. This to David Ricardo was of primary interest.
What were the laws which governed the distribution of product or income between the landlords, entrepreneurs, and workers who had claim to it? "Political Economy you think is an
inquiry into the nature and causes of wealth—I think it
should rather be called an enquiry into the laws which determine the division of the produce of industry amongst the

[7] Alexander Gray, *The Development of Economic Doctrine* (London:
Longmans, Green, 1931), p. 163.

classes who concur in its formation."[8] These laws as Ricardo formulated them worked with ferocious inequality.

Like Malthus, Ricardo regarded population as a dependent variable—it "regulates itself by the funds which are to employ it, and therefore always increases or diminishes with the increase or diminution of capital."[9] Advancing wealth and productivity thus bring more people; but they do not bring more land from which to feed these people. As a result those who own land are able to command an ever greater return, given its quality, for what is an increasingly scarce resource. Meanwhile, in Ricardo's view, profits and wages were in flat conflict for the rest of the product. An increase in profits, other things being equal, meant a reduction in wages; an increase in wages must always come out of profits. "Every rise of profits," on the other hand, "is favourable to the accumulation of capital, and to the further increase of population, and therefore would, in all probability, ultimately lead to an increase of rent."[10] The effect of these compact relationships will be clear. If the country is to have increasing capital and product, profits must be good. But then as product expands the population will increase. The food requirements of the population will press on the available land supply and force up rents to the advantage of the landowner. In other words, capitalists must prosper if there is to be progress and landlords cannot help reaping its fruits. The children of this inescapable misfortune are the people at large. Ricardo summarized that prospect in, perhaps, the most quoted passage in economic literature: "Labour, like all other things which are purchased and sold, and which may be increased or diminished in quantity, has its natural and its market price. The natural price of labour is that price which is necessary to enable the labourers, one with another, to subsist and perpetuate their race, without either increase or diminution."[11]

This was the iron law of wages. As with Smith (and Malthus on population) Ricardo followed the proposition with qualifications. In an "improving" society the market wage might be above the natural wage for an indefinite period and were Ricardo still alive he could show with little

---

[8] Letter to Malthus, October 9, 1820. In *The Works and Correspondence of David Ricardo*, ed. by Piero Sraffa (Cambridge, Eng.: Cambridge University Press), vol. VIII, p. 278. These volumes are henceforth cited as *Works and Correspondence*.

[9] *Ibid.*, vol. I, p. 78.

[10] *Ibid.*, p. 411.

[11] *Ibid.*, p. 93.

difficulty that the conditions necessary for the rule of the iron
law have been in abeyance ever since the nineteenth day of
April, 1817, when *On the Principles of Political Economy
and Taxation* was published. But although the truth rarely
overtakes falsehood, it has winged feet as compared with a
qualification in pursuit of a bold proposition. The iron law,
in its uncompromised clarity, became part of the intellectual
capital of the world.

Moreover, as with Malthus, nothing could be done about
it. Ricardo brought his analysis to a close with the unbending
observation that "These then are the laws by which wages
are regulated, and by which the happiness [a word to be duly
noted] of far the greatest part of every community is governed. Like all other contracts, wages should be left to the
fair and free competition of the market, and should never
be controlled by the interference of the legislature."[12] Nor
may anyone be blamed. On a number of occasions Ricardo
complained that Malthus was unfairly accusing him of being
hostile to landlords—"one would suppose from his language
that I considered them enemies of the state."[13] The landlords
were merely the passive and natural beneficiaries of their
great good fortune. This was the nature of things. Such was
the Ricardian legacy.

There were many contradictions and ambiguities in Adam
Smith. There were also flaws in the Ricardian logic as it
applied to the Ricardian world. His treatment of capital and
profits left much to be desired. And he preoccupied himself
with land at almost the point in history when, because of
the opening of a new world, it had begun to lose its ancient
preoccupying importance. Yet it is hard to think that economists ever came much closer to interpreting the world in
which they lived than did Smith, Ricardo, and Malthus.
None was committed to preconceived doctrine. They had
broken decisively with the conventional wisdom of the tradi-
tionalist and mercantilist society. They had no public opinion
to appease. The result was a formidable interpretation of,
and prescription for, the world as they found it.

In a world that had for so long been so poor nothing was
so important as to win an increase in wealth. The prescription—to free men from the restraints and protection of
feudal and mercantilist society and put them on their own—
was sound, for it was already proving itself. This was not a

[12] *Ibid.*, p. 105.
[13] *Ibid.*, vol. II, p. 117.

compassionate world. Many suffered and many were destroyed under the harsh and unpredictable rule of competition and the market. But many had always perished for one reason or another. Now some were flourishing. This was what counted. One looked not at the peril and misfortune, for there had always been peril and misfortune, but at the opportunity. In any case nothing could be done about the inequality, for it was not rooted in mutable social institutions but in biology. This was fortunate, for the state was excluded from intervention by its prior commitment to freedom of enterprise.

Remarkably little that concerned contemporary economic society was left unbuttoned. It is hardly surprising that a system, seemingly so complete and practical and so subject to test against the realities of the world, made an indelible dent on men's minds.

V

For thirty years following the death of Ricardo the development of economics continued firmly in the tradition he had established. Lesser men together with the conscientious and immeasurably learned John Stuart Mill refined, developed, and organized the ideas. Their thoughts remained centered on the liberal economic society—that in which economic life was regulated by the market and not by the state. On the continent men did talk about socialism but in England and in the Anglo-Saxon tradition they took the market very nearly for granted.

Then at mid-century the economic ideas in the descent from Ricardo came to the great divide. The central tradition continued in its course. It continued to provide the skeletal framework for economic ideas down to our own day. In so doing it gave them system and continuity and went far to make economic life comprehensible. But now, branching off to the left but with a common debt to Ricardo, was the revolutionary tradition of Karl Marx. Henceforth, in shaping attitudes toward economic life, it was both a massive competitor of, and a powerful influence on, the central tradition.

The purpose of these chapters is not to trace the evolution of the individual ideas. That is the task of other volumes and even more of other authors. Rather it is to see what economics assumed in its origins about the ordinary individual and his fate. As between the early Ricardian world and that of Marx, there was in this respect no difference. For both the prospect, given the uninterrupted working out of the underlying forces, combined peril with hopelessness. The difference was that Ricardo and his immediate followers expected the system to survive and Marx did not. But for Ricardo the system survived not because it served the ordinary man. Obviously it did not. It survived only because there was no evident alternative and certainly none that was better. Any effort to modify it made it less efficient.

In time the case for the continuation of the liberal economic society changed. Its superior efficiency was still argued. But by almost imperceptible degrees it came to be argued, or at least implied, that it was also tolerable. It provided a reasonable prospect for the ordinary man and something better for the individual of exceptional capacities. This was widely taken as ushering in an age of optimism on man's material prospects. On closer examination, to which we now turn, we shall see how much of the natal pessimism survived.

CHAPTER IV

The Uncertain Reassurance

As IT WAS LEFT by Malthus and Ricardo the economic prospect for the ordinary individual was remarkably dull. His normal expectation was to live on the edge of starvation. Anything better was abnormal. Progress would enhance the wealth of those who, generally speaking, were already rich but not of the masses. Nothing could be done about it. And these are more than the casual conclusions of two men. They have claim to be considered the propositions on which modern economic thought was founded.

In the usual view, from the middle of the nineteenth century on economists became more sanguine, even optimistic. England was the center of the influential discussion. She was in her great era of commercial and industrial expansion. Real wages were rising. There was a clear and apparently enduring margin over mere subsistence. In Western Europe and America the Malthusian horror was also receding, although it was still possible to suppose that this was the result of the fortuitous opening, all in a few decades, of the North American prairies and plains, the Pampas and the Veld, the New Zealand pastures and the endless Australian outback. These could rescue the world once but not twice. When population had caught up with these new areas population would again press upon the food supply. Only in the present century, as the relation between real income and the rate of population increase has become increasingly unreliable, has there ceased to be fear that the ghost of Malthus might return to haunt western countries as it still roams the villages of Asia.

In the more specific realm of economic theory, the latter half of the last century saw the rejection of the iron law. For a time the income of those who worked was thought to be limited by the amount of working capital somehow dedicated to the employment of labor in agriculture and industry.

This was the famous wages fund which John Stuart Mill first espoused and then rejected. Doubts then began to arise as to whether a single generalization on wages would suffice. Education and special skills came to be regarded as having costs of production that had to be paid for. Special abilities, it was concluded, would, like land, command a rent. Finally, by the end of the century, the worker's return—bearing always in mind that by this is meant the income of the masses of the people—was being related to the value of his marginal product; i.e., he received what he added to the value of his employer's product. Were he paid less than the value of his contribution it would be open to a competitor to offer him more, for in a competitive world there would be other employers whose product he could increase by more than his wage. As a result—a result that might be greatly aided by effective bargaining by a union—wages would tend to be equated with the marginal productivity. This might be high if workers were scarce and highly productive and low if they were redundant and incompetent. But obviously this was a long distance from the iron law, and the break became complete when it no longer seemed certain that well-being brought a self-liquidating flood of children.

With the development of the marginal productivity theory, the effort to construct a general theory of remuneration came pretty much to an end. Having satisfied themselves, as it were, that poverty for those who toiled was not the natural order of things, economists turned to other questions. Most recent work has concerned itself with unions and with the bargaining power which the prescient Adam Smith identified as the real problem.

Yet it would be a great mistake to suppose that economics in the central tradition had escaped from its history. For one thing the notion of an upper limit on the incomes of the masses of the people died very slowly: perhaps these incomes might not be pressed remorselessly down to the floor but they would still be under a ceiling. At the end of the last century Alfred Marshall (1842-1924), whose *Principles* educated the older members of the present generation of economists, was still impelled to argue that if "economic conditions of the country remain stationary sufficiently long . . . both machines and human beings would earn generally an amount that corresponded fairly with their cost of rearing and training, conventional necessaries as well as those things which are strictly necessary being reckoned for."[1] In other words, wages would cover the cost of producing the children, as these costs are conventionally reckoned, and no more. As with Ricardo the tendency was still to a minimum. In the United States in the early decades of the present century, the leading figure in the central tradition and the most respected teacher of his time was Professor Frank W. Taussig of Harvard. His summary of the prospect for the ordinary individual which he republished as late as 1936 was as follows: "The usual rate of wages for ordinary labor in the United States was during the first decade of the twentieth century not far from $800 a year. This is much better than savagery . . . [but] . . . If no more is in prospect, the institution of private property stands not only on the defensive but in a position that cannot long be defended. Yet something better is by no means incompatible with the system."[2] He was not yet prepared to assert categorically that something better was wholly compatible with the system.

II

There remained down to our own time, in short, the lingering conviction that while economic life for the masses might not be intolerable it would still not be very good. In this degree Ricardo still ruled. He ruled in another respect. For it was also believed that if men were poor not much could be done about it. By skill, diligence, and training the individual could raise his marginal product and hence the wage he could claim. As the most obvious avenue of escape for the individual from poverty, this became a factor of great importance in shaping economic attitudes. There will be occasion to return to it later. But if a worker's wage was low it was because his marginal product had remained low. To raise his wage without raising his marginal productivity would be to put his pay above his contribution. This would make it profitable for his employer to fire him. Thus the alternative to low wages was unemployment. Nor is this an antique view. "Each worker receives the value of his marginal product under competition. If a minimum wage is effective, it must therefore have one of two effects: first, workers whose services are worth less than

---

[1] Alfred Marshall, *Principles of Economics* (8th ed.; London: Macmillan, 1927, p. 577. The highly infelicitous expression is exceptional.
[2] F. W. Taussig, *Principles of Economics* (3d ed.; New York: Macmillan, 1936), p. 223. The first edition was published in 1911.

the minimum wage are discharged (and thus forced into unregulated fields of employment or into unemployment . . .) or, second, the productivity of low-efficiency workers is increased."[3] The second likelihood was discarded. The legislation was thus shown to be damaging to those for whom it was designed. This analysis was offered by an able and young scholar in 1946.

The marginal productivity theory, moreover, provided no reassurance on the other malign tendency of the Ricardian system which was for the rich to become very rich indeed. Capital like labor was compensated at a rate corresponding to its marginal product. However appropriate and just this arrangement of things might be, it followed that if the capital were owned in large amounts by few individuals it would be to these that its income would accrue. The resulting inequality might be very great. Observation suggested that this would be the case. In the half century following the Civil War in the United States, men accumulated fortunes of incredible size. Between 1892 and 1899 Rockefeller's personal dividends from Standard Oil amounted to between $30,000,000 and $40,000,000. In 1900 Andrew Carnegie had an income from his steel companies of $23,000,000.[4] These revenues were not subject to tax, and the dollar then was worth rather more than now. In addition to oil and steel, railroads, real estate, copper, banking, and other pursuits returned vast rewards. While some of it represented a return on capital, some could readily be related to a strategic grip on "original and (not perhaps entirely) indestructible powers of the soil" and of the subsoil from which, precisely, Ricardo expected vast wealth would be derived.

There was uneasiness in the central tradition over this inequality. The inheritance of wealth was a special source of discomfort. Perhaps one could justify riches as the reward for the skill, diligence, foresight, and cunning of the original creator. None of this justified its highly fortuitous devolution on the individual who happened to be the son. Monopoly was also regarded with grave misgiving. This rewarded not production but the ability to control production. Moreover, the rule of competition, a point to be emphasized in a moment, was fundamental. Nothing else so completely and utterly underwrote the logic of the system.

[3] G. J. Stigler, "The Economics of Minimum Wage Legislation," *American Economic Review*, vol. XXXVI, no. 3 (June 1946), p. 358.
[4] *New York Times,* March 4, 1957.

Inequality resulting from monopoly might be the warning of fatal flaws in the system itself.

Those who might themselves be subject to equalization have rarely been enthusiastic about equality as a subject of social comment. As a result there has anciently been a muted quality about debate on the subject. Still the economists in the central tradition stated their position with some clarity. There is, Marshall observed, "no moral justification for extreme poverty side by side with great wealth. The inequalities of wealth, though less than they are often represented to be, are a serious flaw in our economic organisation."[5] In the United States Taussig was more specific. "No stretch of psychological analysis concerning the spur of ambition, the spice of constant emulation, the staleness and flatness of uniformity, can prevail against the universal conviction that the maximum of human happiness is not promoted by great, glaring, permanent inequality."[6]

III

The economy of the central tradition presupposed competition. This, also, was the source of misgiving—a misgiving that was often elaborately disguised but nonetheless acute.

The role of competition in the central tradition was fundamental and it became increasingly precise. Numerous firms competed to supply markets at prices which none controlled. The efficient and the progressive were rewarded with survival and growth. The inefficient and unprogressive were penalized by extinction. The employees obviously were involved in the rewards and penalties of their employers and had something of the same inducements to efficiency.

Competition was also the instrument of change. As the tastes of the sovereign consumer altered, the demand for some products rose and so did their prices. The demand and prices of products that were less in vogue declined. Firms in the areas favored by the new demand expanded and others were attracted in. Where demand was shrinking, firms would close down or lay off workers and contract operations. To the extent that this might be possible some would follow the market into the areas of expanding demand. Capital as well as labor and entrepreneurial talent was distributed according to need by the same process.

[5] Marshall, *Principles of Economics,* p. 714.
[6] Taussig, *Principles of Economics,* p. 207.

In the closing decades of the last century and the early years of the twentieth century economists became increasingly preoccupied with the operation of the model of a competitive society. As it was developed and idealized, it was a thing of precision and symmetry, almost of beauty. The hold which it came to exercise on men's minds has often been remarked.[7] There was no equally explicit appreciation of the fact that it committed men to a remarkable measure of uncertainty. The penalty for falling behind in the race for increased efficiency was bankruptcy. This could also be the penalty of mere bad luck in the case of the producer whose product was no longer wanted. And in the case of the worker the component of luck, as opposed to the role of penalty and reward for performance, was multiplied. The most oaken worker could turn up in the employ of an inadequate entrepreneur. The just misfortunes of the employer would then be visited quite irrationally upon this faithful servant. He could lose his job and his livelihood equally through his own shortcomings and those of others. Needless to say, the competitive model had no place for individuals who, as the result of age, infirmity, industrial injury or congenital incompetence, had only a low or negligible marginal productivity.

These misfortunes did not go entirely unperceived. It was ever necessary to assert that they were "part of the system." And it was also made clear by the prophets of the competitive model, not without a certain ruthless logic, that to seek to mitigate the risks and uncertainties of the system would be to undermine the system itself. The race for increased efficiency required that the losers should lose. If consumers were to rule, there must be rewards for those producers who were in the path of current tastes and penalties for those who were left behind. To seek to mitigate the penalties was to undermine the incentives—to separate the stick from the carrot.

Abridgment of the rigors of competition might even be unjust and immoral. "The traders or producers, who find that a rival is offering goods at a lower price than will yield them a good profit, are angered at his intrusion, and complain of being wronged; even though it may be true that those who buy the cheaper goods are in greater need than themselves,

---

[7] I have done so in *American Capitalism: The Concept of Countervailing Power* (Boston: Houghton Mifflin, 1952), especially Chapter II. On the reasonable assumption that the only individual less to be forgiven than the man who repeats others is the man who repeats himself, my comment here on the competitive model is brief.

and that the energy and resourcefulness of their rival is a social gain."[8] Indeed there is a curious likelihood that the competitive model, as it was adumbrated by the textbooks, was intrinsically more insecure and dangerous than anything produced by competition in real life. In the real world competition was abridged by custom, monopoly, trade unions, torpor, legislation, and even a degree of compassion. Thus the penalties for falling behind in the race were exacted less relentlessly in practice than in principle.

The basic impact of these ideas will be clear. The economic system pictured in the central tradition was a thing of peril for those who participated in it and so, *pro tanto*, was economic life at large. This peril was a virtue, and the purer the peril the better the performance of the system. Yet the intrinsic insecurity was disturbing and in two respects. The vulnerability of the weakest members of the society could not entirely be ignored. An economic system which of constitutional necessity was so unfeeling, so intolerant of weakness, was troubling. Even in the best of causes compassion is difficult to control. And equally disturbing was the unwillingness of ordinary men—businessmen, farmers, workers, reformers—to live with that peril. At every turn they showed their inclination to press collectively or with the aid of government for measures designed to make their life more secure. Even if the insecurity of the competitive model was not a damaging flaw, the efforts at self-protection that it induced almost certainly were.

In addition, there was the gnawing doubt as to whether competition, in fact, existed. As the nineteenth century wore along, both firms and fortunes grew. Control over economic life seemed to be passing into fewer hands—a development which was heralded by Marx as marking the system's doom. As the notion of competition became intellectually more precise the behavior of the economy became empirically more at odds with the competitive model. Where the latter called for many firms in a market there were in real life often few. Where the competitive model called for a price that no firm controlled, in real life some firms, at least, seemed to have quite considerable discretionary power over price. And unions were not without power of their own.

In the twentieth century economists in the central tradition began to accommodate the competitive model to these seeming facts of life. Instead of pure competition there was

[8] Marshall, *Principles of Economics*, p. 8.

monopolistic competition or imperfect competition. But who could be sure that a blending of competition and monopoly would be benign? Would not such oddly assorted parents produce a misshapen progeny?[9]

IV

There was a final source of disquiet in the central tradition. That was the serious depression. Depression through the nineteenth and the first decades of the twentieth century had become ever more difficult to ignore. Business suffered a sharp setback in the seventies following the resumption of specie payment after the Civil War. There was a period of comparative stagnation in the nineties and a brief interruption following the financial panic in 1907. There was a short but severe depression following World War I. Then came the vast disaster of the nineteen-thirties. What was the meaning of these recurring misfortunes for the future of the system? Perhaps men might not starve amidst Malthusian scarcity, but might it not still be their fate to starve amidst an abundance they could not buy? Was it not a fair conclusion that by whatever means they were predestined to poverty?

Nothing in the history of social ideas is more interesting than the treatment of the so-called business cycle in the central tradition of economic thought. Its study was isolated in a separate compartment. (To some extent the quarantine still continues.) Prices, wages, rents and interest, all of which were profoundly affected by depressions, were studied on the assumption that depressions did not occur. Normal conditions were assumed; normal meant stable prosperity. In the separate study of the business cycle emphasis was placed on the peculiar and nonrecurring conditions which lay back of each depression—the retirement of the greenbacks prior to 1873, the readjustments following World War I, the breakdown of international trade and capital movements and the collapse of the stock market in 1929. But, paradoxically, there was an equal emphasis—sometimes in the same work—on the rhythmic and normal character of the succession of good times and bad. The etymology emphasized the rhythm—as noted, the study was not of depressions but of the business cycle which served to remind everyone that just as bad times

---

[9] I have also dealt with this source of uneasiness, which I regard as of prime importance, in *American Capitalism*.

followed good, so good times would follow the bad. Even the word depression itself was the terminological product of an effort to soften the connotation of deep trouble. In the last century the term crisis was normally employed. With time, however, this acquired the connotation of the misfortune it described. And Marx's reference to the "capitalist crisis" gave the word an ominous sound. The word panic, which was a partial synonym a half century ago, was no more reassuring. As a result the word depression was gradually brought into use. This had a softer tone; it implied a yielding of the fabric of business activity and not a crashing fall. During the Great Depression the word depression acquired from the event it described an even more unsatisfactory connotation. Therefore the word recession was substituted to connote an unfearsome fall in business activity. But this term eventually acquired a foreboding quality and the recession of 1953-1954 was widely characterized as a rolling readjustment. Should we have a really serious rolling readjustment this phrase would become taboo.

To view the business cycle as a normal rhythm was to regard it as self-correcting. Hence nothing needed to be done about it. Remedies are unnecessary if the patient is certain to recover and they are also unwise. Writing in 1934, Joseph A. Schumpeter, then with Wesley C. Mitchell one of the world's two most eminent authorities on the business cycle, surveyed the experience of the preceding century and concluded, "In *all* cases . . . recovery came of itself. . . . But this is not all: our analysis leads us to believe that recovery is sound only if it does come of itself. For any revival which is merely due to artificial stimulus leaves part of the work of depressions undone and adds, to an undigested remnant of maladjustment, new maladjustments of its own."[10]

Had depressions always remained mild, the notion of a normal rhythm, which wisdom required be undisturbed, would have been reassuring. But as depressions became more violent such a view was the very reverse of reassuring. Workers lost their jobs. Farm prices fell and some farmers lost their farms. Investors lost their savings and some businessmen, more particularly the smaller ones, went bankrupt. And all this was insouciantly described as normal. The conclusion was inevitable: there must be something very wrong with a

[10] J. A. Schumpeter, *Essays,* ed. by Richard V. Clemence (Cambridge, Mass.: Addison-Wesley, 1951), p. 117. This essay was originally published in 1934 in *The Economics of the Recovery Program* (New York: Whittlesey House, McGraw-Hill). The italics are in the original.

system in which such faults were normal. Especially in the early thirties the ideas in the central tradition acted powerfully to breed such doubts. And those who were immune to such uneasiness had another reason for disquiet. Although it was unwise to do anything about depressions, ignorance and popular passion might easily force some action. This could only serve to make things worse. In face of a really bad depression, the notion of a normal self-correcting cycle was calculated to provide uneasiness tailored for every temperament.

There is little need to stress the consequences. To the lingering fear that poverty might be normal, the increasing conviction that inequality was inevitable and the sense of individual insecurity which was inherent in the competitive model, the orthodox view of the business cycle added a much more general sense of disquiet. This was the insecurity of a householder who is told that in the normal and regular course of events he must expect his house to catch fire and his property to be partially or wholly destroyed. The fire cannot be prevented or arrested for it has its work to do; to call for a fire department is to invite an attempt to drown the flames by drenching them with gasoline.

Such was the legacy of ideas in the great central tradition of economic thought. Behind the façade of hope and optimism there remained the haunting fear of poverty, inequality, and insecurity. Partly latent, partly in the suppressed background of conviction, these doubts could easily be aroused by such an occurrence as the Great Depression.

But the reader will surely ask if there was not a more confident stream of ideas—one more completely purged of all traces of the Ricardian gloom. The question will occur especially to Americans: surely in the American tradition there must have been a more consistently optimistic current. Here there must have been some who rejected doubt—who reflected an indigenous and abounding confidence. Perhaps among those who neither read nor wrote there was such confidence. But those who gave voice to the American ideas were far from confident.

CHAPTER V

The American Mood

ONLY WITHIN very narrow limits can one speak of a separate American tradition in economics. Ideas do not respect national frontiers, and this is especially so where language and other traditions are in common. The precepts of the central tradition were accepted equally by Englishmen and Americans. It was from Smith, Ricardo, Mill, and Marshall that American economic ideas were derived. The ideas were written by Americans into the textbooks and enlarged or amended as to detail. But in the last century not much was added by American theorists. Just as the ideas were common to both countries so were the worries, uncertainties, and doubts which the ideas engendered.

This is not to say there were no distinctively American figures but, as compared with the majestic authority of the central tradition, their influence was comparatively small. There would be a measure of agreement on who were the three that were most heard. They were not the total of the American voice but they were also far more than a mere sample. Of the three, two did nothing to offset the presumption of privation and the sense of foreboding which lingered in the central tradition. On the contrary they did a good deal to accentuate it.

The exception was Henry Charles Carey (1793-1879) who did voice the buoyant optimism which one is obliged to think appropriate to the new republic. Ricardo, he observed, had never seen from his window the progress of a new settlement; had he done so he would have had a different view of the prospects for mankind. Drawing on such observation he argued that, with the passage of time, men were not forced as Ricardo claimed to poorer and poorer land with ever lower return to their labor and, for any land that was better than the worst, ever higher rents to the landlords. On the contrary they first cultivated the thin but unencumbered

47

soil on top of the hills. Then at a later period they tackled the thick vegetation in the valleys; having cleared away the trees they proceeded to work this richer alluvial soil. The returns to their toil were not less but more. In his first book in 1835 which, like those of his English contemporaries, centered on the problem of wages and thus as ever on the mass prospect for poverty or well-being, he argued that real wages during the previous forty years had shown a tendency to rise. This, too, was in contrast with Ricardian expectations.

But even Carey was not an unqualified optimist. He more than half agreed with Malthus on the procreative power of mankind and in his earlier books he hazarded the guess that the time might come when "there will not even be standing room."[1] And the influence of Carey, whether as an optimist or pessimist, was not great. Of this he himself was aware. He complained bitterly of the small attention that was paid to his ideas in his own country. In Europe he felt that he was discussed more seriously, and this may well have been so.[2] Little or nothing of Carey passed into the tradition of American economic thought. His books moldered and died. In the last fifty years he has been mentioned only as a curiosity—an early American economist who had the fortitude to disagree with Ricardo on rent and with Adam Smith on the virtues of free trade.

II

The two other distinctively American figures had more enduring influence. These were Henry George and Thorstein Veblen. But so far from manifesting the exuberant attitudes of the frontier, both were prophets of a gloom that was, in some respects, more profound than that of Ricardo. Henry George (1839-1897) was like Marx the founder of a faith, and the faithful still assemble to do honor to their prophet. Like Adam Smith he made clear his view of the social prospect in the title of his remarkable book: *Progress and Poverty. An Inquiry into the Cause of Industrial Depressions and of Increase of Want with Increase of Wealth*. In the opening chapter he posed his basic questions: Why in a time of general economic advance—he was writing in the depression years following 1873—should so much labor "be

---

[1] Quoted by Gray, *The Development of Economic Doctrine*, p. 256.
[2] See Joseph Dorfman, *The Economic Mind in American Civilisation, 1606-1865* (New York: Viking, 1946), p. 804.

condemned to involuntary idleness," should there be so much "pecuniary distress among businessmen," and so much "want, suffering and anxiety among the working classes?"[3] Why, to press things further, should there be so little gain to the poorest classes from increased productive power? "Nay, more," why should its effect be "still further to suppress the condition of the lowest classes?"[4]

The reason for this perverse aspect of progress was again part of the almost infinite legacy of Ricardo. Labor and capital increased in productivity; the land supply remained constant in quality and amount. Rents, as a result, increased more than proportionately and made the landlords the undeserving beneficiaries of advance. The anticipation of rent increases and attendant speculation in land values was also the cause of depression. (It is worth recalling that the nineteenth century was marked by recurrent outbreaks of real estate speculation, especially in the West, and that Henry George spent much of his life in California. Economic ideas, as ever, have their nexus with their environment.) So long as there was private property in land, poverty and depressions were the prospect. Progress would make them worse.

In one respect Henry George was radically more optimistic than Ricardo. On his title page were the further words *The Remedy;* this phrase had no place in the Ricardian lexicon. If land were nationalized—more precisely if a tax were imposed equal to the annual use value of real property *ex* its improvements, so that it would now have no net earnings and hence no capital value—progress would be orderly and its fruits would be equitably shared. But this, obviously, was a very drastic prescription. Were the remedy not applied, and this was a reasonable prospect given the predictable reaction of property owners to the proposal, then the consequence would be continuing poverty combined with increasing inequality and increasing insecurity. If this was the American dream, it had little to commend it as compared with the meager classical prospect. And in fact the mood of Henry George's followers was often one of misanthropic or frustrated radicalism.

---

[3] Henry George, *Progress and Poverty* (Fiftieth Anniversary Ed.; New York: Robert Shalkenbach Foundation, 1933), p. 5.
[4] *Ibid.*, p. 9.

III

In the tradition of American popular radicalism there were other influential figures besides Henry George—Henry Demarest Lloyd and Edward Bellamy come especially to mind as important figures of the latter decades of the last century. Their conclusions, however, were broadly similar: great inequality and great poverty were inevitable in the absence of great reform. And unlike Henry George their words mostly died with them. There remains, however, the man whom many regard as the uniquely American economist, Thorstein Veblen (1857-1929).[5]

For the eager search for reassurance that followed the Ricardian gloom, Veblen substituted a grandiloquent iconoclasm. Ricardo had forecast a disagreeable fate for most mankind. His followers hoped against hope that it might not be. Veblen took a position above the debate. The fate of man was something with which, at least for purposes of posture, he chose not to identify himself. But he also made clear his view that those who talked of progress were mostly idiots or frauds.

To this end he made specific many of the misfortunes that lurked in the background of the central tradition. Poverty, or more accurately both the moral and material debasement of man, was part of the system and would become worse with progress. There is an inescapable conflict between industry and business—between the "excessive prevalence and efficiency of the machine industry" and its "deplorable" tendency to overproduce and thus to threaten the basic goal of business which is to make money.[6] In this conflict business always wins. Monopolistic restrictions are imposed where, on purely technical grounds, there could be abundance. This channels

[5] A case might be made for the influence of three other men who were generally outside the central tradition; namely, Simon N. Patten (1852-1922), John R. Commons (1862-1945), and Wesley C. Mitchell (1874-1948). However, Patten, a singularly interesting and original figure, has joined Carey in the neglect reserved for American heretics. Commons and Mitchell, as a matter of principle or method, largely avoided any overall theoretical formulation of man's prospects and hence could not be said to have contributed to the attitudes with which we are here concerned.

[6] Thorstein Veblen, *The Theory of Business Enterprise* (1932 ed.; New York: Scribner), p. 234.

income to the owners. The public pays with relative impoverishment.

The economic costs of progress are, however, even less severe than its cultural consequences. Machine industry does not necessarily call for less intelligence on the part of the workers. But it does require a peculiarly narrow and mechanical process of thought and it discourages all other. It also undermines family and church and (here the unions play a key role) the ancient foundations of law and order. The massing together of the workers is a great inducement to "socialist iconoclasm" which is the threshold to anarchy.

Serious depressions are not accidental misfortunes. They are inherent in the conflict between industry and business and hence are organic aspects of the system. They occur "in the regular course of business."[7]

Finally, in his immortal *The Theory of the Leisure Class,*[8] Veblen dramatized, as no one before or since, the spectacle of inequality. The rich and successful were divorced from any serious economic function and denied the dignity of even a serious or indignant attack. They became, instead, a subject for detached, bemused and perhaps subtly contemptuous observation. One observes the struggle between hens for social pre-eminence in the chicken yard as an interesting phenomenon but in so doing one does not do much to underwrite the social values of the birds. So with Veblen on the rich.

But equally with Ricardo, wealth and poverty were made inherent. And so, moreover, were their least ingratiating aspects. The ostentation, waste, idleness, and immorality of the rich were all purposeful: they were the advertisements of success in the pecuniary culture. Work, by contrast, was merely a caste mark of inferiority. "During the predatory culture labour comes to be associated in men's habits of thought with weakness and subjection to a master. It is, therefore, a mark of inferiority, and, therefore, comes to be accounted unworthy of man in his best estate."[9] In the central tradition the worker was accorded the glory of honest toil. Veblen denied him even that.

Nor was there any hope for change. These things were part of the pecuniary culture. Where Marx looked forward hopefully to revolutionary reconstruction, Veblen did not.

[7] *Ibid.,* p. 183. The conclusions sketched above are principally developed in *The Theory of Business Enterprise.*

[8] Published in 1899. This is available in the Modern Library.

[9] *Ibid.,* p. 36.

In his latter years he comforted himself only with the thought that the evolving economic society was destroying not only itself, but all civilization as well. Such was the view of the greatest voice from the frontier.

There will always be debate as to how influential Veblen was. He is the indubitably indigenous figure in American economic thought. This has always commended him to those who—failing to see the enormous authority of the orthodox-classical tradition—have supposed that the dominating influence in American thought must be an American.[10] This must still be true even though, as in the case of Veblen, no one could worse fit the cultural stereotype of the optimistic, extrovert American. In fact Veblen's strictly economic conclusions were not widely read or taught. They never entered the textbooks in competition with the ideas of the central tradition. Yet he was no Carey. He influenced a generation of scholars, writers, and teachers. These, in turn, brought something of his iconoclasm to the ideas of the time. Teachers influenced by Veblen taught the doctrines of the central tradition but they brought to it a disbelief, even a contempt, for the notion that economic progress could much benefit the masses or, indeed, that there was such a thing. Veblen thus precipitated the doubts and pessimism which lurked in the central tradition. In American social thought before the Great Depression there was a strong feeling, manifested for example in such liberal journals as *The Nation* and *The New Republic*, that the hard-headed intellectual was never beguiled by notions of reform or advance under capitalism. These when offered were either a façade, a trap, or an illusion which would quickly bring disenchantment. These attitudes faded with the New Deal, but not until the Roosevelt reforms had been similarly and repeatedly discussed and dismissed. These attitudes were in no small measure the legacy of Veblen.

IV

Such was the distinctively American contribution. However, we must take note of the impact of another set of social ideas —ideas which though not American in origin came almost uniquely to root in the American soil. Toward the close of the last century and in the early years of this they deeply

[10] This is a criticism which, I think, can fairly be made of Professor Commager. Cf. his discussion of Veblen in *The American Mind* (New Haven: Yale University Press, 1950), pp. 227-246.

influenced attitudes on the fate of the ordinary man. These were the doctrines of the Social Darwinists.

Ricardo and Malthus did not conceal from anyone that theirs was a world of struggle. In that struggle some, and perhaps many, succumbed and there was no hope in public measures to ameliorate the lot of those who were to fall. Speaking of the poor laws, then supported by a fund subscribed by each parish for the support of the indigent, Ricardo concluded that no scheme for their amendment "merits the least attention, which has not their abolition for its ultimate object," adding that "the principle of gravitation is not more certain than the tendency of such laws to change wealth and power into misery and weakness."[11]

However, Ricardo's case for leaving everything to the market—for not allowing compassion to interfere with economic process—was essentially functional. Idleness not being subsidized and substance not being wasted, more was produced and the general well-being would thus be raised. Struggle and misfortune were not themselves to be welcomed.

The position of the Social Darwinists was different. Economic society was an arena in which men met to compete. The terms of the struggle were established by the market. Those who won were rewarded with survival and, if they survived brilliantly, with riches. Those who lost went to the lions. This competition not only selected the strong but developed their faculties and insured their perpetuation. And in eliminating the weak it insured that they would not reproduce their kind. Thus the struggle was socially benign and, to a point at least, the more merciless the more benign its effects, for the more weaklings it combed out.

The birthplace of these ideas was nineteenth-century England, and their principal source and protagonist was Herbert Spencer (1820-1903). It was Spencer and not Charles Darwin who gave the world the phrase "the survival of the fittest," and it was first applied not to the lower animals but to mankind. Spencer believed that acquired as well as inherited traits were genetically transmitted.

Spencer was a decidedly uncompromising exponent of a very uncompromising creed. He opposed state ownership of the post office and the mint. He was opposed to public education, for it interfered with parental choice between different schools and, indeed, with the choice between wisdom and ignorance for their children. Public aid to the needy and

---

[11] *Principles of Political Economy*, pp. 107-8.

even public sanitation tended to perpetuate the more vulnerable members of the race.

> *Partly by weeding out those of lowest development, and partly by subjecting those who remain to the never-ceasing discipline of experience, nature secures the growth of a race who shall both understand the conditions of existence and be able to act up to them. It is impossible in any degree to suspend this discipline by stepping in between ignorance and its consequences, without, to a corresponding degree, suspending the progress. If to be ignorant were as safe as to be wise, no one would become wise.*[12]

Spencer was restrained from a condemnation of all private charity only by the disturbing thought that this would abridge the liberty of the giver as surely as it would winnow out the weaklings of the race. Misery and misfortune are not misery and misfortune alone but the rungs of a ladder up which man makes his ascent. To seek to mitigate misery was to put in abeyance the fundamental arrangements by which nature insured progress. "What can be a more extreme absurdity than that of proposing to improve social life by breaking the fundamental law of social life."[13]

Although Spencer was an Englishman, Social Darwinism had much of its greatest success in the United States. Here, in William Graham Sumner (1840-1910) of Yale, it found its major prophet. Here too it found a host of minor ones. Spencer's own books were widely read, or at least widely discussed, in the closing decades of the nineteenth century and the opening years of the present one. When Spencer visited the United States in 1882, he was accorded a welcome by the faithful befitting a messiah. In 1904, when the Supreme Court struck down a New York State law limiting the hours of labor of bakers to ten a day, Justice Holmes observed that "The Fourteenth Amendment does not enact Mr. Herbert Spencer's Social Statistics."[14] It was a dissenting opinion.

There were a number of reasons for this popularity in the new republic. By the time of Spencer, England was already moving away from the unhampered rule of the market. Unions, factory inspection, the regulation of the hours of

[12] *Social Statics* (New York: D. Appleton, 1865), p. 413.
[13] *Principles of Ethics*, vol. II (New York: D. Appleton & Co., 1897), p. 260.
[14] Lochner v. New York, 1904.

women and children had gained acceptance. In the United
States the race was still being more ruthlessly improved.

And there were many who wished to see the improvement
continue with all it implied for those who had been selected.
"The peculiar conditions of American society," Henry Ward
Beecher told Spencer as early as 1866, "has made your writ-
ings far more quickening here than in Europe."[15] In fact,
ideas were never more marvelously in the service of circumstance.

The rise of Social Darwinism in the United States coincided
with the rise of the great fortunes. It was a time not only of
heroic inequality but of incredible ostentation. Great lime-
stone mansions were rising in New York. Even more stately
pleasure domes were being built in Newport. Mrs. William
K. Vanderbilt gave her $250,000 ball in 1883. That of
Bradley Martin in 1897 was rather more lavish. For this the
ballroom of the old Waldorf-Astoria was transformed into a
replica of Versailles. One guest appeared in a suit of gold
inlaid armor valued at an estimated $10,000. A little earlier
at Delmonico's—where Spencer had been entertained—
guests were given cigarettes wrapped in hundred-dollar bills
which they lighted with a legitimate sense of affluence.

It was also a time of widespread poverty and degradation.
The distant workers who supported this wealth lived in
noisome slums. There were numerous beggars near at hand.
Nor could it always be said that the wealth was being acquired
without cost to others. The techniques were sometimes very
rude. But none of this need lie on anyone's conscience.
Natural selection was at work. The rich could regard themselves as the product of its handiwork—as Chauncey Depew
was pleased to remind those who attended one of the great
dinners of the successful in New York. So, an important
point, would be their sons for the superior qualities were
genetically transmitted. This legitimized inherited wealth,
for it blessed only the biologically superior. The problem of
poverty, meanwhile, was being solved by the only means by
which it could be solved. The unfit were being weeded out.
Public and even private succor, which if compelled by compassion could be inconveniently expensive, was banned not
by callousness but by a perceptive adherence to the laws of
nature. "The law of the survival of the fittest was not made
by man. We can only by interfering with it produce the

[15] Quoted by Richard Hofstadter. *Social Darwinism in American
Thoughts* (Boston: Beacon Press, 1955), p. 31.

survival of the unfittest."[16] How much better to resist taxation and charity and, incidentally, keep one's money. To
this day the man who refuses a beggar and righteously
observes, "I'm told it's the worst thing you can do," is still
finding useful the inspired formula of Spencer and Sumner.

Nor need one reflect, uncomfortably, on the methods by
which growth had been achieved and wealth acquired. As
John D. Rockefeller explained to a fortunate Sunday-school
class: "The growth of a large business is merely the survival
of the fittest. . . . The American Beauty rose can be produced in the splendor and fragrance which bring cheer to its
beholder only by sacrificing the early buds which grow up
around it." As with the rose, so with the Standard Oil
Company. "This is not an evil tendency in business. It is
merely the working-out of a law of nature and a law of
God."[17] This aligned God and the American Beauty rose
with railroad rebates, exclusive control of pipelines, systematic
price discrimination, and some other remarkably aggressive
business practices.

V

In 1956 the retiring president of the National Association of
Manufacturers, Mr. Cola G. Parker, called solemnly in the
name of Herbert Spencer on the workingmen of the country
to reject the slavery of their unions and on businessmen to
renounce the paternalism of Washington. Concerning the
latter he said in a dynamic sentence: "Before we can build
solidly into the glorious future this is another unsound part
of our structure which we'll have to get rid of, even though
it causes severe pain to us businessmen to forego the federal
crutches we have been leaning on." Neither workers nor
businessmen took any concrete steps in response to his plea.

However, the names of Spencer and Sumner had long
before ceased to evoke response. Both democracy and the
modern corporation had dealt crippling blows. The masses
of the people had shown a marked unwillingness to vote for
the self-denying policies which would contribute to their own
combing out. Individuals were always coming forward with
ideas for abridging the struggle and winning elections on this
platform. If Social Darwinism was to work, there all too

[16] William Graham Sumner, *Essays in Political and Social Science*
(New York: Henry Holt, 1885), p. 85.
[17] Hofstadter, *Social Darwinism in American Thought*, p. 45.

obviously had to be some curtailment of popular government. To enforce acquiescence in misfortune there also needed to be a constabulary whose loyalty was properly insured by social security and seniority.

The corporation dealt a different kind of blow. The competitive struggle, as a device for separating the strong from the weak, at least had elements of plausibility in the world of the individual entrepreneur. And conceivably the rugged traits which permit of survival in this contest are passed on to strengthen the generations that follow. It is not so easy to apply this reasoning to the case of General Electric or General Motors. These show marked indications of immortality. And it is not clear how selection works through reproduction to bring a new generation of young and vigorous companies reflecting the strong bloodlines of their corporate parents. Perhaps it could be argued that natural selection operates to bring to the top those who are most effective in the struggle for promotion—that it rewards with survival those who are most skilled in the tough, complex, and ingenious talents that such advance so often requires. If so, then Social Darwinism would work just as selectively in government where the bureaucratic struggle is reputedly severe. This could not be.

Yet Social Darwinism bore importantly on the attitudes which Americans brought into the age of affluence. This was the country where wealth was increasing most rapidly. It was the one where the reassurance of the central tradition might seem to be most plausible. Here, if anywhere, the ordinary man had a chance. Perhaps he did, but he also had to face the fact that all economic life was a mortal struggle. He might win but he also might lose, and for him to accept the full consequences of loss—hunger, privation, and death —was a social necessity. Poverty and insecurity thus became inherent in the economic life of even the most favored country. So, of course, did inequality, and this was firmly sanctified by the fact that those who enjoyed it were better. If observation suggested that economic life might be less severe in the United States, Social Darwinism emphasized the contrary.

It had another lasting effect. American thought has always been prone to attribute a mystique to the market. More than mere efficiency is involved in uninhibited operation of supply and demand. Other values are at stake. The Social Darwinists identified the vigor of the race with the market. This notion withered and disappeared. But it was easy for others to identify yet other and equally extraneous values with the

market and to warn, accordingly, of the pervasive consequences of anything which, in the name of welfare or compassion, might interfere with the free play of market forces.
Biological progress is no longer threatened by measures which
lessen the perils of economic life for the individual. But
liberty still is. So, in one fairly substantial view, is Christianity
and the chance for eternal salvation. To a considerable degree
it was Social Darwinism which led the way in so broadening
the claim for the market. In so doing it narrowed the scope
for social measures designed to rescue the individual from the
privation or to protect him from the hazards of economic life.

One would not care to claim that this chapter exhausts the
influences which have borne distinctively on American economic attitudes. As noted, the frontier and the West had
their own expansive mood. So, on the whole, did a good deal
of American political debate in the latter part of the last
century and the early decades of the present one. Without
question much of this expressed the conviction that any
American—at a minimum any properly energetic American
of Anglo-Saxon and Protestant antecedents—could by his
own efforts be comfortably opulent. But the ideas which
were taught and read, and by which the properly qualified
were guided, were far from sanguine. The most influential
critics were either misanthropic or committed to the need for
massive reform. The established right pictured and praised a
struggle that improved on that of Ricardo only in being more
heroic and spectacular and in rejoicing over the immolation
of the unfortunate.

CHAPTER VI

The Marxian Pall

IN THE DESCENT from Ricardo the Social Darwinists were an eddy to the right. Marx was a massive eruption to the left. But the roots of Marx were deep in the central tradition. There were socialists before Marx, but there have been a great many more since. One reason is that Marx built socialism on Ricardo's orderly arrangement of economic ideas and, in particular, on his bold conception of the problem of income distribution. At least partly as a result, his work carried an authority and conviction that was incomparably greater than any of his socialist predecessors.

For seventy-five years following his death, Ricardo's admirers were concerned to defend him from the charge, leveled among others by Ruskin, that he was a cold-blooded stockbroker who took a totally detached view of the misery he foresaw for all eternity. The charge may have been unfair, but no one has suggested that Ricardo was a man of passion. Karl Marx (1818-1883) was a man of passion and of Jovian wrath, and this is a matter of first importance. For the Ricardian conclusions—the inevitable impoverishment of the masses, the progressive enrichment of those who own the natural means of production, the inevitable conflict between wages and profits and the priority of the latter for progress —could become, in the hands of an angry man, a call to revolution. As noted, Marx's conception of capitalism was no more gloomy than that of Ricardo or of Malthus. But unlike Ricardo and Malthus, Marx's mission was to identify fault, place blame, urge change and, above all, to enlist disciplined belief. In the latter his success exceeded that of any man since Mohammed.

II

The iron law of wages continued in Marx but in a modified form. The worker is kept on the margin of destitution less

59

because he breeds up to this point than because of his utter weakness in dealing with the capitalist employer and because the system won't work if he is well paid. On occasion he may get more than the bare minimum, but it is for the same reason that the dairyman feeds his cows more than the maintenance ration—they give him more milk. The bargaining position of the worker vis-à-vis the employer is the same as that of the cows vis-à-vis the dairyman.

This is partly so because the labor force is a reservoir into which, with the passage of time, independent craftsmen and farmers are also forced. Helplessness is assured by the industrial reserve army—by the rising and falling but enduring margin of unemployment which is part of the system. Any worker at any time can be flushed into this reserve which insures that he will be cooperative and will accept the wage that is offered him.

The advance of the arts and the accumulation of capital bring no benefit to the average man. On the contrary, in some of Marx's characteristic prose, they ". . . mutilate the labourer into a fragment of a man, degrade him to the level of appendage of a machine, destroy every remnant of charm in his work and turn it into hated toil . . . drag his wife and child beneath the Juggernaut . . . [they bring] misery, agony of toil, slavery, ignorance, mental degradation. . . ."[1]

Resorting to a device which many others have found useful, Marx dug up a candid opponent to help him make his case. A prominent conservative, Destutt de Tracy, had observed: "In poor countries the people are comfortable, in rich nations they are generally poor."[2]

Further, and in its ultimate influence perhaps the most important of all, the system had an inherent tendency to devastating depression. Sismondi, the great French historian, philosopher and economist, had published at the beginning of the century a book which reflected much of the hopeful attitude of Adam Smith. Then, sixteen years later and after extensive travels over Western Europe, he returned to the subject impressed by the importance of industrial crisis and persuaded that they would get worse. The trouble was that the purchasing power of the workers did not keep abreast of what they produced. As a result, goods accumulated for which there were no buyers. A crisis became inevitable. Marx's view of depressions, which he was still working out

[1] *Capital* (London: William Gliesher, 1918), pp. 660-61.
[2] *Ibid.*, p. 664.

when he died, was roughly similar and so, in recent times, has been that of almost everyone.

However, Marx stressed other causes too. As capital accumulated, the rate of return would fall. This would weaken incentives and lead to periods of torpor and stagnation. Also in boom times the industrial reserve army—the unemployed—would be reduced, and the resulting competition for labor would force up wage rates, and hence costs of production, and this would bring the boom to an end.[3] Nothing so well suggests Marx's intransigent pessimism on the outlook for the worker under capitalism as this. A temporary betterment of his position is the cause of a prompt worsening of it. Depressions are caused both by the poverty of the workers (and their insufficient purchasing power) and equally by temporary improvements in their well-being.

Since the government, for Marx, was the handmaiden of the bourgeoisie, there was small likelihood that it would be impelled to succor the unemployed by making jobs for them. But were it to do so the effect would be only to reduce the industrial reserve army, raise wage costs, and cause a depression. To correct the deficiency of purchasing power—the deficiency that kept workers from buying the products of their labor—by public measures to put more purchasing power in the hands of the people, as by spending for public works, would be futile for the same reasons. Also there are deeper disorders in the process of "production and reproduction" which such superficialities leave untouched and which render them worthless.[4] This point is one of considerable importance to Marx and even more to his followers. Were it possible to prevent depressions by compensating for the deficient purchasing power of the worker with (say) public spending, then capitalism might be workable. Instead of revolution there would be a budget deficit. Every acute Marxian has seen the danger and denied the possibility of such an easy escape. In one of those developments which make economics such an engaging study in odd bedfellows, the Marxists have

[3] Marx's explanation of the business cycle is scattered through his work and is in some respects, as Professor Schumpeter has observed, rather casual. This summary owes much to Mrs. Joan Robinson's indispensable book, *An Essay on Marxian Economics* (London: Macmillan, 1952).

[4] I should, perhaps, remind the reader that I am here concerned with a characterization of the Marxian position and of its impact on attitudes and not with a critique. Marxian critiques are still very, very long.

been joined in this contention by the most stalwart conservatives.[5]

With the longer-run Marxian prospect everyone is familiar. Capitalist concentration proceeds; productive plant and resources come to be owned by ever fewer people of ever greater wealth. The Marxian capitalist has infinite shrewdness or cunning on everything except matters pertaining to his own ultimate survival. On these he is not subject to education. He continues willfully and reliably down the path to his own destruction. The worker, by contrast, whom he degrades and beats to a hopeless pulp, is gifted with quick perception and the capacity to learn. He is reinforced by ". . . fresh elements of enlightenment and progress" from the sections of the ruling class who are extruded by the process of capitalist concentration.[6] In the end the centralization of production produces hopeless weakness in face of the masses of the workers who by now have become a disciplined industrial army. Then the knell sounds and the expropriators are expropriated. At the next stage Marx joins the optimists. The path is now open to a laissez-faire more complete by far than that of Ricardo. For government was occasioned by the needs of capitalism and the acquisitive mentality which capitalism produced. With no further need to police the masses or curb the larceny which is the manifestation of acquisitive modes of thought, the state can begin to wither away. But first, unhappily, there was the revolution. A very large number of people were never able to project their minds much beyond this discomforting prospect. And as Marx billed it—". . . the forcible overthrow of all existing social condition. Let the ruling classes tremble . . ."[7]—it was discomforting.

III

Nothing has ever been so badly understood as the influence of Marx. That he seized the minds of millions is, of course,

[5] Question: Then you don't believe in compensatory spending?
Secretary Humphrey: What do you mean by that?
Question: In other words, increasing the level of government spending during a period in which business generally is declining . . .
Secretary Humphrey: No; I don't think so, Joe. I don't think you can spend yourself rich.
— Transcript of Press Conference by former Secretary of the Treasury George M. Humphrey, *Congressional Record*, January 17, 1957, p. 695.
[6] *Communist Manifesto.*
[7] *Ibid.*

agreed. But it is widely supposed that Marx's influence ends with these faithful. In the conventional wisdom his ideas are a kind of infection like smallpox. Either men get it and are permanently scarred, or they escape it because of effective inoculation and are untouched. Nothing could be further from the truth. Marx profoundly affected those who did not accept his system. His influence extended to those who least supposed they were subject to it.

In part this was the result of the breath-taking grandeur of Marx's achievement as an exercise in social theory. No one before, or for that matter since, had taken so many strands of human behavior and woven them together—social classes, economic behavior, the nature of the state, imperialism, and war were all here and on a great fresco which ran from deep in the past to far into the future. On class conflict, or imperialism, or the causes of national war, Marx was bound to be influential, for he was the only man who had offered an explanation which was at all integrated with the rest of human experience. Thus all American thought has been deeply influenced by a Marxian view of imperialism. It could not be otherwise. The break with British imperialism came on economic issues. To this day the principal alternative to explaining imperialism in terms of economic self-interest is to argue the benevolence of the imperial power, its commitment to the white man's burden, and its feeling that the natives are not ready for independence. No one in the United States is more suspicious of such a defense by the colonial power than the right-wing Republican who is conditioned to search for the economic motivation back of any argument.

"As an economic theorist Marx was first of all a very learned man."[8] His goals were those of a revolutionist, but his method was that of a scholar and scientist. Accordingly his concepts helped all social scientists in their perception of reality. In a world but little removed from poverty, and where great store was set by wealth, it was inevitable that most conflict would have an economic cause. Nothing else was nearly so worth quarreling about. Even where there was some other ostensible cause—love, honor, patriotism, or religion—a more penetrating or cynical view could be expected to discern some economic motive. This in simple outline was Marx's materialistic conception of history.

[8] Joseph A. Schumpeter, *Capitalism, Socialism and Democracy* (2d ed.; New York: Harper, 1947), p. 21.

Though it was not original with Marx—as he made clear—
he made it famous. It is something that the modern businessman accepts as a matter of course. When he sees someone
agitating for change, either at home or abroad, he inquires,
almost automatically: "What is there in it for him?" He
suspects that the moral crusades of reformers, do-gooders,
liberal politicians, and public servants, all their noble protesta-
tions notwithstanding, are based ultimately on self-interest.
"What," he inquires, "is their gimmick?"

Marx foresaw, in the process of capitalist concentration,
the tendency for the control of the capital resources of the
community to pass into fewer and fewer hands. As the
materialistic view of human motivation is fundamental in
American conservatism, so capitalist concentration is a prime
tenet of American liberalism. It is Marx, in considerable
measure at least, who agitates year in and year out for the
enforcement of the antitrust laws.

In the central tradition of economic theory, the existence
of social classes—of capitalists, middle class, and proletarians
—was only surreptitiously conceded if at all. Yet classes
obviously existed; so did something that looked suspiciously
like class conflict. For a perception of these matters the world
had also to rely on Marx.

Finally, Marx gained influence by heralding the truly terrifying depression. In the central tradition, as noted, the
depression was a routine affliction. For Marx it was an increasingly devastating fact of capitalist life. In the end a
depression would destroy (or at least mark the destruction of)
the system. On this, of all matters, it was difficult to say that
Marx was wrong for plainly by the nineteen-thirties depressions were not routine. In 1934, in the third year of the
Great Depression, John Strachey, then the most articulate
contemporary English Marxist, surveyed the current economic
situation and concluded, not without satisfaction, that "the
whole capitalist world is on its way to barbarism."[9] But the
judgment of the most orthodox of English economists in the
same year, except in being tinged with regret, was not different. Sir Arthur Salter concluded that "the defects of the
capitalist system have been increasingly robbing us of its
benefits. They are now threatening its existence."[10]

[9] John Strachey, *The Coming Struggle for Power* (4th ed.; London:
Gollancz, 1934), p. 8.
[10] Arthur Salter, *Recovery: The Second Effort* (London: G. Bell &
Sons, 1934), p. 209.

IV

Had Marx been mostly wrong, his influence would quickly have evaporated. The thousands who have devoted their attention to demonstrating his errors would have turned their attention elsewhere. But on much he was notably right, especially in relation to his time. The latter point is worth emphasizing. Most economic philosophers needed only to be right as regards their own time. No one defends Adam Smith in his conviction that corporations—joint stock companies— had no future. But the Marxists require that Marx be right not only for his own time but for all time. This is a truly formidable test.

And it was because Marx was so manifestly right on some things that few could suppress the insistent question: Might he not be right on other things—including the prospect for capitalism itself? Might it be that Marx faced facts while others sought the dubious shelter of wishful thinking? Such thoughts, as much as the convictions of his converts, were the measure of Marx's influence. In those who resisted belief he still had an unparalleled capacity to inspire doubts. Lurking just beneath the surface in the mind of every non-Marxian— everyone at least who was sensitive to any form of thought —was the question: Am I Dr. Pangloss?

And to this doubt the converts also contributed. Whereas those who remained in the central tradition of economics wondered, the Marxists did not. They were certain. No wish for a comfortable and nonviolent future fathered *their* thoughts. They were willing to face the prospect of the progressive immiseration of the masses, worsening economic crises and, in the end, bloody revolution. The unloveliness of these prospects, and the fact that they were being faced, established the Marxist as the profound realist, the man who was entirely without illusion. This evident realism was reinforced by moral passion. "The religious quality of Marxism . . . explains a characteristic attitude of the orthodox Marxist toward opponents. To him, as to any believer in a faith, the opponent is not merely in error but in sin. Dissent is disapproved of not only intellectually but also morally."[11] The

---

[11] Schumpeter, *Capitalism, Socialism and Democracy,* p. 5. In the central tradition, by contrast, such passionate belief was thought inconsistent with scientific rationalism. Not exclusively, to be sure. Marx once observed with some justice that "Economists are like theologians. . . . Every religion other than their own is the invention of man, whereas their own particular brand of religion is an emanation from God." (From *The Misery of Philosophy,* quoted by Strachey, *The Coming Struggle for Power.*)

man who argues with a Marxist has always been assaulting a rock fortress with a rubber flail.

Lastly, it was always possible to dismiss those who believed Marx wrong as being guilty of a failure of understanding. Marx is not easy to understand. Those who thought him wrong had failed to do so. Thus one of Marx's reasons for the capitalist crisis, as noted, was the tendency for the rate of profit to fall with continuing capital accumulation. Marx was as insistent on the importance of profit for investment and production as any president of the National Association of Manufacturers. The falling rate of profit would lead to recurrent interruptions of expansion and these would be of increasing severity and duration.

In this century profits have shown no tendency to fall, and capital accumulation has continued apace. As a result, the declining rate of profit cannot be taken seriously as a cause of depression. One of Marx's sympathetic modern interpreters has been moved to conclude that "his explanation of the falling tendency of profits explains nothing at all."[12] But few Marxists make this concession. Marx was not in error; nor was it because he based his observation on the last century when the rate of return seemed to be showing a tendency to fall. Rather the dissenter has failed to see the full subtlety and complexity of Marx's argument. He has somehow oversimplified or vulgarized Marx's position.

Much has been written of the appeal of Marx—and, in somewhat the same vein, of communism—to intellectuals. How, in particular, can a doctrine that has so obviously acquired the standing of a dogma be attractive to inquiring, rational minds? The answer is a complex one. Apart from the obvious fact that Marx for Marxists is the conventional wisdom, there is the seeming realism, the certainty and security of the defenders and the large component of vivid truth. But much of Marx's strength has always been in the contention of his followers that those who thought him wrong were really themselves obtuse, simple—or literal-minded. These are terrible charges; innumerable intellectuals have been unwilling to risk them. How much better to persuade oneself and others of one's ability to see below the surface. This might mean agreeing that Marx meant what he did not say, but it was proof that one wasn't incapably dull. Thus acceptance of Marx became not a matter of willingness to follow dogma into obvious unreality and error. Rather it was a

---

[15] Joan Robinson, *An Essay on Marxian Economics*, p. 42.

question of whether the individual was willing to adventure into the subtle and inverted as distinct from the surface implications of Marx's words, and had the ability to do so. For intellectuals the lure was strong. This too was a source of Marx's influence.

V

The time has come for a summing up. Up to twenty or twenty-five years ago—say the middle years of the thirties—the broad impact of economic ideas is clear. It could not but leave a man with a sense of the depth, pervasiveness, and burden of the economic problem and, on the whole, with the improbability of a happy outcome. "Depend on it," Dr. Johnson observed, "when a man knows he is going to be hanged in a fortnight, it concentrates his mind wonderfully."[18] For the same reasons men's minds were focused on the perils of economic life.

In particular, although it was no longer the lesson of the central economic tradition that men would starve, neither was it the lesson that they would do very well. Privation was still normal. Men might lift themselves by lifting their marginal product; with increasing efficiency and increasing supplies of capital, marginal productivity and hence wages might rise. But no one could suppose that the result could be more than barely adequate. Certainly no one could suggest that any opportunity for such improvement could be overlooked. On the contrary, to relax such effort in the slightest would be extreme social dereliction. The privation, already great, would be greater—and unnecessarily so. The man of conscience and compassion must see that efficiency is increased by all possible means. To do less was to be profoundly callous, even cruel.

Privation is also enhanced by the intransigent inequality of the income. The miserable consumption of the poor is partly the result of the ostentatious demands of the rich. There isn't enough for both, and the latter get far more than they need. If possible, something should be done about inequality, for no sensitive man could be indifferent to the social strains and conflicts that it was producing and seemed likely to produce as the proletariat became increasingly conscious

[18] The saying owes its modern fame to Winston Churchill, who noted that his mind had been so focused by the prospect of the invasion of Britain in 1940.

of its inferior position. But could anything serious really be done about it?

Finally, there was the nerve-racking problem of insecurity. The competitive model made episodic unemployment for the worker, and occasional insolvency for the farmer or businessman, a part of the system. This insecurity was enhanced by the growing severity of depressions and now in the thirties by the most devastating depression of all. This latter was especially troublesome because the contemporary theory dismissed it as self-correcting. If self-correcting it was inevitable, and if inevitable it was intolerable.

Clearly there was much to bring productivity, inequality, and insecurity to the center of men's minds and to make them a preoccupying concern. And if there was any tendency in the central tradition of economics to conclude that all might in the end work out for the best, there were also voices from the wings to say it couldn't be so. From the right was the echo of the Social Darwinists saying struggle is not only inevitable but good. From the Marxist world, in tones of thunderous conviction, came the warning that the inequality and the insecurity would increase and increase until, in the end, their victims would destroy the whole edifice and, by implication, quite a few of its favored inhabitants.

These—productivity, inequality, and insecurity—were the ancient preoccupations of economics. They were never more its preoccupations than in the nineteen-thirties as the subject stood in a great valley facing, all unknowingly, a mountainous rise in well-being. We have now had that mountainous rise. In very large measure the older preoccupations remain. We should scarcely be surprised. This pre-eminently is an occasion when we would expect the conventional wisdom to lose touch with the reality. It has not disappointed us.

That is not to say that the change has had no effect on conventional attitudes. Especially on equality and insecurity there have been important modifications. To these we now turn.

CHAPTER VII

Inequality

FEW THINGS have been more productive of controversy over the ages than the suggestion that the rich should, by one device or another, share their wealth with those who are not. With comparatively rare and usually eccentric exceptions, the rich have been opposed. The grounds have been many and varied and have been principally noted for the rigorous exclusion of the most important reason, which is the simple unwillingness to give up the enjoyment of what they have. The poor have generally been in favor of greater equality. As the last chapters have shown, the economic and social preoccupation with inequality is deeply grounded. In the competitive society—the society of the central tradition of economics in descent from Ricardo—there was presumed to be a premium on efficiency. The competent entrepreneur and worker were automatically rewarded. The rest, as automatically, were punished for their incompetence or sloth. If labor and capital and land were employed with high efficiency then, *pro tanto*, nothing more, or not much more, could be got out of the economy in the short run by way of product. And longer run progress did not necessarily benefit the average man; in the original doctrine its fruits accrued to others.

So if people were poor, as in fact they were, their only hope lay in a redistribution of income, and especially that which was the product of accumulated wealth. Much though Ricardo and his followers might dissent, there were always some—and the number steadily grew—who believed that redistribution might be possible. (Ricardo and those who followed him in the central tradition were never immune from the suspicion that they were pleading a special interest.) All Marxists took a drastic redistribution for granted. Consequently, throughout the nineteenth century the social radical had no choice but to advocate the redistribution of wealth and income by one device or another. If he wanted to change things this was his only course. To avoid this issue was to avoid all issues.

The conservative defense of inequality has varied. There has always been the underlying contention that, as a matter of natural law and equity, what a man has received save by overt larceny is rightfully his. For Ricardo and his immediate followers the luxurious income of landlords and of capitalists was the inevitable arrangement of things. One could tamper with it but only at the eventual price of disrupting the system and making the lot of everyone (including the poor) much worse.

This was essentially the passive defense. With time (and agitation) the case for inequality became a good deal more functional. The undisturbed enjoyment of income was held to be essential as an incentive. The resulting effort and ingenuity would bring greater production and greater resulting rewards for all. Inequality came to be regarded as almost equally important for capital formation. Were income widely distributed, it would be spent. But if it flowed in a concentrated stream to the rich, a part would certainly be saved and invested.

There were other arguments. Excessive equality makes for cultural uniformity and monotony. Rich men are essential if there is to be an adequate subsidy to education and the arts. Equality smacks of communism and hence of atheism and therefore is spiritually suspect. In any case, even the Russians have abandoned egalitarianism as unworkable. Finally, it is argued that by means of the income tax we have achieved virtual or (depending on the speaker) entirely excessive equality. The trend for the future must be toward restoring an adequate measure of inequality by well-conceived tax reductions affecting the upper surtax brackets.

The cultural misfortunes from excessive equality cannot be pressed too far. As Tawney observed: "Those who dread a dead-level of income or wealth . . . do not dread, it seems, a dead-level of law and order, and of security of life and property. They do not complain that persons endowed by nature with unusual qualities of strength, audacity, or cunning are prevented from reaping the full fruits of these powers."[1] And in fact in the conventional wisdom the defense of

[1] R. H. Tawney, *Equality* (4th ed.; London: Allen & Unwin, 1952), p. 85.

inequality does rest primarily on its functional role as an incentive and a source of capital.

Thus the egalitarianism of the present tax structure is thought to be seriously dampering individual effort, initiative, and inspiration or is in danger of doing so. It "destroys ambition, penalizes success, discourages investment to create new jobs, and may well turn a nation of risk-taking entrepreneurs into a nation of softies. . . ."[2] "It destroys the incentive of people to work. . . . It makes it increasingly difficult, if not impossible, for people to save. . . . It has a deadening effect on the spirit of enterprise . . . which has made America."[3]

However, this case is not an impeccable one. Income taxes have been at present levels for approaching two decades. These in general have been years of rapid economic growth. Those who view the taxes with most concern point to this progress with most pride. Nor would many businessmen wish to concede that they are putting forth less than their best efforts because of insufficient pecuniary incentive. The typical business executive makes his way to the top by promotion over the heads of his fellows. He would endanger his chance for advancement if he were suspected of goldbricking because of his resentment over his taxes or for any other reason. He is expected to give his best to his corporation, and usually he does.

To give individuals large incomes to encourage savings also has elements of illogic. The rich man saves because he is able to satisfy all his wants and then have something over. Such saving, in other words, is the residual after luxurious consumption. This obviously is not an especially efficient way to promote capital formation. Moreover, the empirical evidence on the effect of egalitarianism on capital formation is uncertain. England is often cited as an unfortunate example. But Norway, an even more egalitarian country, has had since the war one of the highest rates of capital formation and of economic growth of any country in the non-communist world.[4] Middle eastern countries where inequality is greatest are among those with the lowest rate of capital formation. All or most gets spent.

[2] "Taxes and America's Future." Address by Fred Maytag II, before National Association of Manufacturers, December 1, 1954.

[3] "The Relation of Taxes to Economic Growth." Address by Ernest L. Swigert, before National Association of Manufacturers, December 6, 1956.

[4] Alice Bourneuf, *Norway: The Planned Revival* (Cambridge, Mass.: Harvard University Press, 1958).

The *formal* liberal attitude toward inequality has changed little over the years. The liberal has partly accepted the view of the well-to-do that it is a trifle uncouth to urge a policy of soaking the rich. Yet on the whole the rich man remains the natural antagonist of the poor. Economic legislation, above all tax policy, continues to be a contest between the interests of the two. No other question in economic policy is ever so important as the effect of a measure on the distribution of income. The test of the good liberal is still that he is never fooled and that he never yields on issues favoring the wealthy. Other questions occupy his active attention, but this is the constant. Behind him, always challenging him, is the cynical Marxian whisper hinting that whatever he does may not be enough. Despite his efforts, capitalist concentration will keep on, and the wealthy will become wealthier and more powerful. They lose battles but win wars.

II

However, few things are more evident in modern social history than the decline of interest in inequality as an economic issue. This has been particularly true in the United States. And it would appear, among western countries, to be the least true of the United Kingdom. While it continues to have a large ritualistic role in the conventional wisdom of conservatives and liberals, inequality has ceased to preoccupy men's minds. And even the conventional wisdom has made some concessions to this new state of affairs.

On the fact itself—that inequality is of declining concern —it is only necessary to observe that for some fifteen years no serious effort has been made to alter the present distribution of income. Although in the semantics of American liberalism there is often a tactful silence on the point, since nothing so stirs conservative wrath, the principal public device for redistributing income is the progressive income tax. Not since World War II has there been a major effort to modify this tax in the interest of greater equality. Loopholes have been opened and a few closed. Liberals have not, however, proposed any important new steps to make the tax more progressive and hence more egalitarian. And conservatives, while they have won numerous secondary victories, have not been able to mount any major attack on the tax itself. On the contrary, although roughly the present nominal surtax rates were put into effect during the war, with the presumption that they were a temporary measure for insuring equality of wartime sacrifice, they are now regarded by many and perhaps by most people as permanent.

As part of the present compromise, liberals do not seek to make current taxes more progressive or even passionately to eliminate existing inequities and loopholes in their application. They would, however, rally in opposition to any general reduction in rates on the higher income brackets. Those who believe the tax has gone too far in enforcing equality are more vocal. Appeals for public sympathy and support, and clarion calls for courage and action, come regularly from the well-to-do. "The hour is late, but not too late. There is no excuse for our hesitating any longer. With all the strength of equity and logic on our side, and with the urgent need for taking the tax shackles off economic progress, initiative is ours if we have the courage to take it."[5] But not even a conservative administration such as that of President Eisenhower thought it wise to tackle the question of surtax reduction on a wide front.

Apart from the income tax almost no legislation has been enacted or even discussed in recent years which has as its main point the reduction of inequality. Fifty years ago, at the height of the debate over socialism and capitalism, it would have been hard to imagine there was any other issue.

The decline in concern for inequality cannot be explained by the triumph of equality. Although this is regularly suggested in the conventional wisdom of conservatives, and could readily be inferred from the complaints of businessmen, inequality is still great. In 1955 the one-tenth of families and unattached individuals with the lowest incomes received after taxes about one per cent of the total money income of the country; the tenth with the highest incomes received 27 per cent of the total, which is to say their incomes averaged 27 times as much as the lowest tenth. The half of the households with the lowest incomes received, after taxes, only 23 per cent of all money income. The half with the highest incomes received 77 per cent. In 1954 only about three per cent of all families had incomes before taxes of more than $15,000. They received, nonetheless, 15.5 per cent of total income. At the other extreme, 16.7 per cent had before tax incomes of less than two thousand and received only 3.6 per cent of the

---

[5] Maytag, "Taxes and America's Future."

income.[6] Vast fortunes are still being made out of natural resources and especially out of oil—where the famous depletion allowance of 27½ per cent effectively frees that proportion of oil income, and sometimes much more, from all taxation. Present laws are also notably favorable to the person who has wealth as opposed to the individual who is only earning it. With a little ingenuity, the man who is already rich can ordinarily take his income in the form of capital gains and limit his tax liability to 25 per cent of his income. In addition, unlike the man who must earn, he is under no compulsion to acquire a capital stake, either for old age, family, or the mere satisfaction it brings, since he already has one. Accordingly he need not save. Yet none of these matters arouses the kind of concern which leads to agitation and action.

III

The first reason inequality has faded as an issue is, without much question, that it has not been showing the expected tendency to get worse. And thus the Marxian prediction, which earlier in this century seemed so amply confirmed by observation, no longer inspires the same depth of fear. It no longer seems likely that the ownership of the tangible assets of the republic and the disposal of its income will pass into a negligible number of hands despite the approving sentiment of those who would abandon the progressive income tax or widen its present loopholes. Meanwhile, there has been a modest reduction in the proportion of disposable income going to those in the very highest income brackets and a very large increase in the proportion accruing to people in the middle and lower brackets. While taxes have restrained the concentration of income at the top, full employment and upward pressure on wages have increased well-being at the bottom. In 1928 disposable income, i.e., income after taxes, of the 1 per cent of the individuals with the highest income was estimated to account for 19 per cent of all income. By 1946 it accounted for a little less than 8 per cent. In 1928 the 5 per cent with the highest incomes received over a third of

[6] U. S. Department of Commerce. *Statistical Abstract of the United States,* 1957, p. 309. The after-tax percentage distributions are from *Board of Governors of the Federal Reserve System* and are based on the surveys of consumer finances. The before-tax data are estimates by the Department of Commerce.

all income; by 1946 their share was about 18 per cent.[7]
The war and postwar years, especially, were a time of rapid
improvement for those in the lower bracket. Between 1941
and 1950 the lowest fifth had a 42 per cent increase in
income; the second lowest fifth had an increase of 37 per cent.
The detailed figures for these years are as follows:

AVERAGE FAMILY INCOME AFTER INCOME TAXES

(In dollars of 1950 purchasing power)[8]

	1941	1950	Per cent change 1941–1950
Lowest fifth of all families	$ 750	$ 1,060	+42
Second lowest	1,730	2,360	+37
Third lowest	2,790	3,440	+24
Second highest	4,030	4,690	+16
Highest	8,190	8,880	+ 8
Highest 5 per cent	15,040	14,740	− 2

Emulation or, when this is frustrated, envy have long
played a large role in the economist's view of human motivation.[9] So long as one individual had more than another, the
second was presumed to be dissatisfied with his lot. He strove
to come abreast of his more favored contemporary; he was
deeply discontented if he failed. It may be, however, that
these disenchanting traits are less cosmic than has commonly
been supposed. Envy almost certainly operates efficiently
only as regards nearby neighbors. It is not directed toward
the distant rich. Hence, at a time when the individual's real
income is rising, the fact that unknown New Yorkers or
Texans are exceedingly wealthy is not, probably, a matter of
prime urgency. It becomes easy, or at least convenient, to
accept the case of the conventional wisdom which is that
the rich in America are highly functional and also much-
persecuted members of the society. Moreover, as noted, to
comment on the wealth of the wealthy, and certainly to
propose that it be reduced, has come to be considered bad
taste. The individual whose own income is going up has no
real reason to incur the opprobrium of this discussion. Why
should he identify himself, even remotely, with soapbox

[7] The data are from National Bureau of Economic Research. Note
that these figures are not for households but for individuals.

[8] From Selma Goldsmith, George Jaszi, Hyman Kaitz, and Maurice
Liebenberg, "Size Distribution of Incomes since the Mid-thirties."
Review of Economics and Statistics, vol. XXXVI (February 1954).

[9] Chapter XI.

orators, malcontents, agitators, Communists, and other un-
desirables?

Things would be different were the incomes of the well-
to-do rising and those of the rest of the people stationary or
falling. This has been well illustrated by the reactions of the
farmers who, though in many cases not badly off by past
standards, during the middle fifties suffered a reduction of
their income at a time when the incomes of nearly all other
groups were rising. They were not reconciled either to
their fate or to a Secretary of Agriculture who sought its
acceptance.

IV

Another reason for the decline in interest in inequality, almost
certainly, is the drastically altered political and social position
of the rich in recent times. Broadly speaking, there are three
basic benefits from wealth. First is the satisfaction in the
power with which it endows the individual. Second is the
physical possession of the things which money can buy. Third
is the distinction or esteem that accrues to the rich man as
the result of his wealth. All of these returns to wealth have
been greatly circumscribed in the last fifty years and in a
manner which also vastly reduces the envy or resentment of
the well-to-do or even the knowledge of their existence.

As recently as a half century ago the power of the great
business firm was paramount in the United States and so,
accordingly, was the power of the individual who headed it.
Men like Morgan, the Rockefeller executives, Hill, Harriman,
and Hearst had great power in the meaningful sense of the
term, which is that they were able to direct the actions and
command the obedience of countless other individuals.

In the last half century the power and prestige of the
United States government have increased. If only by the
process of division, this has diminished the prestige of the
power accruing to private wealth. But, in addition, it has also
meant some surrender of authority to Washington. Furthermore, trade unions have invaded the power of the entrepreneur
from another quarter. But most important, the professional
manager or executive has taken away from the man of wealth
the power that is implicit in running a business. Fifty years
ago, Morgan, Rockefeller, Hill, Harriman, and the others
were the undisputed masters of the business concerns they
owned, or it was indisputably in their power to become so.

Their sons and grandsons still have the wealth, but with rare exceptions the power implicit in the running of the firm has passed to professionals. Nor has any equivalent new generation of owning entrepreneurs come along.

When the rich were not only rich but had the power that went with active direction of corporate enterprise, it is obvious that wealth had more perquisites than now. For the same reasons it stirred more antagonism. J. P. Morgan answered not only for his personal wealth but also for the behavior of the United States Steel Corporation which he had put together and which he ultimately controlled. As a man of corporate power he was also exceedingly visible. Today shares of the United States Steel Corporation are still the foundation of several notable fortunes. But no sins of the Corporation are visited on these individuals, for they do not manage the company and almost no one knows who they are. When the power that went with active business direction was lost, so was the hostility.

The power that was once joined with wealth has been impaired in a more intimate way. In 1194 the crusading knight, Henry of Champagne, paid a visit to the headquarters of the Assassins at the castle at al-Kahf on a rugged peak in the Nosairi Mountains. The Assassins, though a fanatical Moslem sect, had, in general, been on good terms with the Christians, to whom they often rendered, by arrangement, the useful service of resolving disputes by eliminating one of the disputants. Henry was sumptuously received. In one of the more impressive entertainments a succession of the loyal members of the cult, at a word from the Sheik, expertly immolated themselves. Before and ever since, the willing obedience of a household coterie has been a source of similar satisfaction to those able to command it. Wealth has been the most prominent device by which it has been obtained. As may indeed have been the case at al-Kahf, it has not always endeared the master to the men who rendered it.

In any case, such service requires a reservoir of adequately obedient or servile individuals. The drying up of this reservoir, no less than the loss of wealth itself, can rob wealth of its prerogatives. The increase in the security and incomes of Americans at the lower income levels has effectively reduced—indeed, for many purposes, eliminated—the servile class. And again the reciprocal is that those who no longer work for the rich (or who have done so or who fear that they might be forced to do so) no longer feel the resentment which such dependence has induced.

V

The enjoyment of physical possession of things would seem
to be one of the prerogatives of wealth which has been little
impaired. Presumably nothing has happened to keep the
man who can afford them from enjoying his Rembrandts and
his home-grown orchids. But enjoyment of things has always
been intimately associated with the third prerogative of
wealth which is the distinction that it confers. In a world
where nearly everyone was poor, this distinction was very
great. It was the natural consequence of rarity. In England,
it is widely agreed, the ducal families are not uniformly
superior. There is a roughly normal incidence of intelligence
and stupidity, good taste and bad, and morality, immorality,
homosexuality, and incest. But very few people are dukes or
even duchesses, although the latter have become rather more
frequent with the modern easing of the divorce laws. As a
result, even though they may be intrinsically unexceptional,
they are regarded with some awe. So it has long been with
the rich. Were dukes numerous, their position would deteri-
orate. As the rich have become more numerous, they have
inevitably become a debased currency.

Moreover, wealth has never been a sufficient source of
honor in itself. It must be advertised, and the normal medium
is obtrusively expensive goods. In the latter part of the last
century in the United States this advertisement was con-
ducted with virtuosity. Housing, equipage, female adorn-
ment, and recreation were all brought to its service. Expensive-
ness was keenly emphasized. "We are told now that Mr.
Gould's '$500,000 yacht' has entered a certain harbor, or
that Mr. Morgan has set off on a journey in his '$100,000
palace car,' or that Mr. Vanderbilt's '$2,000,000 home' is
nearing completion, with its '$50,000 paintings' and its
'$20,000 bronze doors.' "[10] The great houses, the great yachts,
the great balls, the stables, and the expensive jewel-encrusted
bosoms were all used to identify the individual as having a
claim to the honors of wealth.

Such display is now passé. There was an adventitious contributing cause. The American well-to-do have long been
curiously sensitive to fear of expropriation—a fear which

[10] Matthew Josephson, *The Robber Barons* (New York: Harcourt,
Brace & Co., 1934), p. 330. Josephson is paraphrasing W. A. Croffut,
Commodore Vanderbilt's biographer, writing in 1885.

may be related to the tendency for even the mildest reformist measures to be viewed, in the conservative conventional wisdom, as the portents of revolution. The depression and especially the New Deal gave the American rich a serious fright. One consequence was to usher in a period of marked discretion in personal expenditure. Purely ostentatious outlays, especially on dwellings, yachts, and females, were believed likely to incite the masses to violence. They were rebuked as unwise and improper by the more discreet. It was much wiser to take on the protective coloration of the useful citizen, the industrial statesman, or even the average guy.[11]

However, deeper causes were at work. Increasingly in the last quarter century the display of expensive goods, as a device for suggesting wealth, has been condemned as vulgar. The term is precise. Vulgar means: "Of or pertaining to the common people, or to the common herd or crowd." And this explains what happened. Lush expenditure could be afforded by so many that it ceased to be useful as a mark of distinction. A magnificent, richly upholstered, and extremely high-powered automobile conveys no impression of wealth in a day when such automobiles are mass-produced by the thousands. A house in Palm Beach is not a source of distinction when the rates for a thousand hotel rooms in Miami Beach rival its daily upkeep. Once a sufficiently impressive display of diamonds could create attention even for the most obese and repellent body, for they signified membership in a highly privileged caste. Now the same diamonds are afforded by a television star or a talented harlot. Modern mass communications, especially the movies and television, insure that the populace at large will see the most lavish caparisoning on the bodies not of the daughters of the rich but on the daughters of coal miners and commercial travelers, who struck it rich by their own talents or some facsimile thereof. In South America, in the Middle East, to a degree in socialist India, and at Nice, Cannes, and Deauville, ostentatious display by the rich is still much practiced. This accords with expectations. In these countries most people are still, in the main, poor and unable to afford the goods which advertise wealth. Therefore ostentation continues to have a purpose. In not

[11] Cf. C. Wright Mills, *The Power Elite* (New York: Oxford University Press, 1956), p. 117. Mr. Mills suggests that in the depression years this effort to provide protective coloration led to the recruiting of technicians and corporate managers as front men behind which the well-to-do could survive in peace. Not uncharacteristically, I think, Mr. Mills reads too much design and contrivance into such change.

being accessible to too many people it has not yet become vulgar.

The American of wealth is not wholly without advantages in his search for distinction. Wealth still brings attention if devoted to cultural and technical pursuits or to hobbies with a utilitarian aspect. A well-to-do American may gain in esteem from an admirably run farm, although never from an admirably manicured estate. He will be honored for magnificent and imaginative cow stables, although not for luxurious horse stables. Although wealth aids a public career those who too patently rely on it are regarded as slightly inferior public citizens. A Harriman or a Lehman who is elected to public office enjoys a prestige far in excess of an Aldrich or a Whitney whose appointment to an ambassadorial position, however justified on merit, might have been less certain in the absence of sizable campaign contributions. In sum, although ostentatious and elaborate expenditure, in conjunction with the wealth that sustained it, was once an assured source of distinction, it is so no longer. The effect on attitudes toward inequality will be evident. Ostentatious expenditure focused the attention of the poor on the wealth of the wealthy, for this of course was its purpose. With the decline of ostentation, or its vulgarization, wealth and hence inequality were no longer flagrantly advertised. Being less advertised they were less noticed and less resented. The rich had helped to make inequality an issue. Now they were no longer impelled to do so.

There were similar consequences from the fact that the rich man now had to compete for esteem. Once the intellectual, politician, or man of general ambition saw the rich man achieve distinction without effort and in contrast with his own struggle. He reacted by helping to focus the resentment of the community as a whole. Now he saw the man of wealth forced to compete for his honors. In this competition the rich man retained undoubted advantages, but he did not automatically excel. Nothing could operate more effectively to dry up the supply of individuals who otherwise would make an attack on inequality a career. By graduating into the ranks of the professional managers, and after making his way up through the hierarchy of the modern corporation, the ambitious man could expect to compete on tolerably equal terms with the grandson of the founder.

It would be idle to suggest that the man of wealth has no special advantages in our society. Such propositions are the one-day wonders of the conventional wisdom, and those who offer them have a brief but breath-taking reputation as social prophets. This itself suggests that such findings assuage some sense of guilt. But it does seem clear that prestige and power are now far more intimately identified with those who, regardless of personal wealth, administer productive activity. The high corporate official is inevitably a man of consequence. The rich man can be quite inconsequential and often is.

VI

In the Ricardian world, as noted, progress required profits, and its fruits accrued to the landlords. Economic advance—expanding output—did not ordinarily help the common man. His only hope lay in reforms that Ricardo and his followers would have considered highly destructive or, alternatively, in a drastic overthrow of the system. Economic advance still holds little promise of betterment for the average man in many if not most countries. On Andean haciendas, in the Arab lands, and in India and China at least until recent times it mattered little to the man who tilled the land whether the product increased. His own share was minute; an increase in product is not important if all but a minute fraction goes to someone else. And matters may be worse: any surplus over the barest need may be absorbed, as the result of an *ad hoc* revision of the rules, by the landlord, merchant, or moneylender. This is still the Ricardian world, and in it the obvious hope for improvement lies in a different distribution of income. For the same reason, until the share of the ordinary man in the product is increased, his incentive to increase production—to adopt better methods of cultivation, for example—is slight or nil. The people of the so-called backward countries have frequently heard from their presumptively more advanced mentors in the economically more advanced lands that they should be patient about social reform, with all its disturbing and even revolutionary implications, and concentrate on increasing production. It can be remarkably inappropriate advice. Reform is not something that can be made to wait on productive advance. It may be a prerequisite to such advance.

In the advanced country, in contrast, increased production is an alternative to redistribution. And, as indicated, it has been the great solvent of the tensions associated with inequality. Even though the latter persists, the awkward conflict which its correction implies can be avoided. How much better to concentrate on increasing output, a program on which both rich and poor can agree, since it benefits both.

That among those who might be subject to redistribution this doctrine has something approaching the standing of divine revelation is perhaps not entirely surprising. For many years the relationship of businessmen to economists in the United States has been characterized by a degree of waspishness. The economist has shown a predisposition to favor low tariffs, the income tax, the antitrust laws, and quite frequently trade unions. This has made him, at the minimum, an inconvenient friend. But increased output as a substitute for greater equality has lately become the basis for a notable *rapprochement*. "From a dollars-and-cents point of view it is quite obvious that over a period of years, even those who find themselves at the short end of inequality have more to gain from faster growth than from any conceivable income redistribution."[12]

Some have reacted with slightly more suspicion. Over the centuries those who have been blessed with wealth have developed many remarkably ingenious and persuasive justifications of their good fortune. The instinct of the liberal is to look at these explanations with a rather unyielding eye. Yet in this case the facts are inescapable. It is the increase in output in recent decades, not the redistribution of income, which has brought the great material increase, the well-being of the average man.[13] And, however suspiciously, the liberal has come to accept the fact. As a result, the goal of an expanding economy has also become deeply imbedded in the conventional wisdom of the American left. The beneficent effects of such an economy, moreover, are held to be comprehensive. Not only will there be material improvement for the average man, but there will be an end to poverty and priva-

[12] "Learning to Multiply and to Divide." Address by Roger M. Blough, Chairman of the Board of the United States Steel Corporation, quoting Professor Henry C. Wallich of Yale University, January 15, 1957.

[13] In the decade 1900-1909 employed workers as a class received an estimated 55 per cent of all income. By the decade of 1930-39 it had increased to 67 per cent since which time it has evidently been more or less stable. A 67 instead of a 55 per cent share of the total income paid out in the first decade would not have meant a very great increase. On the other hand a 55 per cent share of present income would still be a huge advance over what workers received in the first decade. Calculations are from Gale Johnson, "The Functional Distribution of Income in the United States, 1850-1952," *Review of Economics and Statistics*, vol. XXXVI (May 1954). The estimates are rough.

tion for all. This latter, in fact, is suspect. Increasing aggregate output leaves a self-perpetuating margin of poverty at the very base of the income pyramid. This goes largely unnoticed, because it is the fate of a voiceless minority. And liberals have long been accustomed to expect the poor to speak in the resounding tones of a vast majority. To these matters it will be necessary to return.

For the moment we need only notice that, as an economic and social concern, inequality has been declining in urgency, and this has had its reflection in the conventional wisdom. The decline has been for a variety of reasons, but in one way or another these are all related to the fact of increasing production. Production has eliminated the more acute tensions associated with inequality. And it has become evident to conservatives and liberals alike that increasing aggregate output is an alternative to redistribution or even to the reduction of inequality. The oldest and most agitated of social issues, if not resolved, is at least largely in abeyance, and the disputants have concentrated their attention, instead, on the goal of increased productivity. This is a change of far-reaching importance. Our increased concern for production in modern times would be remarkable in itself. But it has also preempted the field once occupied by those who disputed over who should have less and who should have more.

CHAPTER VIII

Economic Security

FEW MATTERS having to do with economic life have been so much misunderstood as the problem of economic security. And in remarkable degree the misunderstanding persists.

In the model of the competitive society such insecurity was inherent. The individual producer or worker might, at any time, suffer a sudden decline in his fortunes. This could be the result of laziness or incompetence which would lose him his customers or his job. But the best of men might suffer from a sudden change in consumer tastes or as the result, not of their own inadequacy but of that of their employer. These unpredictable changes in fortune were both inevitable and useful. They were inevitable, for they were part of the capacity of the system to accommodate itself to change. As requirements and wishes changed, men were employed in new places and disemployed in the old. Capital was sought in the new industries and written off as a loss in the old. The insecurity was useful, for it drove men—businessmen, workers, the self-employed—to render their best and most efficient service, for severe punishment was visited impersonally on those who did not.

However, this insecurity, valuable though it seemed in principle, was cherished almost exclusively either in the second person or in the abstract. Its need was thought urgent for inspiring the efforts of other persons or people in general. It seldom seemed vital for the individual himself. Restraints on competition and the free movement of prices, the principal source of uncertainty to business firms, have been principally deplored by university professors on lifetime appointments. Such security of tenure is deemed essential for fruitful and unremitting thought. The preoccupation of workers with unemployment insurance or old-age pensions has usually seemed most supine and degenerate to business executives who would be unattracted by companies in which they were subject to arbitrary discharge or which lacked adequate pension arrangements. Farmers have been regularly reproached for their lack of fealty to the free price system by entrepreneurs whose own prices have not been changed for some years.

In the conventional wisdom of conservatives, the modern search for security is regularly billed as the greatest single threat to economic progress. These fears have been strongest at a time when great advances in social security were coinciding with great economic progress. Among liberals the prospect for finding new forms of social protection with wide appeal to the masses remains the highest hope both for social progress and for political preferment. When liberals in the United States deplore, as they regularly do, their lack of new ideas, they have reference, almost invariably, to the lack of new and politically attractive forms of social security. This is disconcerting to conservatives who also suppose that an endless number of new ideas for protecting the individual from economic misfortune are lurking just around the corner. Yet in fact there have been few really new proposals for many years.

II

The first step in penetrating this bedlam is to recognize that while risk was indeed inherent in the economic society of the central tradition, it has long been regarded with equanimity by almost no one. And all who were subject to insecurity sooner or later set about eliminating it as it affected themselves. In large measure they were successful. The devices by which they did so have varied much. This has led those who were using one device to see it as a necessary precaution while they deplored the iniquitous measures devised by others. And, as will by now be scarcely surprising, while insecurity was eliminated in the real world, it survived more or less intact in the ideological underpinning of the conventional wisdom and continued therein to play its all but indispensable role.

The elimination of economic insecurity was pioneered by the business firm in respect of its own operations. The greatest source of insecurity, as noted, lay in competition and the free and unpredictable movement of competitive market prices. From the very beginning of modern capitalist society, businessmen have addressed themselves to the elimination or the mitigation of this source of insecurity. Monopoly or the full control of supply, and hence of price, by a single firm was the ultimate security. But there were many very habitable halfway houses. Price and production agreements or cartels, price-fixing by law, restrictions on entry of new firms, protection by tariffs or quotas, and many other devices have all had the effect of mitigating the insecurity inherent in the competitive economy. Most important, where the number of firms is small, a characteristic feature of the modern industry, interdependence is recognized and respected, and firms stoutly avoid price behavior which would enhance uncertainty for all.

These efforts have been long and widely remarked. However, the tendency of these measures to focus directly or indirectly on price, which, as stated, is the greatest source of uncertainty, has led economists to regard the management of prices as being of unique importance. And they have far more frequently related such management to the maximization of profits than to the minimization of risks. The specter that has haunted the economist has been the monopoly seeking extortionate gains at the public expense. This has dominated his thoughts. The less dramatic figure, the businessman seeking protection from the vicissitudes of the competitive economy, has been much less in his mind. That is unfortunate, for the development of the modern business enterprise can be understood only as a comprehensive effort to reduce risk. It is not going too far to say that it can be understood in no other terms.

Specifically, it falls within the power of the modern large corporation to mitigate or eliminate (with one exception) every important risk to which business enterprises have anciently been subject. Consumer taste and demand may shift. The modern large corporation protects itself by its advertising. Consumer taste is thereby brought at least partly under its control. Size makes possible a diversified line. This provides further protection. There is danger that technological change will render obsolete a product or method of production. The modern corporation is able, through its research and technological resources, to insure that it will be abreast of such change. Therefore technological change will occur under its own auspices or within its reach. A measure of control over prices means a measure of control over earnings. This means at least partial independence of the capital market for funds. Size, moreover, greatly diversifies the opportunities of the firm in raising money. In the large organization even the risks associated with the selection of leadership are reduced. Organization replaces individual authority; no individual is powerful enough to do much damage. Were it otherwise, the stock market would pay close attention to retirements, deaths, and replacements in the executive ranks of the large corporations. In fact, it ignores such details in tacit recognition that the organization is independent of any individual.[1]

The massive reduction in risk that is inherent in the development of the modern corporation has been far from fully appreciated. This is partly because the corporation, unlike the worker, farmer, or other individual citizen, has been able to reduce its insecurity without overtly seeking the assistance of government. It has required elaborate organization, but this has been the product of continuous evolution from the original entrepreneurial enterprise. Farmers, workers, and other citizens, by contrast, have had to seek the assistance of government or (as in the case of the unions) they have had to organize specially for the purpose of reducing insecurity. Consequently their search for greater security has been notorious. By contrast the corporate executive, whose concern pioneered the escape from insecurity, has been able to suppose that security is something with which only workers or farmers are preoccupied.

Myth has also played a part in concealing the effort of the modern corporation to minimize insecurity. There is a remarkable conviction, even on the part of the executives of the largest business corporations, that they live dangerously. As this is written, no large United States corporation, which is also large in its industry, has failed or been seriously in danger of insolvency in many years. The security of tenure of corporation executives is remarkably high. So is their remuneration. Certainly these bear no resemblance to the insecurity of the fortunes of the business entrepreneur of the competitive model. Individual decisions of corporate management may still turn out to have been wrong. But in the large, diversified corporation—in contrast with the small and more specialized firm—such decisions are rarely fatal.

The riskiness of modern corporate life is in fact the harmless conceit of the modern corporate executive, and it is vigorously proclaimed. Precisely because he lives an orderly and careful life the executive is moved to identify himself

---

[1] These are matters which I hope to treat in much greater detail in a forthcoming book on the corporation and the corporate personality.

with the dashing entrepreneur of economic literature. For much the same reason, the commander of an armored division, traveling in a trailer and concerning himself with gasoline supplies, sees himself as leading an old-time cavalry charge. Nothing has been more central to the purpose of General Motors or General Electric than to encompass and eliminate the perils to which the one-time entrepreneur was presumed to be subject. Nothing would be more damaging to an executive reputation in General Motors or General Electric than to launch a product without testing the market, to be caught napping by a technological development, to be unprotected on one's raw material supply or to be caught in a foolish price war. These were once the commonplace risks of entrepreneurship.

But the large corporation has been only the leader in the retreat from risk. Nearly everyone else has participated to the best of his ability and ingenuity, and in the thirties there was an especially widespread effort to mitigate the economic perils of the average man. The federal government intervened for the first time with relief and welfare funds to protect the individual from economic misfortune. This was followed by social security—unemployment insurance and old-age and survivors' pensions. Farmers, through public payments and support prices, were protected from some of the insecurity associated with competitive market prices. The unions developed rapidly during this decade. Along with their redress of bargaining power, they provided the worker with protection against capricious or adventitious firing or demotion and thus increased his security in his job. Even the smaller businessman, through the Robinson-Patman Act, the Fair Trade laws, legislation against below-cost selling, and through trade associations, won a measure of security from the uncertainties of market competition for which he shared the universal distaste.

The foregoing measures were microeconomic. They protected the individual, firm, or group from the specific adversities to which it was subject. But the effective mitigation of insecurity required another and parallel effort of a far more general sort. The position of the worker who is protected against arbitrary firing by a sound seniority system is far from ideal if he receives an entirely nondiscriminatory discharge as the result of an insufficiency of demand for the product he is making. This is especially so if a general shortage of demand keeps him from finding a job elsewhere. While unemployment compensation is better than nothing, a job is better than either. Even with an effective enforcement of the laws preventing price discrimination—roughly the use by a large firm of its size to exact and offer prices which small competitors cannot obtain or quote—the competitive position of the small retailer in a time of depression is not happy. Regardless of the conditions of competition, it is much better when the demand for everyone's product is good. Farm support prices are a useful protection against sudden adverse price movements. But a demand for farm products that holds such prices reliably above support levels will be preferred by every rational farmer.

At a time, as during the thirties, when there was great interest in the microeconomic measures to increase security, it would have been surprising indeed had there been no macroeconomic effort with its greater efficiency to the same end. The two efforts would be in the highest degree complementary. In fact, the reduction of insecurity by macroeconomic measures was central in the economic policy of the time. Efforts to eliminate or mitigate the business cycle and to stabilize the economy at a level where the labor force would be more or less fully employed were a principal goal of public policy. Then, as since, economic stabilization was regarded as an end in itself, but it will now be clear that it was only one part of the broad effort to escape the insecurity which was assumed to be inherent in economic life. The change in attitudes on macroeconomic security during the thirties was remarkable. At the beginning of the decade it was almost uniformly assumed that cyclical fluctuations with accompanying price and employment uncertainties were inevitable. It was hoped by many that they would not be violent. But there was no general confidence that depressions could be tempered by government action without the risk either of eliminating the self-corrective features of the cycle or simply making things worse. By the end of the decade, under the combined influence of Keynes and the sanguine and experimental mood generated by the New Deal, there was a widespread belief that depressions could be at least partially prevented. The notion that they must be allowed to run their course was virtually extinct.

III

These measures to enhance security in the thirties, the microeconomic and the macroeconomic together, were numerous and massive in their effect, and they were concentrated in the brief span of a few years. (While it is convenient to speak of a decade, most of the drive for increased economic security occurred in the five years from 1933 to 1938.) Conservatives and liberals alike looked at the measures, and at the mass approval they evoked, and concluded that something new and different had been added in economic motivation. Conservatives struggling, however unconsciously, to reconcile this drive for security with the inherent and seemingly indispensable insecurity of the competitive society were profoundly alarmed. For perhaps the first time in history they worried not about the turbulent ambitions of the masses but about their yearning for peace and contentment. Liberals, observing the political magic in this desire for security, accepted it and rationalized it. Modern industrial life, they concluded, was a thing of exceptional hazard; the worker lived in constant danger of being torn to pieces by the increasingly complex social machine which he served. Given this image, it was possible to argue that he needed much more elaborate protection than in the simpler economic society assumed by earlier economists. These economists could not have foreseen the risks of advanced industrial capitalism. With further advance ever more protection would be required.

We are now able to see the matter in a clearer light. In the thirties the average man was simply showing the commonplace reaction to the insecurity of the competitive system. In doing so he was following a path that had been pioneered by the modern business firm. He was showing, as ever, that insecurity is something that is cherished only for others.

It was inevitable that farmers and workers in general would be the last to concern themselves with security. Before a man will try to protect himself from sudden changes in his economic fortune, he must have some fortune to protect. Businessmen were first to develop a stake in economic society. They were first, as a result, to become concerned with means, explicit or unrecognized, for safeguarding that stake. In the grim world of Ricardo and Malthus the ordinary citizen could have no interest in social security in the modern sense. If a man's wage is barely sufficient for existence, he does not worry much about the greater suffering of unemployment. Life is a heavy burden in either case. Men who are engaged in a daily struggle for survival do not think of old age, for they do not expect to see it. When the normal expectation of life is very low, sickness and death are normal hazards. A man of eighty does not take out life insurance.

He reconciles himself as best he can to the prospect of death. To the landless worker in an Indian village, one of the world's most unfortunate individuals, unemployment is not even a misfortune. It is his normal fortune.

With increasing well-being all people become aware, sooner or later, that they have something to protect. In the very early stages of the evolution of a business concern, the entrepreneur is not much concerned with security. He has little equity to conserve. Only later do he or his descendants begin to talk about their responsibilities to their stockholders. Henry Ford could gamble on the untested idea of producing in a single model the cheapest possible car for the people. It was a breath-taking step. His colleagues discouraged him, but he had nothing much to lose. His grandsons would indeed be derelict were they similarly to risk the present assets of the Ford Motor Company. No criticism attaches to the effort of the modern corporation to minimize risk. It would be delinquent in its responsibilities if it failed to do so. It would be gambling where it could be sure.

The development in the labor market is similar. As the real wage of the worker increases and also as employment becomes more certain, unemployment and the absence of income acquires its contrasting horror. With increasing income it also becomes possible to think of old age: the individual expects to survive, and old age without income is differentiated, as it was not before, by the prospect of discomfort. And as health and physical hazard decline, men come to think of them as abnormal rather than normal afflictions. It is not the poor but the well-to-do farmers who find onerous the uncertainties of the market. In the mountain country of Kentucky and Tennessee a depression is not a grievous hazard. Farmers have little to sell; their property has small value. They are therefore little affected by declining prices and not much concerned about declining property values. In the well-to-do regions things are different. In the nineteen-thirties it was the comparatively rich farmers of Iowa who threatened the judges who presided over foreclosure proceedings. From these farms came the demands for farm relief. Unlike those of the Appalachian plateau, these farmers had something to lose.

Thus the notion, so sanctified by the conventional wisdom, that the modern concern for security is the reaction to the peculiar hazards of modern economic life could scarcely be more in error. Rather it is the result of improving fortune— of moving from a world where people had little to one where they had much more to protect. In the first world misfortune and suffering were endemic and unavoidable. In the second they have become episodic and avoidable. And as they became episodic and avoidable, reasonable men saw the merit of measures to avoid them and the possibilities for so doing.

Increased economic well-being was not the sole cause of the increased interest in economic security. Allowances must be made for differences in national temperament and political development. These may well explain why a comprehensive system of social insurance first appeared in Imperial Germany and why, in the non-Communist lands, it has had its greatest development in Scandinavia and the United Kingdom. The Great Depression which struck with especial severity in the United States and Canada greatly quickened the interest in economic security in these countries.

The Great Depression has, in fact, often been cited as evidence of the growing insecurity of modern industrial life. There was, it is said, no comparable hazard before the Industrial Revolution. This, it will now be clear, is a superficial view. The Great Depression was severe partly because there was so much wealth and income to lose. The hazard was greatest in the United States and Canada where the per capita wealth was greatest. And the depression stimulated concern for economic security in precisely the same way that a conflagration stimulates an interest in fire insurance and a flood in flood control. These also have an effect on individuals which is roughly proportionate to the amount of their property that lies in the path of the flames or the water.

IV

Men of property—the Forsytes of the world—have always known that it is as important to safeguard their wealth as to increase it. But they have never equated the two. Property can be increased without limit; the efforts to safeguard it are subject to sharply diminishing returns. Having insured against fire, theft, and high winds, a man has removed the major hazards to his possessions. Protection against earthquakes and falling airplanes may also be worth while, but it is not of equal urgency and it does not bring an equivalent increase in peace of mind.

The problem of economic security is much the same. There are more serious hazards and less serious ones; as the more serious are covered there will be a declining sense of urgency about the less serious ones and indeed, also, about the entire problem of economic security. For the worker, in the past, the greatest hazard was the loss of his job and income. Thereafter, the uncertainties of old age, sickness, accident, and death may well have ranked next in importance. As and when these risks were mitigated, although others remained, none was of comparable importance. For the farmer protection against a severe decline in his prices was (and remains) of paramount urgency. Such decline threatens both his income and his assets. After that, depending on the region, come the dangers of drought and crop failure. There are no other hazards of similar importance. For the businessman the situation is much the same. The overwhelming uncertainty concerns product prices and markets. This accounts for the attention it has received from economists, indeed why, in the theory of market behavior, efforts to remove this dimension of risk have been regarded as more or less unique and also, not infrequently, as uniquely reprehensible. There are further hazards—those of cost movements, raw material supplies, labor relations—which it is desirable to eliminate, but their potential for damage is less devastating. Other sources of uncertainty are of still less importance.

The meaning of this is that elimination of insecurity in economic life can be a finished business. Nothing is more completely accepted in the conventional wisdom than the cliché that economic life is endlessly and inherently uncertain. In fact, the major uncertainties of pristine economic life (subject to a major qualification concerning the control of depressions) have already been eliminated. The ones that remain are of much reduced urgency.

The corollary is that parties and governments cannot, as the conventional wisdom so devoutly assumes, go on "inventing" new kinds of security. This would be possible were it merely a matter of invention or were the hazards of modern economic life increasing. But the hazards are finite in number; they increase only in the sense that people have more to lose. This is not to say that no economic insecurity remains. For the average individual in the United States sickness—which may mean large expenditures at a time when there is no income—is a considerable hazard. Smaller business and agriculture are still economically insecure vocations. Nonetheless, subject always to the major qualification that depressions are to be prevented, the preoccupation with economic security is largely in the past. No hazards remain that are comparable in importance with those that have been covered. And protection once achieved is quickly taken for granted. It ceases to be a matter for discussion or even of thought. Henceforth, in pursuing the goal of greater economic security, we will be completing and perfecting a structure that in all its major features now exists.

One cannot stress too strongly, however, that if economic security is to be considered finished business, or largely finished business, depressions, or even any serious failure to provide full employment must be prevented. A depression could always break down the micromeasures that have so laboriously been erected by (or for) businessmen, workers, farmers, and other citizens for their protection. Business arrangements for modifying and controlling competition in the interests of market stability then turn into cutthroat competition. Unemployment insurance becomes not a transitional protection for the worker who is changing jobs, but an inadequate livelihood. Farm price supports become low maximum rather than high minimum prices. The prevention of depressions remains the *sine qua non* for economic security.

V

The desire for economic security was long considered the great enemy of increased production. This attitude was firmly grounded in the belief that the insecurity of the competitive model was essential for efficiency. Along with the carrot of pecuniary reward must go the stick of personal economic disaster. Both were essential. To remove the stick, which must be the consequence of increasing economic security, would be to remove half the incentives by which men were inspired. This belief still has a considerable role in the conventional wisdom. The efforts of farmers to minimize uncertainty, although in many respects far less effective than those of larger corporations or trade unions, have inspired especial alarm. In the recent view of a leading agricultural economist, "When millions of able [farm] entrepreneurs have regained the self-confidence to operate without the social harness of bureaucratic guidance and universal risk insurance, it is an event that may amount to a decisive victory in the free, anti-collective world."[2] But even in modern corporate life, the

[2] Karl Brandt, "Agricultural Price Policy During Rearmament," *Journal of Farm Economics*, vol. XXXIV (May 1952), p. 198. Professor Brandt is a past president of the American Farm Economic Association.

conventional wisdom gives great credit to the threat of adversity. "The characteristic of European businessmen as a class as distinguished from Americans is their complacency, their timidity, and their instinctive looking to each other and to government for protection against the rude shocks of the contemporary world. And the thing they fear most is price competition."[8]

Plainly, however, the notion that economic insecurity is essential for efficiency and economic advance was a major miscalculation—perhaps the greatest in the history of economic ideas. (It was the common miscalculation of both Marxian and orthodox economists. Marx and his followers were deeply persuaded that capitalism would be crippled by efforts to civilize it. To cite one obvious example, unemployment compensation would ruin the operation of the industrial reserve army in regulating wages.) In fact the years of increasing concern for economic security have been ones of unparalleled advance in productivity. Those spokesmen who have been most alarmed over the debilitating effects of the search for security have often remarked most breathlessly on the improvements in productivity which have occurred at the same time. The economist whose views were just cited on the alarming dangers of "universal risk insurance" in agriculture characteristically observed in the same paper that, "During the last few decades, breath-taking technological evolution has been opening new frontiers in agriculture, and the progress has been most spectacular in the United States and Canada. Not only did it assist greatly in World War II, but it also kept millions of people in Europe and Asia alive. . . ."[4] Part of this technological advance in agriculture may have been the result of price support legislation which reduced price and income uncertainty. Farmers were thus able to invest in new technology with increased confidence. But this notably plausible possibility has no standing in the conventional wisdom. Hence it is forthrightly ignored.

The data on what has happened to output in the age of security could scarcely be more impressive. In the twenty

[8] Randall, *A Creed for Free Enterprise,* p. 23. Mr. Randall was for many years an executive and after 1949 the very articulate president of the Inland Steel Company. In the steel industry overt price competition is virtually unknown, the elimination of this source of insecurity having been accomplished many years ago. But in the liturgy of the conventional wisdom the praises of price competition are still vigorously sung. As a result, it is strongly recommended even by those who have most successfully eliminated it.

[4] Brandt, "Agricultural Price Policy During Rearmament," pp. 185-86.

years prior to the nineteen-thirties, the decade when the concern for security first became a source of uneasiness, labor productivity—national income produced per man-hour—increased from 89.6 cents in 1900 to 113.3 cents in 1929. This was a total of 23.7 cents or at a rate of about 1.2 cents a year. In the ten years following the thirties the total increase was from 131.5 cents to 179.2 cents or by 47.7 cents. This was by an average of 4.8 cents a year or four times the amount of the earlier period. The increases continued in the decade of the fifties. Plainly the increased concern for security, so far from being in conflict with increased productivity, was consistent with a greatly accelerated rate of advance.[5] The most impressive increases in output in the history of both the United States and other western countries have occurred since men began to concern themselves with reducing the risks of the competitive system.

It must be repeated that in the conventional wisdom such empirical evidence is not necessarily decisive. The consequences truly depicted by the conventional wisdom are, it is held, lurking just out of sight. To respect the evidence is only to evince an unsubtle mind. Yet in this instance the reality is somewhat difficult to evade. The increase in economic security and the increase in economic product are accomplished facts. The conflict between security and progress, once billed as the social conflict of the century, doesn't exist.

VI

Not only is there no inconsistency between the mitigation of insecurity and the increase of production, but the two are indissolubly linked. A high level of economic security is essential for maximum production. And a high level of production is indispensable for economic security. So compulsive, indeed, is the pressure to maintain output as a requisite of economic security that the economy is impelled to a level of performance which, as things now stand, it can sustain only with difficulty and at some cost and danger. But this is running ahead of the story. We must press a step further the relation first of economic security to production and then the reciprocal relation of production to economic security.

[5] Estimates are in 1950 prices. They are from *America's Needs and Resources, A New Survey*, by J. Frederick Dewhurst and Associates (New York: Twentieth Century Fund, 1955), p. 40.

The major threat to production in our day is not, as the more nostalgic exponents of the conventional wisdom still so fondly imagine, the lazy and malingering workman or the unenterprising boss. These wastrels unquestionably exist. Payments designed to bridge periods of involuntary unemployment do provide modestly for some wholly voluntary idleness in Florida. We have featherbedding unions and gold-bricking workmen and slothful supernumeraries everywhere. Indeed it is possible that the ancient art of evading work has been carried in our time to its highest level of sophistication, not to say elegance. One should not suppose that it is an accomplishment of any particular class, occupation, or profession. Apart from the universities where its practice has the standing of a scholarly rite, the art of genteel and elaborately concealed idleness may well reach its highest development in the upper executive reaches of the modern corporation.

What is certain, however, is that the loss of production from this conventional and cherished shirking is small as compared with what can be lost from the involuntary idleness of workers and the far more ruthless frustration of entrepreneurial initiative as the result of depression. For the same reason the potential gain in production from eliminating such involuntary idleness, and from widening entrepreneurial opportunity by expanding markets, is far greater than anything that could be hoped for from the most sweeping strengthening of individual incentives resulting in the most radical increase in the willingness of individuals to work or expend executive energy.

Between 1929 and 1932 the Gross National Product, roughly the total production of the nation, expressed in constant (1950) dollars, dropped by $44 billions from $157.8 to $113.6 billions. No diminution in the energy or initiative of workmen or their employers could have an effect comparable with this massive increase in forced idleness by individuals who would have much preferred to work. (Between 1929 and 1932 unemployment increased from 1.55 million to 12.1 million; nonagricultural employment decreased trom 35.1 million to 28.8 million.)[6] This was a demonstration of historic magnitude of the inefficiency of depression. But there have been more modest if still striking demonstrations in more recent times. In late 1953 and 1954 there was a mild depres-

[6] *Economic Indicators,* Historical and Descriptive Supplement, 1955. Joint Committee on the Economic Report.

sion and in the latter year output was slightly below the previous year. ($360.5 billions as compared with $364.5 billions. Prices were the same.) Unemployment increased from 1.6 million in 1953 to 3.2 million in 1954. If instead of this slight decline there had been the commonplace increase of immediately preceding years, and which the labor force could have sustained, production would have been about $20 billions greater. That was equal to nearly a third of the current outlays of the federal government and approached the total of all state and local outlays. This production was not missed and, indeed, its loss was little remarked. We shall see later that there were very good reasons for such equanimity —the goods so sacrificed were not, in fact, of high urgency. But the figures do show the inefficiency of even the mildest depression.

The immediate although not the ultimate cause of depression is a fall in the aggregate demand—meaning in the purchasing power available and being used—for buying the output of the economy. Unemployment insurance means that a man's purchasing power is protected when he loses his job. It falls, but no longer to zero. Thus a measure designed to reduce the insecurity associated with unemployment also acts to counteract the loss of output—the economic inefficiency—associated with depression. And, to the confusion of the conventional wisdom, it acts on a central cause of inefficiency, one that is far more important than isolated malingering which unemployment insurance might conceivably have encouraged.

This effect, of course, is not peculiar to unemployment insurance. Farm support prices, which force compensatory public outlays when farm prices, income, and purchasing power fall, have the same effect. So do public welfare payments. Old-age and survivors' insurance insure a modest but steady flow of purchasing power from those who are no longer able to work. This flow is unaffected by an ebb in economic activity and thus acts as a stabilizing influence. In the aggregate these measures to minimize insecurity comprise a considerable part of what economists have come to call the "built-in stabilizers" of the economy. Thus measures thought by the conventional wisdom to be hostile to productivity all support it at the most crucial point.

But the reciprocal effect is equally clear and the pressures back of it are much more demanding. As noted above, a high level of production is essential for the economic security of workers, farmers, and businessmen. With it there is a tolerable level of security for all. Without a high level of output, the microeconomic measures, in their present form at least, are only a second best. Moreover, although it has been a point in favor of unemployment compensation, old-age pensions, and other measures for microeconomic security that they enhance economic stability, this has never been their central purpose. They have been centrally designed with the individual recipient in mind.

By contrast, to a very large degree in recent times increased output has been sought not for the goods involved but for the effect on economic security. Whether we need or even wish the goods that are produced, their assured production means assured income for those who produce them. This serves the goal of economic security. Nothing else serves it so well. To falter on production, even though that production serves the most unimportant of requirements, is to expose some individuals somewhere to loss of employment and income. This cannot be allowed.

The facts here are a matter of common observation. In the political life of western countries—the United States, the United Kingdom, and the older British Commonwealths—nothing counts so heavily against a government as allowing unnecessary unemployment. It is not the lost production that is mentioned. It is always the unemployment. The remedy is, of course, more employment and higher production. Thus the effort to enhance economic security becomes the driving force behind production.

The reader scarcely needs to be reminded of the point at which this essay has arrived. The ancient preoccupations of economic life—with equality, security, and productivity—have now narrowed down to a preoccupation with productivity and production. Production has become the solvent of the tensions once associated with inequality, and it has become the indispensable remedy for the discomforts, anxieties, and privations associated with economic insecurity. Here we have the explanation, or more precisely the beginning of the explanation, of a modern paradox: Why it is that as production has increased in modern times concern for production seems also to have increased. Production has become the center of a concern that had hitherto been shared with equality and security. For these reasons, and supported, we shall see, by an elaborately synthetic reinforcement, it has managed at least superficially to retain the prestige which

inevitably it had in the poor world of Ricardo. The nature
of the present preoccupation with production, and the devices
by which this preoccupation is sustained, are the next order
of business.

CHAPTER IX

The Paramount Position of Production

IN THE AUTUMN OF 1954, during the Congressional elections of that year, the Republicans replied to Democratic attacks on their stewardship by arguing that this was the second best year in history. It was not, in all respects, a happy defense. Many promptly said that second best was not good enough —certainly not for Americans. But no person in either party showed the slightest disposition to challenge the standard by which it is decided that one year is better than another. Nor was it felt that any explanation was required. No one would be so eccentric as to suppose that second best meant second best in the progress of the arts and the sciences. No one would assume that it referred to health, education, or the battle against juvenile delinquency. There was no suggestion that a better or poorer year was one in which the chances for survival amidst the radioactive furniture of the world had increased or diminished. Despite a marked and somewhat ostensible preoccupation with religious observances at the time, no one was moved to suppose that 1954 was the second best year as measured by the number of people who had found enduring spiritual solace.

Second best could mean only one thing—that the production of goods was the second highest in history. There had been a year in which production was higher and which hence was better. In fact in 1954 the Gross National Product was $360.5 billion; the year before it had been $364.5. This measure of achievement was acceptable to all. It is a relief on occasion to find a conclusion that is above faction, indeed above debate. On the importance of production there is no difference between Republicans and Democrats, right and left, white or colored, Catholic or Protestant. It is common ground for the general secretary of the Communist Party, the Chairman of Americans for Democratic Action, the President of the United States Chamber of Commerce, and the President of the National Association of Manufacturers.

We are, to be sure, regularly told that production is not everything We set no small store by reminders that there is a spiritual side to life; those that remind are assured a respectful hearing. But it is significant that these are always reminders; they bring to mind what is usually forgotten. No one doubts that in the general course of life one must be sensible and practical. It is an index of the prestige of production in our national attitudes that it is identified with the sensible and the practical. And no greater compliment can be paid to the forthright intelligence of any businessman than to say that he understands production. Scientists are not without prestige in our day, but to be really useful we still assume that they should be under the direction of a production man. "Any device or regulation which interferes, or can be conceived as interfering, with [the] supply of more and better things is resisted with unreasoning horror, as the religious resist blasphemy, or the warlike pacifism."[1]

The importance of production transcends our boundaries. We are regularly told—in the conventional wisdom it is the most frequent justification of our civilization, even our existence—that the American standard of living is "the marvel of the world." To a very considerable extent it is.

II

As Tawney observed, we are rarely conscious of the quality of the air we breathe. But in Los Angeles, where it is barely sufficient for its freight, we take it seriously. Similarly those who reside on a recently reclaimed desert see in the water in the canals the evidence of their unnatural triumph over nature. And the Chicagoan in Sarasota sees in his tanned belly the proof of his intelligence in escaping his dark and frozen habitat. But where sun and rain are abundant, though they are no less important, they are taken for granted. In the world of Ricardo goods were scarce. They were also closely related, if not to the survival, at least to the elemental comforts of man. They fed him, covered him when he was out of doors, and kept him warm when he was within. It is not surprising that the production by which these goods were obtained was central to men's thoughts.

[1] Geoffrey Gorer, *The Americans* (London: Cresset Press, 1948), p. 121.

Now goods are abundant. More die in the United States of too much food than of too little. Where the population was once thought to press on the food supply, now the food supply presses relentlessly on the population. No one can seriously suggest that the steel which comprises the extra four or five feet of purely decorative distance on our automobiles is of prime urgency. For many women and some men clothing has ceased to be related to protection from exposure and has become, like plumage, almost exclusively erotic. Yet production remains central to our thoughts. There is no tendency to take it, like sun and water, for granted; on the contrary, it continues to measure the quality and progress of our civilization.

Our preoccupation with production is, in fact, the culminating consequence of powerful historical and psychological forces—forces which only by an act of will we can hope to escape. Productivity, as we have seen, has enabled us to avoid or finesse the tensions anciently associated with inequality and its inconvenient remedies. It has become central to our strivings to reduce insecurity. And as we shall observe in the next chapters its importance is buttressed by a highly dubious but widely accepted psychology of want; by an equally dubious but equally accepted interpretation of national interest; and by powerful vested interest. So all embracing, indeed, is our sense of the importance of production as a goal that the first reaction to any questioning of this attitude will be, "What else is there?" So large does production bulk in our thoughts that we can only suppose that a vacuum must remain if it should be relegated to a smaller role. Happily, as we shall see in the concluding chapters, there are other things. But first we must examine more closely our present preoccupation with production. For nothing better suggests the extent to which it is founded on tradition and social myth than the highly stylized attitudes with which we approach it and, in particular, the traditional and highly irrational emphasis we accord to the different methods of expanding economic product.

III

Production—the output of the economic system—can, in principle, be increased in five different ways. These are worth listing formally and are as follows:

(1) The productive resources that are available, in partic- ular the labor and capital (including available raw materials), can be more fully employed. In other words, idleness can be eliminated.

(2) Given the technical state of the arts, these resources can be more efficiently employed. Labor and capital can be used in the most advantageous combination, one with the other, and the two can be distributed to the greatest advantage, consumer tastes considered, between the production of various things and the rendering of various services.

(3) The supply of labor can be increased.

(4) The supply of capital, which also serves as a substitute for labor, can be increased.

(5) The state of the arts can be improved by technological innovation. As a result more output can be obtained from a given supply of labor and capital and the capi- tal will be of better quality.

On a purely *a priori* grounds there is no reason for suppos- ing that any one of these methods of increasing production is more effective than any other.[2] A serious effort to increase output would emphasize all five. Yet it is the truly remarkable fact that we concern ourselves seriously with only one of these methods of increasing output and give, at the very most, only passing attention to another two or three.

Thus even in the conventional wisdom no one questions the importance of technological advance for increasing the production (and also multiplying the products) from the available resources. These gains are regularly viewed with great and even extravagant pride. Improvements in tech- nology do not come by accident. They are the result of investment in highly organized scientific and engineering knowl- edge and skills. Yet we do very little to increase the volume

[2] In the period between 1869-73 and 1944-53 net national output in- creased at an average annual rate of 3.5 per cent of which about half (1.7 per cent) can be attributed to the increase in capital and labor supply. The remainder can reasonably be imputed to technological im- provement in capital and the parallel improvement in the people who devise the better capital equipment and operate it. In recent times a growing share of the increase is attributable to such technological ad- vance and a declining share to mere increases in capital and labor supply. Cf. Moses Abramovitz, *Resources and Output Trends in the United States Since 1870*, and John W. Kendrick, *Productivity Trends: Capital and Labor*. Occasional papers 52 and 53 of the National Bureau of Economic Research, New York, 1956.

of this investment, except perhaps where some objective of military urgency is involved. Rather we accept whatever investment is currently being made and applaud the outcome.

The investment almost certainly could be much greater and far more rational. Even on the most superficial view, the scientific and engineering resources by which modern technology is advanced are most unevenly distributed between industries. In industries where firms are few and comparatively large—oil, metallurgy, automobiles, chemicals, rubber, heavy engineering—the investment in technological advance is considerable. The research and developmental work on which this advance depends is well financed and comprehensive. But in many industries where the firms are numerous and small—coal mining, home construction, clothing manufacture, the natural-fiber textile industry, the service industries —the investment in innovation is negligible. No firm is large enough to afford it on an appreciable scale; there is real question as to whether it is worth while for such firms.[3] Unlike agriculture, where innovation is extensively supported by the federal and state governments, there is little or no publicly financed research and development. Yet the absence of investment in innovation in these industries, much though we value its fruits in other industries in which it occurs, excites not the slightest attention. We attach profound importance to the fact that some industries advance. We attach almost no importance to the fact that others do not.

It is easy to overlook the absence of appreciable advance in an industry. Inventions that are not made, like babies that are not born, are rarely missed. In the absence of new developments, old ones may seem very impressive for quite a long while. Until the combine appeared, the self-binder had been the mechanical marvel of the farm machinery industry for forty years. But if we were serious about increased output, we would be much more searching in these matters. Certainly we would regard the absence of investment in innovation in an industry as intolerable. But in fact large numbers of industries make little or no such investment, have little or none made on their behalf, and we are quite untroubled.

[3] I have discussed this point in some detail in my *American Capitalism: The Concept of Countervailing Power*, pp. 84-94.

IV

In everyday economic discourse nothing is more frequently taken as an index of economic growth than the volume of capital formation. This is the product of saving from current consumption and companion investment. As with technological advance, we content ourselves with whatever volume of capital formation we are getting. An occasional scholar may observe that we are not investing enough—possibly that the proportion of current income invested by the Russians is much greater. We have routine preachments on the virtues of thrift. But none of this is assumed to call for any practical action. On the contrary, there is a more general conviction that the current volume of investment in the American economy is never less than adequate and is rarely less than remarkable.

As with capital so with the labor force. Once princes and feudal lords who wished to increase the productive wealth of their domains imported craftsmen as a matter of course. So far as there is a single current limitation on the rate of growth in the American economy, it is the size of the labor force. (Substitution of capital for labor is ordinarily possible with slight effect on cost over a considerable range of output, but some time is required.) The world contains a great many potential recruits for our labor force. But nothing would be viewed with more suspicion than this method of expanding output. Even to suggest that efforts be made to expand the labor force by increasing the domestic birthrate would seem slightly artful. The resistance arises partly from the belief, not wholly justified, that an increase in population might increase total but not per capita production. No nice philosophical point has ever been so decisively resolved as this: that those who are not conceived do not miss the pleasure of consuming the goods they do not get born to enjoy. But whatever the effect of increasing population on standards of living, it is clear that we are not sufficiently interested in increased output, or sufficiently rational about the means of getting it, to seek it by increasing the labor supply.

Even the production that is lost during a depression—and as noted in the last chapter the loss from even a mild setback can be considerable—though it is the subject of a certain amount of erudite regret by economists is not a matter of any general concern. The menace of depressions is not the production that is sacrificed but the jobs and income that are lost—in short, the threat to economic security.

On the other hand, we do take very seriously loss of production which is the result of the deliberate holding of labor or capital out of production or which is the result of any inefficiency in their combination and use. We deplore the malingering workman. We become deeply aroused by the featherbedding union. A monopoly leads to a less than optimum employment of labor and capital in a particular industry and therefore a higher than necessary price for the product. The resources not employed in the monopolized industry are employed in larger quantity and to less advantage in other industries, which means that their distribution is less than ideal. Considerable enthusiasm can be aroused for measures that increase output by eliminating monopoly. Economists have never been loath to give their leadership to the effort.[4] There is equal antipathy to and similar popular concern about inefficient use of resources resulting from tariffs and excessive investment in inherently costly industries; about subsidies to favored but inefficient industries or firms; and about the forms of industrial organization which lead to heavy advertising or sales costs or similar seeming waste. Although, curiously, there is no especial concern about the industry that does no research and makes little technological progress from one year to the next, nothing inspires indignation like a firm which, having made an invention, holds it out of use.

None of this is specifically to decry concern for monopoly, tariffs, subsidies, or organized and unrepentant idleness. Also, although productive efficiency is the central, it is not the sole issue where these matters are concerned. Rather, my purpose is to show how partial and indeed eccentric is our concern for increased production. Nor are its roots very difficult to uncover. A hundred years ago in mid-nineteenth-century Britain, an economist surveying the possibilities for increasing the production on his islands would have found one important and two or three much less important things to recommend. Most obviously and most importantly, he could urge that by attacking monopolies, lowering tariffs, and

[4] Although there have been competent expressions of doubt as to the losses. Cf. in particular "Monopoly and Resource Allocation" by Arnold C. Harberger, *American Economic Review, Proceedings,* vol. XLIV, no. 2 (May 1954), and "The Social Cost of Corporate Monopoly Profits" by Henry H. Villard, *Political Science Quarterly,* vol. LXXII, no. 3 (September 1957).

promoting competition and the free and unhampered movement of labor and capital the efficiency with which labor and capital were employed would be increased. Much less importantly, he could urge that people be thrifty and save so that the rate of capital formation might be increased. And, of course, he could always urge workers to be diligent, and he could condemn anything that might involve restrictions on their effort or impairment of their incentives.

Few of the modern possibilities for raising production were relevant. In a world that was still under the shadow of Malthus he could hardly propose adding more people. There were presumed to be as many as the food supply could sustain. This was well before the age of the large industrial corporation. Only with the arrival of the latter were investment decisions removed from the hands of numerous independent entrepreneurs, responding individually to market incentives, and made subject to a measure of corporate administration. And until this happened it was not really possible to think of the rate of investment and the consequent rate of growth as anything that might be within range of social interest and decision.

The nineteenth-century scholar could scarcely have been occupied with the volume of research and development in an industry. This is a modern phenomenon and also related to the growth of modern corporate enterprise. In his day invention was a largely adventitious matter save as it might be encouraged by the patent office. (The patent office, appropriately, was taken very seriously.) The loss of production during depressions was not an issue in a world which lacked good unemployment and output statistics and in which depressions, in any case, were regarded as inevitable.

The lesson will be evident. Our operative concern for increasing production is confined to the measures—for getting greater resource use efficiency and promoting thrift and diligence—which were relevant a century ago. The newer dimensions along which there might be progress attract our attention scarcely at all. The shortcomings and opportunities here are undoubtedly great. But they are outside the formal and stylized concern of the conventional wisdom for the problem of production.

There is an interesting proof of the point in the increase in production which, in the past, we have regularly achieved during war or under the threat of war. Under the stress of circumstance the conventional wisdom is rejected. We set about expanding output along all the relevant dimensions.

Serious efforts are made to expand the labor force. It becomes permissible to import toilers with swarthy skins who speak unintelligible languages. The drive for increased saving becomes serious. Where investment is inadequate more is made. There is no involuntary idleness. As in the case of alloy steels, synthetic rubber manufacture, and ship construction in World War II, technology is brought purposefully to play to permit of expanded output with available resources. It is at least amusing (though not too much store should be set by the point) that during both World Wars the enforcement of the antitrust laws, the traditional design for insuring greater resource-use efficiency, was suspended. Because of a rational concern for production war has brought an astonishing expansion in output, and this despite the withdrawals from the labor force for military purpose.

Though we have been astonished we should not have been. Our peacetime concern for production, central though it is to our thoughts, is selective and traditional. As a result, at any given time both our total output and its rate of increase are only a small part of what it might be, perhaps indeed only a minor fraction. Nor would the necessary measures to expand labor force, expand the rate of capital formation, and perhaps most important to bring technology to bear on presently backward industries require any very revolutionary change in our economic and political system. It would only require that production have the priority in all public policy which it now has in the traditional areas of resource use and combination.

V

There is another respect in which our concern for production is traditional and irrational. We are curiously unreasonable in the distinctions we make between different kinds of goods and services. We view the production of some of the most frivolous goods with pride. We regard the production of some of the most significant and civilizing services with regret.

Economists in calculating the total output of the economy —in arriving at the now familiar Gross National Product— add together the value of all goods and all services of whatever sort and by whomsoever produced. No distinction is made between public and privately produced services. An increased supply of educational services has a standing in the total not different in kind from an increased output of television receivers. Nothing, however, could be more in conflict with popular attitudes, and indeed it is rather surprising that economists have not been reproached by the rather considerable number of individuals who, if they fully understood the nature of the calculation, would regard the inclusion of government spending as subversive.

In the general view it is privately produced production that is important, and that nearly alone. This adds to national well-being. Its increase measures the increase in national wealth. Public services, by comparison, are an incubus. They are necessary, and they may be necessary in considerable volume. But they are a burden which must, in effect, be carried by the private production. If that burden is too great, private production will stagger and fall.

At best public services are a necessary evil; at worst they are a malign tendency against which an alert community must exercise eternal vigilance. Even when they serve the most important ends, such services are sterile. "Government is powerless to create anything in the sense in which business produces wealth. . . ."[5]

Such attitudes lead to some interesting contradictions. Automobiles have an importance greater than the roads on which they are driven. We welcome expansion of telephone services as improving the general well-being but accept curtailment of postal services as signifying necessary economy. We set great store by the increase in private wealth but regret the added outlays for the police force by which it is protected. Vacuum cleaners to insure clean houses are praiseworthy and essential in our standard of living. Street cleaners to insure clean streets are an unfortunate expense. Partly as a result, our houses are generally clean and our streets generally filthy. In the more sophisticated of the conventional wisdom, this distinction between public and private services is much less sharp and, as I have observed, it does not figure in the calculation of Gross National Product. However, it never quite disappears. Even among economists and political philosophers, public services rarely lose their connotation of burden. Although they may be defended, their volume and quality are almost never a source of pride.

There are a number of reasons for these attitudes, but again tradition plays a dominant role. In the world into which economics was born the four most urgent requirements of

[5] Francis X. Sutton, Seymour E. Harris, Carl Kaysen, and James Tobin, *The American Business Creed* (Cambridge, Mass.: Harvard University Press, 1956), p. 195.

man were food, clothing and shelter, and an orderly environment in which the first three might be provided. The first
three lent themselves to private production for the market;
given good order, this process has ordinarily gone forward
with tolerable efficiency. But order which was the gift of
government was nearly always supplied with notable unreliability. With rare exceptions it was also inordinately expensive.
And the pretext of providing order not infrequently afforded
the occasion for rapacious appropriation of the means of
sustenance of the people.

Not surprisingly, modern economic ideas incorporated a
strong suspicion of government. The goal of nineteenth-century economic liberalism was a state which did provide order
reliably and inexpensively and which did as little as possible
else. Even Marx intended that the state should wither away.
These attitudes have persisted in the conventional wisdom.
And again events have dealt them a series of merciless blows.
Once a society has provided itself with food, clothing, and
shelter, all of which so fortuitously lend themselves to private
production, purchase, and sale, its members begin to desire
other things. And a remarkable number of these things do
not lend themselves to such production, purchase, and sale.
They must be provided for everyone if they are to be provided for anyone, and they must be paid for collectively or
they cannot be had at all. Such is the case with streets and
police and the general advantages of mass literacy and sanitation, the control of epidemics, and the common defense.
There is a bare possibility that the services which must be
rendered collectively, although they enter the general scheme
of wants after the immediate physical necessities, increase in
urgency more than proportionately with increasing wealth.
This is more likely if increasing wealth is matched by increasing population and increasing density of population. Nonetheless these services, although they reflect increasingly urgent
desires, remain under the obloquy of the unreliability, incompetence, cost, and pretentious interference of princes. Alcohol, comic books and mouth wash all bask under the superior
reputation of the market. Schools, judges, and municipal
swimming pools lie under the evil reputation of bad kings.

Moreover, bad kings in a poorer world showed themselves
to be quite capable, in their rapacity, of destroying or damaging the production of private goods by destroying the
people and the capital that produced them. Economies are
no longer so vulnerable. Governments are not so undiscrimi-
nating. In western countries in modern times economic

growth and expanding public activity have, with rare exceptions, gone together. Each has served the other as indeed they must. Yet the conventional wisdom is far from surrendering on the point. Any growth in public services is a manifestation of an intrinsically evil trend. If the vigor of the race is not in danger, liberty is. And this may be threatened even by the activities of the local school board. The structure of the economy may also be at stake. In one branch of the conventional wisdom the American economy is never far removed from socialism, and the movement toward socialism may be measured by the rise in public spending. Thus even the most neutral of public services, for one part of the population, fall under the considerable handicap of being identified with social revolution.

Finally—also a closely related point—the payment for publicly produced services has long been linked to the problem of inequality. By having the rich pay more, the services were provided and at the same time the goal of greater equality was advanced. This community of objectives has never appealed to those being equalized. Not unnaturally, some part of their opposition has been directed to the public services themselves. By attacking these, they could attack the leveling tendencies of taxation. This has helped to keep alive the notion that the public services for which they pay are inherently inferior to privately produced goods.

While public services have been subject to these negative attitudes, private goods have had no such attention. On the contrary, their virtues have been extolled by the massed drums of modern advertising. They have been pictured as the ultimate wealth of the community. Clearly the competition between public and private services, apart from any question of the satisfactions they render, is an unequal one. The social consequences of this discrimination—this tendency to accord a superior prestige to private goods and an inferior role to public production—are considerable and even grave.

VI

By way of summary, then, while production has come to have a goal of pre-eminent importance in our life, it is not a goal which we pursue either vigorously or even very thoughtfully. We take production as the measure of our achievement, but we do not strive very deliberately to achieve. Our efforts to increase production are stylized. We stress the evils of idleness and bad resource allocation which were relevant to efforts to increase output a century ago. We do little or nothing in peacetime to increase the rate of capital formation or the rate of technological progress in backward industries despite the clear indication that these are the dimensions along which large increases in output are to be expected. We rarely deplore the production we lose in depression. We are protected from this loss far more by the threat of depression to economic security. Last of all, on ancient and traditional grounds, we relegate one important class of production to a second-class citizenship.

The predictable reaction of many readers will be that we should by all means address ourselves to the measures for increasing output that we now ignore. However, a closer look is called for. We need to understand the reasons for our passivity in this matter. In the past, under conditions of emergency, we have addressed ourselves seriously to the measures by which output is seriously increased. Perhaps we fail to do so in present circumstances less because of ignorance or inertia than because the additional production is not of sufficient urgency to justify the effort. Our preoccupation with production, in other words, may be a preoccupation with a problem of rather low urgency. We are not sufficiently concerned about it to have recourse to the measures by which production could be efficiently increased. We are content with what we get, which comes close to saying that we are deeply concerned with production only so far as the problem solves itself. We set great store by doing what, in a manner of speaking, comes naturally.

None of this would be possible if the goods we produced were of great and urgent importance. Then we would be searching vigorously for ways of increasing the supply instead, as at present, of regarding with approval the increases we obtain. All this becomes intelligible, and in degree even obvious, when we contemplate the elaborate myth with which we surround the demand for goods. This has enabled us to become persuaded of the dire importance of the goods we have without our being in the slightest degree concerned about those we do not have. For we have wants at the margin only so far as they are synthesized. We do not manufacture wants for goods we do not produce.

CHAPTER X

The Imperatives of Consumer Demand

> In an economy, such as that of the United States of America, where leisure is barely moral, the problem of creating sufficient wants . . . to absorb productive capacity may become chronic in the not too distant future. In such a situation the economist begins to lead a furtive existence.
>
> —W. BECKERMAN[1]

BOTH THE ancient preoccupation with production and the pervasive modern search for security have culminated in our time in a concern for production. Increased real income provides us with an admirable detour around the rancor anciently associated with efforts to redistribute wealth. A high level of production has become the keystone of effective economic security. There remains, however, the task of justifying the resulting flow of goods. Production cannot be an incidental to the mitigation of inequality or the provision of jobs. It must have a *raison d'être* of its own. At this point economists and economic theory have entered the game. So, rather more recently, have those who profess to be the philosophers on problems of defense and national security. The result has been an elaborate and ingenious defense of the importance of production as such. It is a defense which makes the urgency of production largely independent of the volume of production. In this way economic theory has managed to transfer the sense of urgency in meeting consumer need that once was felt in a world where more production meant more food for the hungry, more clothing for the cold, and more houses for the homeless to a world where increased output satisfies the craving for more elegant automobiles, more exotic food, more erotic clothing, more elaborate entertainment—

[1] "The Economist as a Modern Missionary," *The Economic Journal*, March 1956.

indeed for the entire modern range of sensuous, edifying, and lethal desires.

Although the economic theory which defends these desires and hence the production that supplies them has an impeccable (and to an astonishing degree even unchallenged) position in the conventional wisdom, it is illogical and meretricious and in degree even dangerous.

II

The rationalization begins with the peculiar urgency of production not to society but to economic science. There will be occasion later for considering the vested interest in production, but it may be noted here that the interest of the economist is unique. The importance of production is central to his scheme of economic calculation. All existing pedagogy and nearly all research depend on it. Any action which increases production from given resources is good and implicitly important; anything which inhibits or reduces output is *pro tanto* wrong. In the choice between two taxes there is a nearly overriding case for the one that least damages efficiency, meaning the output from a given stock of labor and capital. If a company seems to be restricting production to enhance returns, or for any other reason, it can safely be condemned as antisocial. This is at least equally so with a trade union. The test of effect on productive efficiency is all but universal.

To assess the effect of a given action or measure, say a new union rule, on production is not always easy. There may be a complicated chain of cause and effect on which opinions will differ. The effect on the short run may be different from that on the long. And where it is necessary to assess the effect on a variety of products, or on the total output of the economy, there are numerous difficulties. The latter must be valued, and the prices at which individual items are valued will reflect the existing income distribution—the prices of mink pelts reflect the demand of an opulent minority—or, in some cases, the more or less arbitrary decision of the firms that administer the prices. Hence to trace and compare the effect of different policies on the output of the economy can be endlessly intricate. But all this provides much of the interest of economics as well as a good deal of its employment. And underlying all is the bedrock agreement on the goal and on the importance of that goal. Anything that increases the product from given resources increases welfare. It is important that it be done. Here is the anchor. To cast doubt on the importance of production is thus to bring into question the foundation of the entire edifice. Action must then be tested by new criteria—criteria which are necessarily difficult and subjective. Nothing could be less welcome. At least in social disciplines, obsolescence and irrelevance are a small price to pay for the privilege of remaining comfortably, even if archaically, with the familiar, the settled, and the safe.

And the profession of economics is not lacking in the instinct of self-preservation. The mother bear sees in the threat to her cubs the ultimate threat to the survival of her kind. She reacts with angry venom. Nothing is more likely to produce a similar reaction from defenders of the conventional economic wisdom than an attack on the edifice which now rationalizes the importance of production and the urgency of consumer need.

The parallel with maternal instinct is important, for the defense of the present value system as it relates to production is largely intuitive. Few economists in recent years can have escaped some uneasiness over the kinds of goods which their value system is insisting they must maximize. They have wondered about the urgency of the longer and lower automobiles. They have been uneasy about the lengths to which it has been necessary to go with advertising and salesmanship to synthesize the desire for such goods. That uneasiness has reflected the crucial weakness of the literature at this point.

Some, moreover, have also noticed the changed position of the economist in the community. Twenty years ago he was in touch with the problems of depression and unemployment. Even though there was less than general certainty that he had the answers, he was a figure of interest and controversy. Now for many years he has been in an intellectual backwater. The dentist who seeks the fluoridation of the city water supply is a more controversial figure than the economist who tells of an expanding economy. Once students were attracted by the seeming urgency of economic problems and by a sense of their mission to solve them. Now the best come to economics for the opportunity it provides to exercise arcane mathematical skills. Could this mean that society itself is losing its sense of the urgency of the economic problem? Does it mean that there is now a subjective realization that increased product is being used to serve rather unimportant ends? Even the vigor and scorn of the denial may reflect uncertainty.

As with the bear and her cubs we must expect the reaction to be increasingly sharp as the danger becomes more threatening. In part it will take the form of a purely assertive posture. "There is still an economic problem"; "We still have poverty"; "It is human nature to want more"; "Without increasing production there will be stagnation"; "We must show the Russians." But the ultimate refuge will remain in the theory of consumer demand. This is a formidable structure; it has already demonstrated its effectiveness in defending the urgency of production. In a world where affluence is rendering the old ideas obsolete, it will continue to be the bastion against the misery of new ones.

III

The theory of consumer demand, as it is now widely accepted, is based on two broad propositions, neither of them quite explicit but both extremely important for the present value system of economists. The first is that the urgency of wants does not diminish appreciably as more of them are satisfied or, to put the matter more precisely, to the extent that this happens it is not demonstrable and not a matter of any interest to economists or for economic policy. When man has satisfied his physical needs, then psychologically grounded desires take over. These can never be satisfied or, in any case, no progress can be proved. The concept of satiation has very little standing in economics. It is neither useful nor scientific to speculate on the comparative cravings of the stomach and the mind.

The second proposition is that wants originate in the personality of the consumer or, in any case, that they are given data for the economist. The latter's task is merely to seek their satisfaction. He has no need to inquire how these wants are formed. His function is sufficiently fulfilled by maximizing the goods that supply the wants.

The examination of these two conclusions must now be pressed. The explanation of consumer behavior has its ancestry in a much older problem, indeed the oldest problem of economics, that of price determination.[2] Nothing originally proved more troublesome in the explanation of prices,

---

[2] The provenance of the theory of consumer behavior is sketched in Mr. I. D. M. Little's interesting article "A Reformulation of Consumer Behavior," *Oxford Economic Papers,* New Series, vol. I, no. 1 (January 1949), p. 99.

i.e., exchange values, than the indigestible fact that some of the most useful things had the least value in exchange and some of the least useful had the most. As Adam Smith observed: "Nothing is more useful than water; but it will purchase scarce anything; scarce anything can be had in exchange for it. A diamond, on the contrary, has scarce any value in use: but a very great quantity of other goods may frequently be had in exchange for it."[3]

In explaining value, Smith thought it well to distinguish between "value in exchange" and "value in use" and sought thus to reconcile the paradox of high utility and low exchangeability. This distinction begged questions rather than solved them and for another hundred years economists sought for a satisfactory formulation. Finally, toward the end of the last century—though it is now recognized that their work had been extensively anticipated—the three economists of marginal utility (Karl Menger, an Austrian; William Stanley Jevons, an Englishman; and John Bates Clark, an American) produced more or less simultaneously the explanation which in broad substance still serves. The urgency of desire is a function of the quantity of goods which the individual has available to satisfy that desire. The larger the stock the less the satisfactions from an increment. And the less, also, the willingness to pay. Since diamonds for most people are in comparatively meager supply, the satisfaction from an additional one is great, and the potential willingness to pay is likewise high. The case of water is just the reverse. It also follows that where the supply of a good can be readily increased at low cost, its value in exchange will reflect that ease of reproduction and the low urgency of the marginal desires it thus comes to satisfy. This will be so no matter how difficult it may be (as with water) to dispense entirely with the item in question.

The doctrine of diminishing marginal utility, as it was enshrined in the economics textbooks, seemed to put economic ideas squarely on the side of the diminishing importance of production under conditions of increasing affluence. With increasing per capita real income, men are able to satisfy additional wants. These are of a lower order of urgency. This being so, the production that provides the goods that satisfy these less urgent wants must also be of smaller (and declining) importance. In Ricardo's England the supply of bread for many was meager. The satisfaction resulting from

[3] *Wealth of Nations.* Smith did not foresee the industrial diamond.

an increment in the bread supply—from a higher money income, bread prices being the same, or the same money income, bread prices being lower—was great. Hunger was lessened; life itself might be extended. Certainly any measure to increase the bread supply merited the deep and serious interest of the public-spirited citizen.

In the contemporary United States the supply of bread is plentiful and the supply of bread grains even redundant. The yield of satisfactions from a marginal increment in the wheat supply is small. To a Secretary of Agriculture it is indubitably negative. Measures to increase the wheat supply are not, therefore, a socially urgent preoccupation of publicly concerned citizens. These are more likely to be found spending their time devising schemes for the effective control of wheat production. And having extended their bread consumption to the point where its marginal utility is very low, people have gone on to spend their income on other things. Since these other goods entered their consumption pattern after bread, there is a presumption that they are not very urgent either—that *their* consumption has been carried, as with wheat, to the point where marginal utility is small or even negligible. So it must be assumed that the importance of marginal increments of all production is low and declining. The effect of increasing affluence is to minimize the importance of economic goals. Production and productivity become less and less important.

The concept of diminishing marginal utility was, and remains, one of the indispensable ideas of economics. Since it conceded so much to the notion of diminishing urgency of wants, and hence of production, it was remarkable indeed that the situation was retrieved. This was done—and brilliantly. The diminishing urgency of wants was not admitted. In part this was accomplished in the name of refined scientific method which, as so often at the higher levels of sophistication, proved a formidable bulwark of the conventional wisdom. Obvious but inconvenient evidence was rejected on the grounds that it could not be scientifically assimilated. But even beyond this, it has been necessary at times simply to close one's eyes to phenomena which could not be reconciled with convenience.

IV

The first step, as noted earlier, was to divorce economics from any judgment on the goods with which it was concerned. Any notion of necessary versus unnecessary or important as against unimportant goods was rigorously excluded from the subject. Alfred Marshall, who on this as on so many other things, laid down the rules to which economists have since adhered, noted that "the economist studies mental states rather through their manifestations than in themselves; and if he finds they afford evenly balanced incentives to action, he treats them prima facie as for his purposes equal."[4] He almost immediately added that this simplification, which indeed has rendered profound scientific service to economics, was only a "starting-point." But economists ever since have been content to stay with his starting point and to make it a mark of scholarly restraint and scientific virtue to do so. Nothing is so thoroughly drilled into the minds of the young as the need for this restraint. Nothing in economics so quickly marks an individual as incompetently trained as a disposition to remark on the legitimacy of the desire for more food and the frivolity of the desire for a more elaborate automobile.

Next, economics took general cognizance of the fact that an almost infinite variety of goods await the consumer's attention. At the more elementary (and also the more subjective) levels of economic analysis it is assumed that, while the marginal utility of the individual good declines in accordance with the indubitable law, the utility or satisfaction from new and different kinds of goods does not diminish appreciably. So long as the consumer adds new products— seeks variety rather than quantity—he may, like a museum, accumulate without diminishing the urgency of his wants. Since even in Los Angeles the average consumer owns only a fraction of the different kinds of goods he might conceivably possess, there is all but unlimited opportunity for adding such products. The rewards to the possessors are more or less proportional to the supply. The production that supplies these goods and services, since it renders undiminished utility, remains of undiminished importance.

This position ignores the obvious fact that some things are acquired before others and that, presumably, the more important things come first. This, as observed previously, implies a declining urgency of need. However, in the slightly more sophisticated theory this conclusion is rejected. The rejection centers on the denial that anything very useful can be said of the comparative states of mind and satisfaction of the

[4] *Principles of Economics*, p. 16.

consumer at different periods of time. Few students of
economics, even in the elementary course, now escape without
a warning against the error of intertemporal comparisons of
the utility from given acts of consumption. Yesterday the
man with a minimal but increasing real income was reaping
the satisfactions which came from a decent diet and a roof
that no longer leaked water on his face. Today, after a large
increase in his income, he has extended his consumption to
include suede shoes and a weekly visit to the races. But to
say that his satisfactions from these latter amenities and
recreations are less than from the additional calories and the
freedom from rain is wholly improper. Things have changed;
he is a different man; there is no real standard for comparison.
That, as of a given time, an individual will derive lesser satisfactions from the marginal increments to a given stock of
goods, and accordingly cannot be induced to pay as much
for them, is conceded. But this tells us nothing of the satisfactions from such additional goods, and more particularly
from different goods, when they are acquired at a later time.
The conclusion follows. One cannot be sure that the satisfaction from these temporally later increases in the individual's stock of goods diminishes. Hence one cannot suggest
that the production which supplies it is of diminishing
urgency.

A moment's reflection on what has been accomplished will
be worth while. The notion of diminishing utility still serves
its indispensable purpose of relating urgency of desire and
consequent willingness to pay to quantity. At any given time
the more the individual might have, the less would be the
satisfaction he would derive from additions to his stock and
the less he would be willing to pay. The reactions of the
community will be the aggregate of the reactions of the individuals it comprises. Hence the greater the supply the less
the willingness to pay for marginal increments and hence the
demand curve familiar to all who have made even the most
modest venture into economic theory. But, at the same time,
the question of the diminishing urgency of consumption is
elided. For, while the question of willingness to pay for
additional quantities is based on a hypothesis as to behavior
in face of these quantities at a given point of time, an increase
in stock of consumer's goods, as the result of an increase in
real income, can occur only over time. On the yield of satisfactions from this the economist has nothing to say. In the
name of good scientific method he is prevented from saying

anything.[5] There is room, however, for the broad assumption —given the large and ever-growing variety of goods awaiting the consumer's attention—that wants have a sustained urgency. In any case, it can safely be concluded that more goods will satisfy more wants than fewer goods. And the assumption that goods are an important and even an urgent thing to provide stalks unchallenged behind, for have not goods always been important for relieving the privation of mankind? It will be evident that economics has brilliantly retrieved the dangers to itself and to its goals that were inherent in diminishing marginal utility.

There has been dissent. Keynes observed that the needs of human beings "fall into two classes—those needs which are absolute in the sense that we feel them whatever the situation of our fellow human beings may be, and those which are relative only in that their satisfaction lifts us above, makes us feel superior to, our fellows." While conceding that the second class of wants might be insatiable, he argued that the first were capable of being satisfied and went on to conclude that "assuming no important wars and no important increase in

---

[5] In the yet more technical analysis of consumer demand, attention has been further diverted from the diminishing urgency of product by the shift from cardinal to ordinal utility as an instrument of analysis. Ordinal analysis treats the consumer's desires strictly in terms of the preferences of one good as against the other. This does not mean either that the notion of diminishing marginal utility of a good or the diminishing urgency of additional products disappears. In the indifference map or surface diminishing marginal utility is what makes the consumer willing, with an increasing stock, to surrender more and more of one product to have a given quantity of another. Recreation will not enter the consumer's preference system except in combination with some minimum quantity of food. Food can be present without recreation.

However, these considerations are not obtrusive in the analysis or its pedagogy. The much more evident fact is that food, gasoline, and pinball all exchange for one another at given rates and thus are equated one with the other. The point most stressed in the pedagogy is that the consumer will always find his highest satisfaction on the highest indifference curve that his income allows him to reach. The effect of higher income or of a larger product at lower prices is to put the consumer on a higher curve. This goal is implicit in the analysis. Thus a line of thought which once might seem to throw doubt on the importance of marginal increments to the stock of goods ends by affirming it. In practice the analytical apparatus excludes from consideration the possibility that the movement to higher and higher indifference curves is of declining urgency.

The unprofessional reader who wishes to acquaint himself with the essentials of this analysis will find a competent and lucid summary in Paul A. Samuelson's chapter appendix "Geometrical Analysis of Consumer Equilibrium," *Economics* (3d ed.; New York: McGraw-Hill, 1955), pp. 432-38.

population the *economic problem* may be solved, or at least within sight of solution, within a hundred years. This means the economic problem is not—if we look into the future— *the permanent problem of the human race.*"[6] However, on this conclusion Keynes made no headway. In contending with the conventional wisdom he, no less than others, needed the support of circumstance. And in contrast with his remedy for depressions this he did not yet have.

---

[6] J. M. Keynes, *Essays in Persuasion,* "Economic Possibilities for Our Grandchildren," pp. 365-66. The italics are in the original. Notice that Keynes, as always little bound by the conventional rules, did not hesitate to commit the unpardonable sin of distinguishing between categories of desire.

CHAPTER XI

The Dependence Effect

THE NOTION that wants do not become less urgent the more amply the individual is supplied is broadly repugnant to common sense. It is something to be believed only by those who wish to believe. Yet the conventional wisdom must be tackled on its own terrain. Intertemporal comparisons of an individual's state of mind do rest on doubtful grounds. Who can say for sure that the deprivation which afflicts him with hunger is more painful than the deprivation which afflicts him with envy of his neighbor's new car? In the time that has passed since he was poor his soul may have become subject to a new and deeper searing. And where a society is concerned, comparisons between marginal satisfactions when it is poor and those when it is affluent will involve not only the same individual at different times but different individuals at different times. The scholar who wishes to believe that with increasing affluence there is no reduction in the urgency of desires and goods is not without points for debate. However plausible the case against him, it cannot be proven. In the defense of the conventional wisdom this amounts almost to invulnerability.

However, there is a flaw in the case. If the individual's wants are to be urgent they must be original with himself. They cannot be urgent if they must be contrived for him. And above all they must not be contrived by the process of production by which they are satisfied. For this means that the whole case for the urgency of production, based on the urgency of wants, falls to the ground. One cannot defend production as satisfying wants if that production creates the wants.

Were it so that a man on arising each morning was assailed by demons which instilled in him a passion sometimes for silk shirts, sometimes for kitchenware, sometimes for chamber pots, and sometimes for orange squash, there would be every reason to applaud the effort to find the goods, however odd, that quenched this flame. But should it be that his passion was the result of his first having cultivated the demons, and should it also be that his effort to allay it stirred the demons to ever greater and greater effort, there would be question as to how rational was his solution. Unless restrained by conventional attitudes, he might wonder if the solution lay with more goods or fewer demons.

So it is that if production creates the wants it seeks to satisfy, or if the wants emerge *pari passu* with the production, then the urgency of the wants can no longer be used to defend the urgency of the production. Production only fills a void that it has itself created.

II

The point is so central that it must be pressed. Consumer wants can have bizarre, frivolous, or even immoral origins, and an admirable case can still be made for a society that seeks to satisfy them. But the case cannot stand if it is the process of satisfying wants that creates the wants. For then the individual who urges the importance of production to satisfy these wants is precisely in the position of the onlooker who applauds the efforts of the squirrel to keep abreast of the wheel that is propelled by his own efforts.

That wants are, in fact, the fruit of production will now be denied by few serious scholars. And a considerable number of economists, though not always in full knowledge of the implications, have conceded the point. In the observation cited at the end of the preceding chapter Keynes noted that needs of "the second class," i.e., those that are the result of efforts to keep abreast or ahead of one's fellow beings "may indeed be insatiable; for the higher the general level the higher still are they."[1] And emulation has always played a considerable role in the views of other economists of want creation. One man's consumption becomes his neighbor's wish. This already means that the process by which wants are satisfied is also the process by which wants are created. The more wants that are satisfied the more new ones are born.

However, the argument has been carried farther. A leading modern theorist of consumer behavior, Professor Duesenberry, has stated explicitly that "ours is a society in which

[1] *Op. cit.*

one of the principal social goals is a higher standard of living. . . . [This] has great significance for the theory of consumption . . . the desire to get superior goods takes on a life of its own. It provides a drive to higher expenditure which may even be stronger than that arising out of the needs which are supposed to be satisfied by that expenditure."[2] The implications of this view are impressive. The notion of independently established need now sinks into the background. Because the society sets great store by ability to produce a high living standard, it evaluates people by the products they possess. The urge to consume is fathered by the value system which emphasizes the ability of the society to produce. The more that is produced the more that must be owned in order to maintain the appropriate prestige. The latter is an important point, for, without going as far as Duesenberry in reducing goods to the role of symbols of prestige in the affluent society, it is plain that his argument fully implies that the production of goods creates the wants that the goods are presumed to satisfy.

III

The even more direct link between production and wants is provided by the institutions of modern advertising and salesmanship. These cannot be reconciled with the notion of independently determined desires, for their central function is to create desires—to bring into being wants that previously did not exist.[3] This is accomplished by the producer of the goods or at his behest. A broad empirical relationship exists between what is spent on production of consumers' goods and what is spent in synthesizing the desires for that production. A new consumer product must be introduced with a suitable advertising campaign to arouse an

[2] James S. Duesenberry, *Income, Saving and the Theory of Consumer Behavior* (Cambridge, Mass.: Harvard University Press, 1949), p. 28.

[3] Advertising is not a simple phenomenon. It is also important in competitive strategy and want creation is, ordinarily, a complementary result of efforts to shift the demand curve of the individual firm at the expense of others or (less importantly, I think) to change its shape by increasing the degree of product differentiation. Some of the failure of economists to identify advertising with want creation may be attributed to the undue attention that its use in purely competitive strategy has attracted. It should be noted, however, that the competitive manipulation of consumer desire is only possible, at least on any appreciable scale, when such need is not strongly felt.

interest in it. The path for an expansion of output must be paved by a suitable expansion in the advertising budget. Outlays for the manufacturing of a product are not more important in the strategy of modern business enterprise than outlays for the manufacturing of demand for the product. None of this is novel. All would be regarded as elementary by the most retarded student in the nation's most primitive school of business administration. The cost of this want formation is formidable. In 1956 total advertising expenditure—though, as noted, not all of it may be assigned to the synthesis of wants—amounted to about ten billion dollars. For some years it had been increasing at a rate in excess of a billion dollars a year. Obviously, such outlays must be integrated with the theory of consumer demand. They are too big to be ignored.

But such integration means recognizing that wants are dependent on production. It accords to the producer the function both of making the goods and of making the desires for them. It recognizes that production, not only passively through emulation, but actively through advertising and related activities, creates the wants it seeks to satisfy.

The businessman and the lay reader will be puzzled over the emphasis which I give to a seemingly obvious point. The point is indeed obvious. But it is one which, to a singular degree, economists have resisted. They have sensed, as the layman does not, the damage to established ideas which lurks in these relationships. As a result, incredibly, they have closed their eyes (and ears) to the most obtrusive of all economic phenomena, namely modern want creation.

This is not to say that the evidence affirming the dependence of wants on advertising has been entirely ignored. It is one reason why advertising has so long been regarded with such uneasiness by economists. Here is something which cannot be accommodated easily to existing theory. More pervious scholars have speculated on the urgency of desires which are so obviously the fruit of such expensively contrived campaigns for popular attention. Is a new breakfast cereal or detergent so much wanted if so much must be spent to compel in the consumer the sense of want? But there has been little tendency to go on to examine the implications of this for the theory of consumer demand and even less for the importance of production and productive efficiency. These have remained sacrosanct. More often the uneasiness has been manifested in a general disapproval of advertising and advertising men, leading to the occasional suggestion that they shouldn't exist. Such suggestions have usually been ill received.

And so the notion of independently determined wants still survives. In the face of all the forces of modern salesmanship it still rules, almost undefiled, in the textbooks. And it still remains the economist's mission—and on few matters is the pedagogy so firm—to seek unquestioningly the means for filling these wants. This being so, production remains of prime urgency. We have here, perhaps, the ultimate triumph of the conventional wisdom in its resistance to the evidence of the eyes. To equal it one must imagine a humanitarian who was long ago persuaded of the grievous shortage of hospital facilities in the town. He continues to importune the passers-by for money for more beds and refuses to notice that the town doctor is deftly knocking over pedestrians with his car to keep up the occupancy.

And in unraveling the complex we should always be careful not to overlook the obvious. The fact that wants can be synthesized by advertising, catalyzed by salesmanship, and shaped by the discreet manipulations of the persuaders shows that they are not very urgent. A man who is hungry need never be told of his need for food. If he is inspired by his appetite, he is immune to the influence of Messrs. Batten, Barton, Durstine & Osborn. The latter are effective only with those who are so far removed from physical want that they do not already know what they want. In this state alone men are open to persuasion.

IV

The general conclusion of these pages is of such importance for this essay that it had perhaps best be put with some formality. As a society becomes increasingly affluent, wants are increasingly created by the process by which they are satisfied. This may operate passively. Increases in consumption, the counterpart of increases in production, act by suggestion or emulation to create wants. Or producers may proceed actively to create wants through advertising and salesmanship. Wants thus come to depend on output. In technical terms it can no longer be assumed that welfare is greater at an all-round higher level of production than at a lower one. It may be the same. The higher level of production has, merely, a higher level of want creation necessitating a higher level of want satisfaction. There will be frequent occasion to refer to the way wants depend on the process by which they are satisfied. It will be convenient to call it the Dependence Effect.

We may now contemplate briefly the conclusions to which this analysis has brought us.

Plainly the theory of consumer demand is a peculiarly treacherous friend of the present goals of economics. At first glance it seems to defend the continuing urgency of production and our preoccupation with it as a goal. The economist does not enter into the dubious moral arguments about the importance or virtue of the wants to be satisfied. He doesn't pretend to compare mental states of the same or different people at different times and to suggest that one is less urgent than another. The desire is there. That for him is sufficient. He sets about in a workmanlike way to satisfy desire, and accordingly he sets the proper store by the production that does. Like woman's his work is never done.

But this rationalization, handsomely though it seems to serve, turns destructively on those who advance it once it is conceded that wants are themselves both passively and deliberately the fruits of the process by which they are satisfied. Then the production of goods satisfies the wants that the consumption of these goods creates or that the producers of goods synthesize. Production induces more wants and the need for more production. So far, in a major *tour de force*, the implications have been ignored. But this obviously is a perilous solution. It cannot long survive discussion.

Among the many models of the good society no one has urged the squirrel wheel. Moreover, as we shall see presently, the wheel is not one that revolves with perfect smoothness. Aside from its dubious cultural charm, there are serious structural weaknesses which may one day embarrass us. For the moment, however, it is sufficient to reflect on the difficult terrain which we are traversing. In Chapter VIII we saw how deeply we were committed to production for reasons of economic security. Not the goods but the employment provided by their production was the thing by which we set ultimate store. Now we find our concern for goods further undermined. It does not arise in spontaneous consumer need. Rather, the dependence effect means that it grows out of the process of production itself. If production is to increase, the wants must be effectively contrived. In the absence of the contrivance the increase would not occur. This is not true of all goods, but that it is true of a substantial part is sufficient. It means that since the demand for this part would not exist, were it not contrived, its utility or urgency, ex contrivance, is zero. If we regard this production as marginal, we may say that the marginal utility of present aggregate output, ex advertising and salesmanship, is zero. Clearly the attitudes and values which make production the central achievement of our society have some exceptionally twisted roots.

Perhaps the thing most evident of all is how new and varied become the problems we must ponder when we break the nexus with the work of Ricardo and face the economics of affluence of the world in which we live. It is easy to see why the conventional wisdom resists so stoutly such change. It is a far, far better thing to have a firm anchor in nonsense than to put out on the troubled seas of thought.

CHAPTER XII

The Illusion of National Security

ON THREE NIGHTS late in July and at the beginning of August 1943, the heavy planes of the RAF Bomber Command droned in from the North Sea and subjected the city of Hamburg to an ordeal such as Germans had not experienced since the Thirty Years' War. A third of the city was reduced to a wasteland. At least 60,000 and perhaps as many as 100,000 people were killed—about as many as at Hiroshima. A large number of these were lost one night when a ghastly "fire storm," which literally burned the asphalt pavements, swept a part of the city and swept everything into itself. Adolf Hitler heard the details of the attack and for the only known time during the war said it might be necessary to sue for peace. Hermann Goering visited the city with a retinue to survey the damage and was accorded so disconcerting a reception that he deemed it discreet to retire.

Yet this terrible event taught a lesson about the economics of war which very few have learned and some, indeed, may have found it convenient to ignore. The industrial plants of Hamburg were around the edge of the city or, as in the case of the submarine pens, on the harbor. They were not greatly damaged by the raids; these struck the center of the city and the working-class residential areas and suburbs. In the days immediately following the raids production faltered; in the first weeks it was down by as much as 20 or 25 per cent. But thereafter it returned to normal. By then the workers had scanned the ruins of their former homes, satisfied themselves that their possessions and sometimes their families were irretrievable, had found some rude clothes and the shelter of a room or part of a room in a still habitable house, and had returned to work. On these three nights of terror their standard of living, measured by houseroom, furnishings, clothing, food and drink, recreation, schools, and social and cultural opportunities, had been reduced to a fraction of what

131

it had been before. But the efficiency of the worker as a worker was unimpaired by this loss. After a slight period of readjustment, he labored as diligently and as skillfully as before.

There is a further chapter to the story. Before the attacks, there had been a labor shortage in Hamburg. Afterward, despite the number killed and the number now engaged on indispensable repairs, there was no shortage. For, as a result of the attacks, thousands who were waiters in restaurants and cafés, attendants in garages, clerks in banks, salesmen in stores, shopkeepers, janitors, ticket takers, and employees in handicraft industries (which, being small and traditional, were more likely to be in the center of town) lost their places of employment. They had previously contributed nothing to war production. Their contribution to the standard of living proved dispensable. Now they turned to the war industries as the most plausible places to find employment.

Even in the presumptively austere and dedicated world of the Third Reich, in the third year of a disastrous war, the average citizen had access to a wide range of comforts and amenities which habit had made to seem essential.[1] And because they were believed to be essential they were essential. On such matters governments, even dictatorships, must bow to the convictions of the people even if—the exceptional case—they do not share them. The German standard of living was far above what was physically necessary for survival and efficiency. The RAF broke through the psychological encrustation and brought living standards down somewhere nearer to the physical minimum. In doing so it forced a wholesale conversion of Germany's scarcest resource, that of manpower, to war production.

In reducing, as nothing else could, the consumption of nonessentials and the employment of men in their supply, there is a distinct possibility that the attacks on Hamburg

---

[1] In fact, in 1943 the Germans were not concentrating their energies with particular severity on war production. In this respect they were almost certainly behind the British at the time. Until not long before there had been a heady mood of victory with, inevitably, some relaxation. Quite a few of the Nazi leaders were sybarites and were thus somewhat handicapped in imposing austerities which they would not practice themselves. A dictatorship which does not quite trust its people is likely to be hesitant in imposing hardships. Finally, the strategy of industrial mobilization was poorly understood in Germany and this strategy assumed a short war. This failure of understanding was most important of all and might be a lesson.

increased Germany's output of war material and thus her military effectiveness.[2]

II

On few matters does the conventional wisdom have such authority as in military policy and international affairs. The problems here are difficult and infinite in their ramifications. Old ideas and old formulas are rocks on which men can stand. They are cherished as much as new thought, which so adds to the complexity of an already uncertain and complex world, is resisted. Moreover, where military policy is concerned, the effect of peace is to exempt the conventional wisdom from any test by experience. Since, as noted, it is ordinarily only experience which exposes error, the conventional wisdom is here admirably protected. Countries have rarely gone to war, at least in the last century, without discovering that the military wisdom which they had treasured in the previous period of peace as the nearest thing to divine revelation, was, when put to the test of circumstance, remarkably foolish. In the thirties few things were so thoroughly accepted as the invincibility of the Maginot Line, the stalwart effectiveness of the French Army, the speed and effortlessness with which American industry could convert to war, the daylight bombing virtuosity of the AAF, the great effectiveness of blockade and economic warfare, and the congenital weakness of Russia. All when put to the test of experience were found wanting. Understanding, as we do, the nature of the conventional wisdom, this will no longer surprise us.

In the years following World War II nothing had such massive standing in the conventional wisdom as the proposition that there is a direct correlation between national power and economic output. National power and therewith defensive capability and external security increased *pari passu* with increases in the Gross National Product. A country with a higher rate of increase was on the way to ultimate victory. "The ultimate survival of the free nations may well turn on their ability to develop their productive power. . . .

[2] These details are based on studies made in 1945 by the United States Strategic Bombing Survey (of which I was a director) which included a detailed investigation of the effect of the Hamburg raids. The Germans had an understandable pride in the speed of Hamburg's industrial recovery and kept detailed records which much facilitated the investigation.

he Soviet rulers are counting heavily on the economic growth of the Soviet Union . . ."[3] "On that day when the non-Communist world finds the way in which it can outrun the Communist world in the rate of growth without using totalitarian means, Communism will be defeated—and until then it will not be."[4]

There was even a degree of quiet pride in the sophistication of such conclusions. Men at last saw the bearing of economics on military capacity. Until Napoleonic times armies freely destroyed the economy of a country, even a friendly one, in order to victual their troops. As late as World War I generals went ahead with military plans in blithe ignorance of the ability of the economy to supply the supporting matériel. Indeed it was the strategic peculiarity of that conflict which first brought home the importance of economics. Men stood shoulder to shoulder in a continuous line from the Channel to Switzerland and had to be supplied. It was the highest military doctrine that they could not advance except after a mighty eruption of steel and explosive. Thus it came to pass that even the most dashing cavalry officer could see that the scale of the supporting economy had something to do with the size of the supporting barrage.[5]

[3] Assistant Secretary of State, before Ninth International Banking Seminar, Rutgers University, July 9, 1956.

[4] Former State Department economist, *New Republic,* April 29, 1947. While the conventional wisdom regularly accepts production, or rather the rate of increase in production, as the single and sufficient measure of national power, independent scholars have on occasion pressed the matter further. An interesting instance is an article by Mr. Peter Wiles ("Growth versus Choice," *Economic Journal,* vol. LXVI [June 1956], pp. 244-55). Mr. Wiles dismisses at the outset the notion that production can catch up with wants. "We need not here consider the possibility of an 'exhaustion of consumption opportunities' . . . when productivity is so great that all consumer needs can be satisfied. . . . Such a state of affairs, if possible at all, is obviously very far off indeed." He then proceeds to argue the urgency of a greater rate of growth in the West so that more resources will be available for domestic investment and capital exports. But obviously, if growth itself fosters the wants—if the two are interdependent—the extra resources will not become available for the purposes for which he seeks them. Indeed the very question he poses, Growth *versus* Choice, is a false one if the promotion and manipulation of the choosing is part of the process of production and growth.

[5] Ludendorff, in a highly rhetorical observation, attributed the German defeat to the "pitiless efficiency" of the American industrialists who he said understood war. In the conventional wisdom his compliment has the standing of canon law. No other observation has been more used to argue the importance of economic performance for military power. In fact, Ludendorff did not know what he was talking about. A man of slight economic knowledge, it would have been surprising if

Aided by this background it became possible in World War II to persuade almost everyone that the might of armies was related to the might of the economies that supplied them. The index of the latter was the Gross National Product. In the end victory did lie with the greatest GNP. This concept was then promptly imbedded in the conventional wisdom as the new dimension of military power. There it remains. And we react with satisfaction to the knowledge that we are aware of something more subtle than merely the bigness of the battalions. We are the victims of a serious and possibly a dangerous new illusion.

III

It will be evident, although this is only a first approximation, that it is not gross output but usable military output which counts. If all that is produced is required to sustain civilian consumption and none remains for military use, then production may be large and military strength can be very small indeed. One must consider both the available economic resources and the demands upon them. To talk of production without talking of related consumption is, obviously, like assessing the capacity of a barrel for catching water by considering its size and ignoring the detail of whether it is already full.

But there is much more to the problem. The size of the barrel becomes almost entirely irrelevant for measuring its ability to hold the rainwater if there are circumstances which tend always to keep it full. And this is the tendency of the economy, given the dependence effect. We increase its size but we do so by increasing, in one way or another, the demand for what it produces. This demand having increased along with the economy, it follows that there will never be much left over. If to increase economic output we must increase the desires for that output, things cannot be otherwise. If one more metaphor may be allowed, a balloon cannot be larger than the gas that is pumped into it.

In part these relationships are simply ignored by the conventional wisdom. Total production is the accepted measure

he had been able to relate economic to military power. British and French industrial power were, in fact, far more effective than our own. The year and a half of our engagement was not sufficient to bring our matériel to the Western Front in decisive quantities and, in fact, our troops were extensively supplied with British and French weapons as veterans of the conflict are aware.

of total resources available for defense, and that is the end of it. There are few enough solid truths in this world. Why doubt those we have?

At a more sophisticated level, however, there is an unquestioned assumption that in any emergency civilian wants can be easily and quickly suppressed and the production that has gone into satisfying them will then be available for public deployment. In fact, as will be argued presently, the resources that best serve peace or survival may be most needed in peacetime—when no emergency has been proclaimed which would justify cutting civilian wants. A society that expands production by expanding wants can never have a large margin available over seeming need. But the notion that production, given the dependence effect, can be readily made available in time of crisis involves appalling contradictions. They might easily have become fatal had modern technology not rendered obsolete the concepts of defense to which they are relevant.

For what is being suggested is that a society which in peacetime attributes the highest importance to the satisfaction of consumer wants—in which people are taught to believe that a great range of goods is essential for existence and elementary happiness—will, in the event of a national emergency, divest itself of these attitudes as simply and naturally as a man removes his nightshirt on arising. Needs so carefully nurtured will be forgotten. As a result, the capacity that supplied the goods can quickly be made available to the common effort. Having come to believe, like the people of Hamburg, that a given standard of living is minimal, and having been brought to this conclusion by the efforts of the world's most capable propagandists and persuaders, supported increasingly by the nation's most competent psychologists, they will divest themselves of this misconception effortlessly and unreluctantly and reduce their standard of living as required.

Patently this is nonsense—or at least a remarkable gamble. It is tantamount to saying that delusion will last until it is about to become fatal, at which point an onset of sanity is certain. It is far more likely that, having been persuaded of the need for automobiles as part of our way of life and that need being further affirmed by a pattern of living that makes us dependent on them, we will remain persuaded of the need for automobiles. That means that we will need the gasoline that powers them, the service stations that service them, the mechanics and the parts that keep them in operation, and even the new vehicles which replace the inevitable casualties of age and accident. As with automobiles so with kitchens, clothes, television, food, dishwashers, recreation, and nearly everything else. If we are committed to oil heat and oil burners in peacetime, will we be quickly uncommitted in time of emergency? Is it practical to suppose we can be? If we believe that fresh frozen orange juice is essential for our peacetime health, will we be quickly unpersuaded under the threat of war? This is not a case of a democracy being unwilling to make sacrifices. It is the very different case of a people who have persuaded themselves that these things are essential and cannot be sacrificed. Though the bamboozling was infinitely costly, we are nonetheless expected to believe that the de-bamboozling will be a simple act of rational will.

This argument must not be carried to extremes. Something can always be squeezed out. Some wants can be suppressed and some can be contracted. There can be savings here and there. And, though let no one seize on this as a serious concession, the savings, other things equal, can be larger in a large economy than in a small one. But the total of such savings cannot be equated with total production. Only a small part of the latter, in an economy where the dependence effect is operative, can be made available. In past periods of crisis, the amount thus made available for defense was comparatively small. Far more impressive was the output that became available as the result of serious and deliberate, as distinct from formal and passive, efforts to increase production.[6] We were saved, not by the size of the economy, but by our unused ability to expand it.

IV

Lest anyone suppose that this argument is academic, it is readily verified from experience, although in the central case of World War II, the lessons have been deeply disguised by the otherwise fortunate fact that we won the war. In 1941, as the danger of war became more and more evident, consumption was growing rapidly. This high and increasing level of consumption, together with domestic rearmament and aid to the British and other allies,[7] could not for long be provided

[6] See pages 103-09.
[7] Domestic rearmament began in a serious way in 1940 following the fall of France. The Lend Lease bill was enacted in early 1941.

out of the current capacity of the economy, at least without subjecting military supply to serious delays. Proposals were made in 1941 to cut back the production of civilian consumers' goods. These were fiercely resisted, most notably by the businessmen who had come to Washington to help mobilize the economy. Motives were mixed, and the passion of the time produced many accusations. Jockeying for competitive position, the fear of loss of peacetime markets, the well-developed tendency of the businessman in government to mistrust the long view and to assume that things will work out, all played a part. But underlying everything was the ultimate fact that people wanted the goods, regarded them as important, and that the men who made the goods shared the latter conviction and wanted to supply them. While there was a certain amount of intellectual resistance to these attitudes, they prevailed throughout 1941 and in an administration not noted for its identification with business. There were no important cutbacks in 1941, nor were any serious efforts made to arrest the increase in consumption. Had the New Deal been a business-oriented administration, the issue would scarcely have arisen.

Nor did the situation change nearly as much as is commonly supposed after the outbreak of war in December of 1941. Although not without difficulty, the production of metal-using goods was cut down or suspended. War, more precisely an old-fashioned war, makes a special demand on metals. But the consumption of goods in the aggregate was not reduced. On the contrary, it increased in every year of the war. Measured in constant (1947) prices the supply of consumers' goods available to and purchased by consumers increased from $122.5 billion to $145.2 billion worth or by about $23 billions from 1940 to 1945. In the next five free and unrestricted peacetime years the increase was not overwhelmingly greater—it was a little under $38 billion.[8] We did not use our productive capacity for war purposes in World War II in any meaningful sense. Rather we made concessions in our metal-producing and metal-using industries—it is significant that the Controlled Materials Plan, the most formidable and far-reaching of the wartime production controls, worked by limiting the use of a handful of scarce metals. We relied principally on our ability, then especially large because of previous unemployment, to increase production. An additional amount of capacity was obtained by the postponement of peacetime civilian investment.

[8] Department of Commerce Estimates. *Statistical Abstract*, 1956.

No one can doubt that it would have been profoundly difficult to arrest the increase in wartime civilian consumption. To reduce it in the absence of the assistance of enemy action as in Hamburg would assuredly have been formidable. This does not presuppose a shortage of patriotism Rather it reflects the attitudes which the dependence effect makes inevitable. If people and their leaders alike are persuaded that goods are important—as they must if production depends on persuasion—they cannot be quickly persuaded that they are unimportant. If a high standard of living is central in the American way of life, it will even be said that it is paradoxical to abandon it in a war to preserve the American way of life With time and effort the paradox can perhaps be resolved, but for that the leaders must have the requisite understanding. And leaders in a democracy are a part of the culture.

During World War II few things were so frequently emphasized as the importance of maintaining civilian morale. In the conventional wisdom of the time this was regarded as exceptionally important and exceptionally frail. It was also regarded as depending, all but exclusively, on the supply of consumer goods and services—on the quality of the housing, the supply of gasoline, the availability of recreation, even, as in the case of Los Angeles and other communities, the continued operation of the racetrack. Leadership attitudes, no less than others, accepted the need for the consumers' goods and services which the dependence effect had made to seem urgent. The process of expanding production insured that the production would not be readily available for other than civilian consumption.

As noted we won the war. We had the good fortune to be on the side of overwhelming manpower and vastly superior strategic position. We were blessed by the time in which to increase output. We had the support of two allies with far smaller productive plants but far greater ability to use them for military purposes. Ever since the war ended it has been a source of the most profound pride in the conventional wisdom that, while winning the greatest war in history, we were able to increase our civilian consumption by nearly twenty per cent. But had we lost there would have been a different, less comforting, though clearer view. Then discreet conversation, after dealing with the uncouth behavior of the occupying army, the ambiguous reactions of a neighboring daughter to rape, the ordeal of the Jews in the Bronx, and the increase in collaboration, would have turned to the man-

agement of the war. Generals might not have escaped rebuke.
But certainly no one would have mentioned with much
approval the record output of clothing in the years before
the final defeat, the expansive food supply supported by
special provisions in the draft, the exceedingly adequate
supply of gasoline, the remarkable expansion of other civilian
goods, the record rail travel, the way the railroads were able,
at the cost of a very large investment in rolling stock and
roadbed, to accommodate the unparalleled volume of civilian
and military business. It would then have been seen how
little of our economic capacity we used for the war. It would
then have been sensed that our presumed civilian needs kept
millions of men from facing the enemy or from supporting
with weapons and supplies those who did. Fortunately we
were saved the lesson. Unfortunately, given the power and
the comfort of the conventional wisdom, it is mostly by such
lessons that nations learn.

V

There is a marked likelihood that the foregoing argument
rests on military assumptions which are obsolete. We have
probably had the last of the conflicts that, even remotely,
could be called a Gross National Product war. It is implausi-
ble to suppose that the United States will for a third time
have a chance to mobilize and deploy its industrial resources
in an orderly, undisturbed fashion while the enemy is fought
by friends on distant fronts. But attitudes on the relation of
production to military power are rooted in the past. As
always, the conventional wisdom must first be attacked on
its own grounds.

If one is condemned to consider the possibilities, there now
remain very broadly two possible kinds of wars. One follows
the pattern of the Korean war where the scale, objectives, and
weapons are all circumscribed. There is also the atomic and
thermo-nuclear holocaust.

The aggregate output of the economy is obviously unimportant for the limited war. The U. S. economy was not
tested by the Korean war, nor would it have been by several.
The defeats in the early months were the result not of a
shortage of ultimate resources, but of a shortage of trained
manpower and weapons either in being or in position. The
problem was not the potential but the preparation.

The lack of preparation rested on two factors. There was the simple miscalculation of the likelihood of the event. But there was the further fact that during the preceding five years from 1945 to 1950, although production had been higher than ever before in peacetime, consumer requirements had been equally high as befits an economy where their level depends on the level of production. In consequence (though as always other forces were at work), military outlays had been kept to a level where they did not interfere appreciably with civilian consumption.

Once the war broke out in Korea, the civilian economy and the effort to protect the conventional standard of living became an immediate and clear-cut threat to the effective prosecution of the war. Consumers, anticipating possible shortages, immediately began to protect themselves against a deprivation which, in light of their peacetime persuasion, they inevitably regarded as painful or even intolerable. They proceeded to the shops to equip themselves with automobiles, radios, kitchen durables, washing machines, irons, furniture, canned goods, and other products in unprecedented volume. From the second quarter of 1950, the last three months of peace, to the third quarter, the first three months of the war, expenditures for national defense increased $1.8 billions. Consumer expenditures increased $13.1 billions. By the first quarter of 1951 defense spending was up $12.9 billions as compared with the last peacetime quarter, but civilian spending had increased $19.0 billions. Under these circumstances the size of the economy was almost irrelevant. The efforts of consumers to sustain (and given the uncertainties of the future, to insure) what persuasion had caused them to regard as a minimum standard of living effectively pre-empted the total output of the economy and more. The result was a damaging inflation. In the early part of 1951 it was necessary to impose price controls. Meanwhile military production was increasing slowly and painfully in the face of the civilian competition for goods. The conventional wisdom continued to emphasize the importance of the size of the economy and its rate of growth in assessing our military power.

Nor has further evidence challenged the cliché.[9] In the years from 1953 until 1957 the Department of Defense was headed by Mr. Charles E. Wilson, a former President of

---

[9] Since this was written, Russian technological advances have indeed challenged the conventional wisdom at this point.

General Motors. The Department of the Treasury was headed by Mr. George M. Humphrey, a former head of the M. A. Hanna Company. Both of these industrialists stoutly maintained throughout this period that what the United States could spend on defense was strictly circumscribed. It would be dangerous, they warned repeatedly, to spend more than we could afford. To do so would only bring comfort to our enemies, distress and consternation to our own people, and serious, though mostly unspecified, damage to our economy.

Their position was widely criticized. Economists and journalists joined in emphasizing their error. The objects of the criticism were not notably impressed. Nor was there particular reason why they should be. They were accepting the position of their critics and carrying it to its inevitable, if absurd, conclusion. The critics themselves asserted the importance of production for military power. In doing so they underwrote, without realizing it, the importance of the civilian goods being produced and hence the unavailability of the capacity for military purposes. Messrs. Wilson and Humphrey merely made this point explicit. They noted, as must be so given the dependence effect, that consumption had grown *pari passu* with production, that to divert some of the latter to military purposes would be at the expense of consumption. And accepting the logic of the situation, along with the importance the society attaches to consumption, they concluded that this could not be afforded. Any other conclusion would have been remarkable. Men who have spent their lives making automobiles, or providing raw materials to that industry, do not easily conclude that automobiles are unimportant.

If production is held in high esteem, then we shall also esteem the goods we produce. As a result there will always be close limits on what we can spare for military purposes. Given the present economic goals, there always will be. The size of the economy, by which so many set store, is quite illusory as a clue to what is available.

If a sizable armed force is necessary for protection against small disputes—if men can devise no better arrangements for conciliation than recourse to arms—then productive virtuosity and growth are no guarantee that we shall have it. On the contrary, the processes of growth, as they now operate *both* on output and on wants, are as likely to be damaging as helpful to such power.

VI

One of the tolerable features of old-fashioned wars was that the military planner could proceed with his task in the reasonably secure knowledge that in the event of hostilities someone else would be killed. This contributed to the interest and the sense of detachment which he brought to his task. Planning for thermo-nuclear warfare, the other type of conflict with which presumably we must reckon, is a more disenchanting task. These weapons make it likely that the planner, along with everyone else, will be extinguished under circumstances which allow for a minimum of graceful gestures at the end.

Yet if only for pressing home a point, it is evident that such conflict will allow for no time-consuming conversion of consumers' goods capacity and productive skills to war purposes, and it thus reduces nearly to irrelevance the bearing of civilian production and capacity on military power.

The perilous strategy of deterrence, on which for the present we rely, places its emphasis on peacetime preparedness—on warning systems, interception, a retaliatory force in being, shelters and, perhaps most of all, a scientific dynamic of the highest order. But here, once again, the question is not the size of the economy but how much can be diverted to public purposes. (This includes not only public spending for weapons and protection but also for schooling and training the highly developed manpower that is required.) The same process which makes the economy large makes large the private demands upon it and makes small what seemingly can be spared for public use. Even the conventional wisdom, with its reiterated emphasis on the all-embracing importance of output, will occasionally concede the difficulty in extracting resources for the present purposes.

VII

The purpose of the foregoing argument is to deal with a myth—the myth that military power is a function of economic output. If peace and survival are to be achieved, the search must almost certainly go beyond the effort to find a balance in thermo-nuclear terror. The present analysis bears strongly on this search. There will be occasion to return to these matters, but a preliminary word is in order.

The role of the rich man in the poor community has never been an easy one although it is noteworthy, considering the number of philosophers who have dwelt on the miseries of riches, that few men of means have found it desirable to exchange their wealth for the more graceful situation of the insolvent. The American rich, as noted in Chapter VII, have long since found it wise, as well as more fashionable, to suppress the cruder manifestation of opulence. They now seek prestige not by determinedly adding to their hoard but in public toil and good works. The number of exceedingly well-to-do Americans who have made a success in politics as the accepted friends of the masses attests to the success of the formula. The rich may have their problems, but they are not insuperable.

The analogy between men and states is an exceedingly perilous one, but here at least there is a parallel. We are led, as a nation, by our present preoccupations, to adopt numerous of the least elegant postures of wealth. Though we have much, and much of the remainder of the world is poor, we are single-mindedly devoted to getting more. This is for the satisfaction of wants which our well-being has induced or which—and the advertising art is not one which by its nature can be concealed—we have synthesized. And we are, on the whole, rather solemn about the whole process.

We do, each year, provide some aid for others. But first we have a prayerful discussion of whether or not we can afford the sacrifice. The question is, indeed, inescapable, since production keeps wants abreast of itself. Elsewhere in the world, however, it is our vast well-being and not the urgency of our need which is evident. The nineteenth-century plutocrat who devoted his energies to expanding his already considerable income; who was led by his competitive position in the plutocracy to live on a suitably ostentatious scale; who found, as a result, that his income was never entirely adequate; who came to the aid of the poor only after a careful consideration of their worth, his ability to spare from his needs and the realistic likelihood of revolt and disorder if he abstained; and who believed withal that God inspired his enterprise and generosity and often said so, was not in all respects an attractive figure. Thus with nations.

Without entering further into the matter it is plain that our wealth is a valuable weapon. No other country has its equivalent. It is, presumptively, a valuable instrument for reducing the tensions that grow out of privation, helping to organize international order and thus possibly to insure survival. But as things now stand it is largely unavailable, and to the extent that it is available its usefulness is gravely impaired.

In recent times no problem has been more puzzling to thoughtful people than why, in a troubled world, we make such poor use of our affluence. Some failure of statesmanship has been regularly assumed. Now it is clear that the trouble lies much deeper. It is an aspect of our economic attitudes. It will persist as long as these remain unexamined.

CHAPTER XIII

The Vested Interest in Output

THE NOTION of a vested interest has an engaging flexibility in our social usage. In ordinary intercourse it is an improper advantage enjoyed by a political minority to which the speaker does not himself belong. When the speaker himself enjoys it, it ceases to be a vested interest and becomes a hard-won reward. When a vested interest is enjoyed not by a minority but by a majority, it is a human right. These conceptual pitfalls notwithstanding, the time has come for a survey of the vested interests in our present attitudes toward production. Who is most dependent on the present illusion? Who will be most affected when, under the onslaught of ideas, circumstances, and time itself, these matters come to appear in a clearer light? As a general makes a reconnaissance of the opposing forces, the author should know who is dug in against him. Moreover, along with the accepted theory of consumer demand and the conventional attitudes on national security, we must allow a place for self-interest as a bulwark of present attitudes. It is known to play a certain role in our society.

Without question the individual with the greatest stake in the present economic goals is the businessman—more precisely, perhaps, the important business executive. If production is of preoccupying importance he, as the man with the traditional and established right to the title of producer, will be the dominant figure in the social constellation. Society will accord him prestige appropriate to the role he plays; what may well be less important, he will be able, without difficulty or criticism, to command an income that is related to his prestige. As production has increasingly monopolized our economic attitudes, the business executive has grown in esteem. So long as inequality was a matter of serious concern the tycoon had, at best, an ambiguous position. He performed a function of obvious urgency. But he was also regularly accused of taking far too much for his services. As concern for inequality has declined, this reaction has disappeared. The businessman is no longer subject to a serious challenge of any sort. Although in his hierarchical role in the large corporation he has, perhaps, been more successful than most in eliminating economic insecurity, both personal and institutional, he has even managed to retain a certain cachet as a risk-taker, a man who lives dangerously. No one questions the superior position of the businessman in American society. But no one should doubt that it depends on the continuing preoccupation with production.

The case of water under conditions of plenty and shortage has been mentioned before. In the year 1950 the City of New York suffered from a potentially troublesome water shortage. Clouds were watched anxiously and seeded in the hope that they might yield their burden. With fanfare a program of water conservation was launched. The washing of automobiles, dripping of faucets, sluicing of streets, and cooling of air were all prohibited. Presiding over the considerable publicity which these results required was the New York City water commissioner, Mr. Stephen J. Carney. For a time he was the most important man in the metropolis. His name was on everyone's tongue. Mr. Carney was a public figure. Then the rains came, and the reservoirs filled. Carney was forgotten. One day he was quietly dropped. No one noticed.

The title of producer in our society seems securely honorific. The head of a distillery, a drive-in theater, or a dog track is a producer. He is not a basic producer which is better, but a producer nonetheless. As such he enjoys a position in the community as one of its supports or pillars and the sources of its wealth, which is not necessarily enjoyed by the high school principal or the parish priest. It is as a producer that the president of the United States Steel Corporation calls on the President of the United States. We are glad to see a department of government in the hands of a production man. Nothing better can be said of any individual than that he knows production. But the prestige of the producer is only the prestige of production. Should production ever come to be taken for granted, so, in some measure, will the producer. Mr. Carney is a warning.

II

Men fight for what is important to them, and the businessman who senses his self-interest will battle vigorously for a value system which emphasizes the importance of production. Indeed, and perhaps more intuitively than otherwise, he already does. The business liturgy now accords an important place to resonant assertions of the vital role of production. "Only the productive can be strong. Only the strong can be free." "Production made America . . ." "Let us stop bickering and produce."

The widespread suspicion and even hostility of businessmen to government, even when, as in the case of the Eisenhower Administration, it was presumptively sympathetic to business, is one of the great constants in our political life. In part this is because the businessman is a sizable taxpayer and hence regards government services as in conflict with his economic interest. But we are too addicted in our social comment to a kind of mechanical economic determinism. Modern government also represents perhaps the major threat to the businessman's prestige. To the extent that problems of military defense, foreign policy, agricultural administration, public works, education, and social welfare are central to our thoughts, so the generals, foreign service officers, administrators, teachers, and other professional public servants are the popular heroes. Businessmen have almost certainly sensed this competiiton in modern times, and it is equally certain that it has conditioned their attitudes toward government. One of its manifestations is a vehement insistence that the government does not produce anything, that it is a barren whore. "Government is powerless to create anything in the sense in which business produces wealth and individuals produce ideas [and] inventions. . . ."[1] The case involves some rather strained argument—it makes education unproductive and the manufacturer of the school toilet seats productive—but, nonetheless, it has a position of considerable prominence in the business liturgy.

A tension, perhaps ultimately more important, has also long existed between businessmen and the intellectuals. "The emergence of a numerous class of . . . frivolous intellectuals is one of the least welcome phenomena of the age of modern

[1] Sutton, *et al.*, *The American Business Creed*, p. 195.

capitalism. Their obtrusive stir repels discriminating people. They are a nuisance."[2] As in the case of the government the basis of the tension has long been assumed to be economic. "The men whose research has given rise to new methods of production hate the businessmen who are merely interested in the cash value of their research work. It is very significant that such a large number of American research physicists sympathize with socialism and communism. . . . University teachers of economics are also opposed to what they disparagingly call the profit system. . . ."[3] However, although the actual or suspected social radicalism of intellectuals may well contribute to hostility between businessmen and intellectuals, it is most doubtful if the tension would disappear even were intellectuals to conform their social attitudes to a line laid down by Senator John W. Bricker of Ohio. Scientists, writers, professors, artists are also important competitors of the businessmen for public esteem.

This competition is especially noticeable in comment on public affairs—economic policy, foreign policy, the effect of government measures on popular morals and behavior. Perhaps the most honorific function in our time is that of social prophecy. No one enjoys quite such distinction as the man who, by common consent, is allowed to look ahead into the unknown and tell us what will happen and advise us as to what we should do to promote or retard a particular occurrence. The intellectual naturally assumes his authority on these matters. He is likely to be gifted well beyond the businessman in erudition and oral capacity. That felicity the businessman counters by stressing his identification with production. He is not a "theorist" but a practical man. He has the forthright approach of the man who knows how to get things done. He has learned about life in his own shop; this has provided him with a unique insight into how things are in the country at large or the world. Nothing is more suggestive in our social attitudes than the notion that almost any issue, however cosmic, can be best appreciated by a man who has had some practical experience with a lathe. Were anything to happen to the prestige of production, it is plain that the businessman, whose mystique is his identification with production, would suffer severely in his competition with the intellectual for the role of social prophet. If he wishes to

[2] Ludwig von Mises, *The Anti-Capitalistic Mentality* (Princeton: Van Nostrand, 1956), p. 107.

[3] *Ibid.*, p. 20. Professor Mises, it should be observed in fairness, would be regarded by most businessmen as rather extreme.

defend himself in his present role, he must defend the importance of production. He can almost certainly be expected to do so.

There will be occasion presently for a further word on the competition between the businessman and the intellectual for contemporary esteem.

III

Politics have long been known to make incongruous bedfellows. More rarely, however, have those between the same sheets remained largely unaware of their intimate if odd companionship. This is the strange case with the vested interests in production. Supporting the businessman on the all-importance of the production of goods is the professional American liberal. The prestige which the businessman derives from production is reinforced by the nearly full weight of American liberal and radical comment. The reason for this alliance, though it requires some explanation, is not essentially complex. Men who hold tenaciously to a life raft may expect to be cast upon strange shores among strange companions. So it is with those who hold long enough to an idea amid changing currents and tides. As so often happens, the course of developments in Britain, in broad contour if not in detail, has been much the same as in the United States.

Until about twenty-five years ago the American liberal, so far as he was concerned with the total output of the economy, addressed himself to the problem of the efficient use of the available resources in capital, manpower, and materials. He insisted not without passion that this goal be not defeated by monopoly, tariffs, labor, or capital immobility, or other interferences with optimal use. To increase output by increasing the rate of capital formation or by expanding the total labor force or by a serious effort to increase the rate of technological innovation was no more in the minds of liberals (or others) than now.[4] Most important of all, the loss of production as the result of depressions was not peculiarly a liberal concern. No one was deeply committed politically on this problem; conservatives had an equal interest with liberals in "smoothing out" the business cycle. During the decade of the twenties the political leadership in discussion of possible means to mitigate the business cycle was assumed by Herbert Hoover.

[4] See p. 111-12.

The classical program of American liberals, until the decade of the thirties, sought the redistribution of the existing income, greater economic security, and the protection of the liberties and immunities of individuals and organizations in face of the highly unequal distribution of economic power. The progressive income tax; the development of government services; the protection of public resources from private appropriation; the extensions of social security; aid to farmers or other especially disadvantaged groups; the strengthening of trade unions; and the regulation of corporations all served these ends. None of these measures was thought much to affect the total output of the economy.

All this changed very much during the decade of the thirties. The Great Depression brought production to a very low level. Between 1929 and 1933 the gross output of the private economy dropped by between a third and a half. The sheer magnitude of this movement focused attention, as never before, on movements in the total output of the economy and on their far-reaching consequences for economic and political fortune. Characteristically, to increase production was less central to men's thoughts than to reduce unemployment. "Our greatest primary task is to put people back to work," Roosevelt said in his first inaugural. But whether directly or as a by-product of the effort to reduce economic insecurity, expanded production began to acquire a growing significance to political liberalism in its American sense.

Then in 1936 came John Maynard Keynes. In the Keynesian system the notion of an aggregate demand for the output of the economy which determined the total production of the economy was central. Depending on various factors, production might find its equilibrium at a high level or a low one. There was no immutable tendency for it to settle at the particular level where all willing workers had a chance for employment. And by manipulating the level of aggregate demand—the most obvious devices were to add to demand by government spending in excess of taxation, or to subtract from it by taxation in excess of spending—the government could influence the level of production.

The rewards from a successful operation on the level of output were breathtaking. To increase production was to ameliorate unemployment, agricultural insecurity, the threat of bankruptcy to the small businessman, the risks of investors, the financial troubles of the states and cities, even the wretched overcrowding which results when people cannot afford to own or rent their own homes and must double up. Scarcely a single social problem was left untouched. And within a few years after Keynes the level of production became the critical factor in war mobilization. It was principally by increased output (pages 137 to 140) that we provided for the war.

As a result, production did more than impress the liberal. It became his program, and it established something akin to a monopoly over his mind. Here was perhaps the nearest thing to alchemy that had ever been seen in the field of politics. Increased production solved, or seemed to solve, nearly all of the social problems of the day.

Furthermore, at least for a time, the practical concern for the total output of the economy was a liberal franchise. Conservatives hesitated to abandon the balanced budget, for so long a canon of the conventional wisdom.[5] To do so was essential. To manipulate the level of production also meant that the role of government must be enlarged. This too was unpalatable to conservatives, for it accorded a prestige to government which had previously been accorded exclusively to private production.

Most important of all for its influence on the liberal mind, the promise to raise production and reduce unemployment won elections. From the late thirties to the early fifties the promise to maintain high production and therewith high employment was the liberal's major claim to votes in the United States, and it was unbeatable. Very nearly the same thing was true of the left in Britain.

Liberal economic policy is still deeply preoccupied with production. As memories of the underproduction of the depression years have faded somewhat, the slogans have ceased to emphasize full employment and have come to stress the expanding economy. Platforms, manifestoes, and speeches develop the vision of a growing, ever more productive America. "We have the resources and machines, the science and skills to expand production and consumption at an accelerating rate, even relative to our rapidly growing population. But we are not seizing boldly this historic opportunity."[6]

---

[5] Although numerous liberals, including unquestionably Roosevelt himself, were also reluctant. And some chose to become conservatives on the issue.

[6] From the introduction to "Consumption—Key to Full Prosperity" by the Conference on Economic Progress, 1957, as printed in *ADA World*, May 1957. However, it should be made clear that the Conference on Economic Progress and its leaders have emphasized the importance of growth not alone for the expansion of private consumption but very specifically as a way of providing for needed and urgent public services.

The economic creed of American liberalism is more production. This, it should be noted, is aggregate output. The question of the distribution of the product so produced—who gets it—is decidedly secondary. To be overly concerned with it is to seem a trifle old-fashioned. There is almost no concern at all over the kinds of private goods and services that are produced. All are important and the total counts.

IV

The preoccupation of the American liberal with production, it may be observed in passing, is an interesting example of the hold of the conventional wisdom in face of changing circumstances. In the two decades and slightly more since Keynes's *General Theory* conservatives, save on the extreme right, have swallowed their distaste for the measures that the Keynesian program requires and have implicitly adopted it. Neither the Eisenhower Administration in the United States nor the Conservative ministries of Churchill, Eden, and Macmillan in Britain were less committed in principle to full employment and economic expansion than their Democratic or Labour opposition. Had it been thought otherwise they could not have won office.

Moreover, the strategic position of conservatives, especially in the United States, is in some respects stronger in relation to this policy than that of liberals. Should it prove possible to maintain full employment for a considerable number of years, people will eventually forget to whom they are indebted for originating the policy. They will cease to be impressed by the liberal claim to a patent on full employment policies. Producers will come to seem the natural custodians of production. Conservative businessmen, not liberal politicians, will have the natural claim to office on this platform.

There is another curiosity of the liberal position. The issue on which he won during the thirties and which continued to bring him victories for another decade was the promise of the increased production that eliminated unemployment. This was something of massive importance. But having discovered production, he has remained with it. He has continued to stress the importance of the increased output in periods when that involved not the elimination of unemployment but the increase in output of the already employed. He has believed, in brief, that increased production remains the touchstone of political success even when it involves additions to an already opulent supply of goods. Between increases in production that cure widespread unemployment and increases in production that add to affluence, there is a difference not in degree but in kind. In continuing to emphasize production, liberals, who once had a great issue, have without realizing it come to possess no issue at all. Yet this is not surprising. No less than any others, liberals accept the elaborate rationalization by which we persuade ourselves of the continued urgency of additions to our stock of consumers' goods.

Nor is there likely to be any change in the liberal position in the near future. Few things are so immutable as the addiction of political groups to the ideas by which they have once won office. Conservatives can be reasonably assured of the continuing if unavowed support of their opposition. Businessmen who depend for their position and prestige, and also for a goodly share of their political power, on the prestige of production will find that prestige eloquently attested by liberal manifestoes. The National Association of Manufacturers should make a token contribution to the treasury of the Americans for Democratic Action.

However, this is a digression. For present purposes we need only observe that Keynes concentrated the eyes of liberals on production, and their political successes gave them a vested interest in it. Keynesian attitudes became, as ever, the new conventional wisdom. The liberal reaction to any questioning of the role we presently assign to production will, one imagines, be little less outraged than that of producers.

V

Browning observed that "Jove strikes the Titans down, not when they set about their mountain-piling but when another rock would crown their work." The position of our present economic goals could scarcely look more secure. Is there a chance, nonetheless, that this is their moment of weakness?

That the security of our present preoccupation with production *qua* production is formidable there can be no doubt. It has inherited the concern once felt for equality. It is powerfully reinforced by the service it renders to economic security. It is rationalized by an elaborate and traditional, even if meretricious, theory of consumer demand. It has the sacred support of national security even though the relation may in fact add to our peril. For businessmen production means prestige. For liberal politicians it is thought to mean public office.

Yet the goals may not be impregnable. There may well be some cracks in the façade. How significant they are no one can guess. But they are worth remarking.

The prestige of production depends on the prestige of goods. In the more censorious social levels of American society there is already a well-developed and even fashionable aversion to gadgetry. (The word gadget is itself a pejorative term for durable goods.) In such circles shiny rumpus rooms, imaginative barbecue pits, expansive television screens, and magnificent automobiles no longer win acclaim. They may even invite mild social obloquy. A degree of shabbiness in personal attire is now occasionally sought, especially among males. We have here what could be an incipient revolt against goods or at least a refusal to allow competitive emulation to be the source of wants.

Even more suggestive is the belief of the businessman that his position in the community is slipping. This is reflected in the recurrent complaints that the country does not appreciate the problems of the business executive, does not sufficiently accept his advice and leadership, and that business is not "selling itself" to the American people. This latter is also, and perhaps more immediately, related to the fear of unpleasant or inimical tax or regulatory legislation or the drift toward "socialism." But even that implies that the country is insufficiently willing to accept the leadership and respect the warnings of businessmen. Neither Carnegie nor the elder Morgan thought it necessary to make such complaints.

Equally suggestive, the businessman who is seriously in search of public esteem must now show that he is something more than a producer of goods.

The rise of the public relations industry, which draws its clientele overwhelmingly from among business executives, shows that business achievement is no longer of itself a source of acclaim. At a minimum the achievement must be advertised. But the first task of the public relations man, on taking over a business client, is to "re-engineer" his image to include something besides the production of goods. His subject must be a statesman, a patron of education, or a civic force. Increasingly some artistic or intellectual facet must be found. A businessman who reads *Business Week* is lost to fame. One who reads Proust is marked for greatness.

These added requirements for esteem are unquestionably related to changing attitudes toward goods. In the early years of the automobile age it was sufficient for Henry Ford or R. E. Olds that they were makers of cars. What indeed could be a source of more acclaim? Now the automobile has become commonplace. And in the more *recherché* attitudes, it is even big, ungainly, and unfunctional in its shape and decoration. It is easy to see why the modern car manufacturer does not enjoy the eminence of a Ford or an Olds.

As noted, the intellectual, along with the public official and politician, is the natural competitor of the businessman for what may be called the solemn acclaim of the community.[7] (Neither competes with Hollywood, baseball, television commentators, or café society for what both agree is the frivolous applause of the community.) In fact the position of the intellectual is almost certainly more secure than that of the businessman. It would hardly occur to a successful poet or scientist to hire a public relations man, just as it would scarcely seem wise for a successful corporation president to do without one. Although the businessman must, increasingly, show that he is at home with ideas, it does not occur to the philosopher or artist that he should show that he is a good businessman. Perhaps most suggestive of all, American intellectuals long ago created what amounts to a second-class citizenship for the intellectual efforts of the business executive. They listen to his speeches, review his books, and receive his ideas with respectful attention. But they do not judge them to be good or bad in themselves. They are good (or on occasion bad) for a businessman. It is well understood that this is a much lower standard.

In Gabriel Chevallier's *Clochemerle* the *curé* was by no means the leading figure in the village by the more ostensible standards of that agreeable community. He was a competent but not a brilliant drinker; he was prevented by the cloth from displaying the amorous enterprise by which the community set such store. But his ultimate triumph was complete, for he alone held the keys to heaven. In the United States no business executive has arrived until, on one sunny summer morning, he walks in procession with the right combination of solemnity and relaxed amiability and receives a reputable honorary degree.

Still these are no more than straws in the wind. The miracle is still the prestige that we associate with production and therewith with producers. Nothing could be more remarkable than the beliefs and the illusions which have kept it intact since Ricardo. In doubting its supreme power we are challenging a phenomenon that is still of heroic proportions.

[7] For a roughly similar conclusion see Russell Lynes, *A Surfeit of Honey* (New York: Harper, 1957).

CHAPTER XIV

The Bill Collector Cometh

THE SITUATION is this. Production for the sake of the goods produced is no longer very urgent. The significance of marginal increments (or decrements) in the supply of goods is slight. We sustain a sense of urgency only because of attitudes that trace to the world not of today but into which economics was born. These are reinforced by an untenable theory of consumer demand, an obsolete, erroneous, and even somewhat dangerous identification of production with military power, and by a system of vested interests which marries both liberals and conservatives to the importance of production.

At the same time production does remain important and urgent for its effect on economic security. When men are unemployed, society does not miss the goods they do not produce. The loss here is marginal. But the men who are without work *do* miss the income they no longer earn. Here the effect is not marginal. It involves all or a large share of the men's earnings and hence all or a large share of what they are able to buy. And, we note, high and stable production is the broad foundation of the economic security of virtually every other group—of farmers, white-collar workers, and both large businessmen and small. The depression also remains the major uncovered risk of the modern large corporation. It is for reasons of economic security that we must produce at capacity.

These simple conclusions will not be well regarded by the conventional wisdom. To urge the importance of production because of its bearing on economic security, and to suggest that the product is in any way incidental, is disturbing. It brings the economic society to the brink of the dubious world of make-work and boondoggling. One of the escapes from this world is to make all wants urgent, and no doubt we have here another reason for the obscurantist rationalization of

consumer demand. It still seems more satisfactory to say that
we need the goods than to stress the real point which is that
social well-being and contentment require that we have
enough production to provide income to the willing labor
force. But if anyone has surviving doubts as to where the
real priorities lie, let him apply a simple test. Let him assume
that a President, or other candidate for re-election to major
public office, has the opportunity of defending a large increase
in man-hour productivity which has been divided equally
between greatly increased total output and greatly increased
unemployment. And let it be assumed that as an alternative
he might choose unchanged productivity which has left everyone employed. That full employment is more desirable than
increased production combined with unemployment would be
clear alike to the most sophisticated and the most primitive
politician.

The foregoing provides the basic rule of procedure for the
remainder of this essay. It shows that we need not be much
concerned with the supply of goods for their own sake. The
urgencies here are founded not on substance but on myth.
And, indeed, our ultimate purpose is to see the opportunities
that emerge as this myth is dispelled. But in all this we must
be exceedingly conscious of the importance of production
for its bearing on the economic security of individuals. As a
source of income for people its importance remains undiminished. This function of production must be carefully
safeguarded.

But myth is rarely benign. And the system of illusions
which causes us to attach such importance to production for
its own sake is itself damaging or dangerous. One danger
arises in the devices by which we fabricate wants and this,
indeed, nurtures a threat to the security of employment and
income which production provides. Our failure to solve the
problem of inflation is also the result of present attitudes
toward the production of goods. And the way that present
attitudes cause us to emphasize the supply of some as distinct
from all goods and services is the source of deeper social
dangers. To these problems, beginning with the dangers
inherent in the present methods of manufacturing wants, the
essay now turns.

II

The immediate danger in the way wants are now created lies
in the related process of debt creation. Consumer demand

thus comes to depend more and more on the ability and willingness of consumers to incur debt. And there are aspects of this debt creation which are inherently unstable.

An increase in consumer debt is all but implicit in the process by which wants are now synthesized. Advertising and emulation, the two dependent sources of desire, work across the society. They operate on those who can afford and those who cannot. With those who lack the current means it is a brief and obvious step from stimulating their desire by advertising to making it effective in the market with a loan. The relation of emulation to indebtedness is even more direct. Every community contains individuals with a wide range of difference in ability to pay. The example of those who can pay bears immediately on those who cannot. They must incur debt if they are to keep abreast. The great increase in consumer indebtedness in our time has been widely viewed as reflecting some original or unique change in popular attitudes or behavior. People have changed their view of debt. Thus there has been an inexplicable but very real retreat from the Puritan canon that required an individual to save first and enjoy later. In fact, as always, the pieces of economic life are parts of a whole. It would be surprising indeed if a society that is prepared to spend thousands of millions to persuade people of their wants were to fail to take the further step of financing these wants, and were it not then to go on to persuade people of the ease and desirability of incurring debt to make these wants effective. This has happened. The process of persuading people to incur debt, and the arrangements for them to do so, are as much a part of modern production as the making of the goods and the nurturing of the wants. The Puritan ethos was not abandoned. It was merely overwhelmed by the massive power of modern merchandising.

Viewing this process as a whole, we should expect that every increase in consumption will bring a further increase—possibly a more than proportional one—in consumer debt. Our march to higher living standards will be paced, as a matter of necessity, by an ever deeper plunge into debt. The evidence is already impressive. The increase in living standards in the twenties was accompanied by a relatively much greater increase in consumer borrowing. The same was true during the years of recovery in the thirties. It has been most spectacularly the case since World War II. In the five years from the end of 1952 to the end of 1956 total consumer debt (not including real estate loans) increased from $27.4 billions to $41.7 billions or by 53 per cent. Installment credit increased by 63 per cent and that for automobiles by nearly a hundred per cent. Although these were years of high prosperity, disposable income of individuals increased by only about twenty-one per cent.[1] In 1955 one family in four of those with incomes between $3000 and $4000 bought an automobile, and 69 per cent of those did so on credit. Of families with incomes between $4000 and $5000, more than one in three bought a car in that year, and 66 per cent did so on credit. Only among the families with incomes in excess of $10,000 did the proportion of cash buyers exceed the proportion of credit buyers. About thirty per cent of those who bought cars on credit in 1955 had bought their previous car the same way and still had debt outstanding on that vehicle.[2]

One wonders, inevitably, about the tensions associated with debt creation on such a massive scale. The legacy of wants, which are themselves inspired, are the bills which descend like the winter snow on those who are buying on the installment plan. By millions of hearths throughout the land it is known that when these harbingers arrive the repossession man cannot be far behind. Can the bill collector be the central figure in the good society?

In 1955 the median income of the American family before taxes was $3960. Of all families within the income range from $3000 to $4000, 48 per cent had installment payments to meet. For nearly a third of those the payments commanded more than a fifth of the family income before taxes. Among families in the next lower bracket—with incomes from $2000 to $3000—42 per cent had payments to make. Of these in turn 42 per cent had committed at least a fifth of their income for installment payments, and one family in nine surrendered 40 per cent or more of its income to the bill collector.[3] On the desirability of this each must decide according to his own values. But there are associated economic dangers which are less subjective.

---

[1] *Economic Indicators,* Washington: U. S. Government Printing Office, June 1957.

[2] These data are all from *Consumer Instalment Credit,* pt. I, vol. 1, *Growth and Import,* Board of Governors of the Federal Reserve System, Washington, D.C., 1957.

[3] *Ibid.,* p. 110.

III

In a society where virtuosity in persuasion must keep pace with virtuosity in production, one is tempted to wonder whether the first can forever keep ahead of the second. For while production does not clearly contain within itself the seeds of its own disintegration, persuasion may. On some not distant day, the voice of each individual seller may well be lost in the collective roar of all together. Like injunctions to virtue and warnings of socialism, advertising will beat helplessly on ears that have been conditioned by previous assault to utter immunity. Diminishing returns will have operated to the point where the marginal effect of outlays for every kind of commercial persuasion will have brought the average effect to zero. It will be worth no one's while to speak, for since all speak none can hear. Silence, interrupted perhaps by brief, demoniacal outbursts of salesmanship will ensue.

Were this heroic eventuality to occur, there would, unquestionably, be some interesting problems of economic readjustment. There would be a counterpart increase in consumer saving as the unpersuaded allowed their bank balances to grow and repaid their debts. Unless these increased savings were speedily offset by increased outlays elsewhere—and the day on which the massed voices of the advertisers brings total cancellation of effect will not be one of supreme business confidence and burgeoning investment spending—the result would be a decline in total spending and, therewith, in the total output of the economy. The further and more painful consequence would be an increase in unemployment and a reduction in other incomes—in brief, a serious curtailment of the social security of which production has become the servant.[4]

The less imaginative dangers arise in connection with consumer borrowing. Here trouble is already foreseeable. Indeed, it has already been accorded a degree of recognition in the conventional wisdom which has taken the usual form of assurances that there are no grounds for concern.

[4] In the conventional wisdom, just as there has been hesitation in stressing the role of advertising and salesmanship in want creation so there has been little tendency to explore our dependence on such persuasion. An exception is Paul Mazur whose book *The Standards We Raise* (New York: Harper, 1953) has a forthright philistinism that, while it doubtless cost him scholarly attention, brought him refreshingly close to the modern role of advertising and related activities.

As we expand debt in the process of want creation, we come necessarily to depend on this expansion. An interruption in the increase in debt means an actual reduction in demand for goods. Debt can be expanded by measures which, in the nature of the case, cannot be indefinitely continued. Periods for payment can be lengthened, although eventually there comes a point when they exceed the life of the asset which serves as the collateral. Down payments can be reduced, but eventually there comes a point when the borrower's equity is so small that he finds it more convenient to allow repossession than to pay a burdensome debt. Poorer and poorer credit risks can be accommodated, but at last it becomes necessary to exclude the borrower who, as a matter of principle, does not choose to pay.

In 1955, a year of especially urgent persuasion in the automobile market, the average repayment period on automobile installment contracts was lengthened from an estimated average of 24.5 months in 1954 to 28 months. The average down payment remained the same in the face of a substantial increase in the average retail price of cars purchased, and the *average* credit granted per installment sale increased from $1960 to $2240.[5] During 1955 the total volume of automobile installment credit outstanding increased by $3.6 billions.

This was a trend that could not be sustained. Although there was some further easing of terms the following year, the rate of increase in the volume of loans subsided. The result was a marked reduction in sales of automobiles— from 7.9 million passenger vehicles in 1955 to 5.8 million in 1956—and in face of a continued increase in disposable income of consumers. Automobile centers experienced a perceptible amount of unemployment in a period of general prosperity.

This experience shows what could occur on a much wider canvass and with more serious consequences. No one can speak with confidence on the extent of the danger. However, few things are more satisfactorily established in economics than that debt creation, whether by producers or consumers, is a major source of uncertainty in economic behavior. It has anciently been recognized that times of high income and employment and a generally sanguine outlook are encouraging to both borrowers and lenders. The spending that results from these transactions adds to the general total of purchasing

[5] *Ibid.*, p. 128.

power when, in effect, it is least needed. Under less sanguine circumstances loans are advanced more cautiously. Instead of spending from new loans, there is repayment of old ones and this, as perversely as in prosperity, occurs at the least propitious time.

Borrowing, in the past, has been mainly by business firms for investment. For this reason business spending was regarded as the most mercurial of the three major categories of spending. Outlays by consumers and by government were, by contrast, regarded as comparatively reliable. "There is . . . general agreement that [general fluctuations in employment] show themselves predominantly in swings in the demand for labour for investment—chiefly for investment in works of construction."[6] ". . . movements in income, output, and employment are mainly characterized by fluctuations in the rate of real investment. Moreover, consumption rises or falls, in large part, in response to real investment."[7] The effect of the expansion of consumer credit is to add an uncertainty, paralleling that which business borrowing brings to business spending, to the hitherto more reliable consumer spending. The instability may be greater, for the terms of consumer credit will be eased—down payments reduced and repayment periods lengthened—as an aspect of competitive merchandising techniques. In the case of business investment this is less likely to occur.

In any case consumers will add the most spending from borrowed funds to their spending from current income during the period when it is least needed. This will exaggerate inflationary pressures. And it is plain that a family that has committed forty or even twenty per cent of its income to installment payments will have to cut its current spending appreciably if one or more of its income earners lose their jobs. Thus an increase in unemployment, accompanied by the fear that it might get worse, could induce a general effort to avoid new debt and reduce the old. The further effect on consumer spending, thereafter on employment, and thence once again in reducing borrowing and magnifying efforts to meet debts, could be considerable and disagreeable.

[6] A. C. Pigou, *Income* (London: Macmillan, 1946), pp. 89-90.

[7] Alvin H. Hansen, *Business Cycles and National Income* (New York: Norton, 1951), p. 17. Professor Hansen goes on to observe that consumer's durables, including automobiles, can be an original source of fluctuation. These are the consumer products principally associated with debt creation.

IV

By virtue of position, certain individuals in our society are accorded the privilege of stating as fact what, in the nature of things, is unknowable. The tycoon and college president have well-recognized rights along these lines. Any candidate for public office may distinguish with clarity between actions which will lead to unlimited prosperity and those which will lead to utter ruin. Secretaries of State may tell us by which actions our lives and liberties will be preserved to near eternity and by which they and we will be destroyed. In all instances those privileged as prophets are permitted to identify salvation with the action which at the moment they find most expedient. To a remarkable extent, considering their much more humble status, economists are allowed to tell what present trends in society will culminate in deep trouble and distress. In consequence, it would be entirely permissible to foresee the gravest results from the way consumer demand is now sustained by the relentless increase in consumer debt.

In the course of its study of consumer credit in 1956, the Board of Governors of the Federal Reserve System concluded that while "relatively little is known about the safety margins in the finances of consumers who borrow on a short-term and intermediate-term instalment basis . . . the evidence of a trend over past decades toward more liberal terms suggests that these margins are less than in earlier years." Then, without throwing caution to the winds, it warned that "the possibility of an episode of drastic and spiraling liquidation [of this credit] should not be dismissed." Thereafter, for purposes of practical action it did dismiss it.

In fact we do not really know the extent of the danger. A tendency to liquidation of consumer debt, with accompanying contraction in current spending, could be offset by prompt and vigorous government action to cut taxes, increase public outlays, and so compensate with spending from other sources. On the other hand, such measures are subject to both psychological and procedural delays. Nothing in our economic policy is so deeply ingrained, and so little reckoned with by economists, as our tendency to wait and see if things did not improve by themselves. In a time of receding income the income tax reduces itself automatically. Social security, farm and other payments have a similarly automatic tendency to expand. But taxation and expenditure beyond the range of these automatic stabilizers require Executive and Congressional action. Such decision and action could be in a radically slower tempo from that of debt liquidation and the consequent slump in spending.

V

In a society in which the production and sale of goods seems sacrosanct there will be extreme hesitation over measures which will seem to restrain the financing of consumers' goods and hence their sale. Measures to prevent the competitive liberalization of consumer credit terms will encounter the heaviest resistance. When regarded in relation to the underlying interest in stability and economic security, such precautionary measures have a much stronger claim for attention. They promise to help keep the process of synthesizing demand and the purchasing power to make it effective from damaging the continuity of production and employment. The regulation of the terms and conditions of consumer credit, while it has been undertaken in the past in wartime, is not a power presently possessed by the United States government. It is, however, a commonplace in the United Kingdom.

However, the more substantial remedy lies deeper. Not all goods and services are subject to sale on the installment plan and to the attentions of the bill collector. Automobiles and radios and wall-to-wall carpeting are; the services of the schools, hospitals, and public libraries are not. To the extent that an economy concentrates its efforts on the first it will be subject to the vagaries of want-*cum*-debt creation. As it devotes its energies to serving itself with health, education, and other like services, it will reduce its danger. We have already seen that the preoccupation with production is a selective one. In particular it is heavily centered on those goods which by their character or by tradition are in the domain of private production. It concentrates energies, in other words, on producing the products which are subject to the greatest instability. It carries this indeed to the point where the manufacture of wants may itself be a tenuous process. A different arrangement for satisfying our needs— one, for example, that allotted a larger proportion of resources to those needs that are in the public domain—would thus be an important step toward stability. In one of the paradoxes with which economics is replete it might even, by contributing to the reliability of production, insure a greater total private product.

However, once again this is to run ahead of the story. We are concerned for the moment only with the tensions and the dangers of a society in which the pursuit of goods is paramount and which does not pause to reflect on the devices —mass persuasion leading on to mass encouragement to indebtedness—which further the chase. We now turn to another of the tensions of this society.

CHAPTER XV

Inflation

THROUGH MOST of man's history the counterpart of war, civil disorder, famine, or other cosmic disaster has been inflation. In recent times inflation has acquired new habits: it persists in periods of peace and high and rising prosperity. This tendency has been strongly manifest in the United States and especially in the decade and more following World War II. In these years the prices of a large range of industrial products—steel and steel products, machinery, machine tools, farm equipment, many nonferrous metals and their products —moved steadily upward. Steel prices, in the mid-fifties, were increasing at a rate sufficient to double their level every decade. In some years, 1955 and 1956 for example, new high levels of living costs were posted month after month with monotonous regularity.

The public response to this recurrent inflation has been interesting. It has been widely deplored and condemned. Politicians of both parties have taken a strong position against it. Conservatives, anciently the self-designated custodians of the "honest dollar," have continued to stress this tenet of their faith. Businessmen, bankers, insurance executives, and nearly every type of professional public spokesman at one time or another have warned of the dangers of continued inflation. Meanwhile liberals have deplored failure to take effective action while proposing none themselves. Next only to the virtues of competition, there is nothing on which the conventional wisdom is more completely agreed than on the importance of stable prices. Yet this conviction leads to remarkably little effort and, indeed, to remarkably few suggestions for specific action. Where inflation is concerned nearly everyone finds it convenient to confine himself to conversation. All branches of the conventional wisdom are equally agreed on the undesirability of any remedies that are effective.

II

There are several reasons for this barren position. First, to be sure, some reap material benefit from inflation. They too oppose it, for reasons of respectability, but their opposition is less than impassioned. Of importance also is the influence of inaction—or postponement—as a policy. This does not reflect mere negativism, as is often supposed and even more frequently charged. As noted, in the nineteenth-century model of the competitive society, a rhythmic sequence of expansion and contraction in economic activity was assumed. The expansion was accompanied by rising prices; in the contracting phase these gave way to falling prices. The movements in either direction were thought to be self-limiting. Thus if prices were rising one had only to wait. Presently they would reverse themselves and begin to fall.

In the course of time confidence in the self-limiting character of these movements was seriously weakened. This was especially true as regards the period of contraction or depression, and the Great Depression dealt a decisive blow. Although as late as the early thirties it was a tenet of the conventional wisdom that in depressions the only appropriate course of action was a severe "hands-off" policy, government intervention against depression is now regarded as inevitable.

However, there was never any equally dramatic assault on the older confidence that rising prices and inflation would cure themselves. Keynes led the attack on the conviction that depressions were self-correcting by picturing the possibility, indeed the probability, that the economy would find its equilibrium with an unspecified amount of unemployment. Dozens seized his point and sought to persuade the politicians and the public. The notion that, in peacetime, prices might as a normal thing rise continuously and persistently has had no Keynes.

Thus the conviction, or more precisely the hope, has remained that peacetime inflation might somehow be self-correcting. This is not a hope in which even conservatives repose very great confidence. But in combination with the belief, so common in recent years, that the behavior of the economic system is bound to be favorable if only earnest and God-fearing men are in command of its destinies, it provides a strong reason for always waiting to see if prices won't turn down by themselves. Even liberals, who are required to advocate although not to specify action to prevent inflation, are in practice likely to be tempted to wait and see.

This disposition to inaction is reinforced by the belief, of strong if diminishing influence ever since the thirties, that the most grievous threat to the American economy is a depression. If this danger lurks, however obscurely, around the corner, then there is all the less reason to act to control inflation. For inflation may any day come to an end in the thunder of economic collapse or the lesser misery of a few million unemployed. These eventualities are much more grave than rising prices. We are especially hesitant, knowingly at least, to invoke measures which might precipitate them. Some inflation remedies might do so or, at any rate, be blamed.

However, the forces which act to make inflation a peculiarly unmanageable problem in our time are imbedded much more deeply in the fabric of our social life. We are impelled, for reasons of economic security, to operate the economy at a level of output where it is not stable—where persistent advances in prices are not only probable but normal. The remedies that would be effective collide with the urgencies of production for purposes of economic security. Or they are in conflict with attitudes which emphasize the importance of economic growth and of unhampered markets for the efficient use of resources. This conflict has been further complicated by what is in part a belief, in part a hope, and in part a faith that the conflict can be evaded. The means to this evasion is the manipulation of the monetary supply—what economists have come to call monetary policy.

We shall look first at the nature of inflation and its consequences and then, in the next chapter, at the hope, never so strong as in recent times, that the conflicts which it presents might somehow be elided by monetary policy. Then we shall examine the unresolved conflict between the other remedies and the store we set by economic security and also by economic growth and unhampered markets.

III

Inflation—persistently rising prices—is obviously a phenomenon of comparatively high production. It can occur only when the demands on the economy are somewhere near the capacity of the plant and available labor force[1] to supply them.[2] When supply cannot be readily increased, as will be the case at capacity production, further increases in demand are capable of bringing price increases. A distinction must be made between two parts of the economy. In that part of the economy where, as with agriculture, there are many producers and an approach to what economists term pure competition, no individual seller controls or influences prices. There prices will move up automatically in response to the increased demand. In the typical industrial market—steel, machinery, oil, automobiles, most nonferrous metals, chemicals—a relatively small number of large firms enjoy, in one way or another, a considerable discretion in setting prices. In these markets—those characterized by what economists call oligopoly—as capacity is approached it becomes possible and profitable to mark up prices. The fact that all firms are at or near capacity is assurance that no firm, by holding back, will capture an increased share of the market. It cannot supply it. Nor under these circumstances is there danger that there will be extra stocks lurking around at a lower price.

---

[1] Capacity use of plant may be defined as that point where any further increase will incur abruptly rising short-run marginal costs. These costs will be above the long-run costs after plant expansion. Full employment or full use of the labor force may be defined as the point where, similarly, additional labor effort is forthcoming only at steeply rising marginal cost. In the ensuing chapters I speak jointly of the capacity of plant and the labor force. In any given situation one or the other can be the limiting factor and the source of the rising marginal costs.

[2] I have written a good deal—more, I suppose, than on any other economic subject—on various aspects of the inflation problem, and I am concerned to avoid repeating myself unnecessarily here. I have dealt with inflation in the general context of big firms and unions in the final chapters of *American Capitalism: The Concept of Countervailing Power*. The theoretical implications of the co-existence of competitive and oligopolistic market structures and the absence of full short-run maximization by the latter are developed in "Market Structure and Stabilization Policy," *Review of Economics and Statistics* (Cambridge, Mass.: May 1957), and summarized in nontechnical form in a statement prepared for the Subcommittee on Antitrust and Monopoly, Committee on the Judiciary, of the United States Senate (*Hearings,* July 11, 1957). My views on the inflation problem have changed (and I trust developed) over the years. In particular I regard the ensuing statement of the causes of inflation, though similar in broad contour, to be somewhat more precise than that in *American Capitalism*. The point of departure that inflation is the central problem of the economy of countervailing power is of course the same. The years since 1952, when this book was published, have, I think, provided a good deal of dismal verification of the point.

At this point it is necessary to foreclose on what is perhaps the commonest error in contemporary attitudes toward inflation, although the point is well understood by economists. This is the almost inevitable temptation to regard increased production as a remedy for inflation. It is the most natural of errors; the first thoughts on the matter are wonderfully simple and forthright. If inflation is caused by output pressing generally on capacity, then one need only get more capacity and more output and thus insure that this tension no longer exists. But as just a moment's further thought will suggest, additional all-round production, even when it can be readily obtained from existing capacity, will pay out, in wages and other costs, the income by which it is bought. We have seen, moreover, that wants do not have an origin that is independent of production. They are nurtured by the same process by which production is increased. Accordingly, the effect of increased production from existing plant capacity is to increase also the purchasing power to buy that production and the desires which insure that the purchasing power will be used.

But there is worse to come. If production is at capacity, increased output will naturally require an increase in capacity. The increased investment that this implies will, in the form of wages, payments for materials, returns to capital and profits, add to purchasing power and the current demand for goods. It does so before the added capacity resulting from the investment is in place to meet the demand. Thus the effort to increase production adds to the pressure on current capacity—and to the prospect for inflationary price increases.

A cat chasing its own tail may, by an extraordinary act of feline dexterity, on occasion succeed in catching it. To overcome inflation by increasing production, while superficially similar, will not so often be successful.

IV

The response of the economy, when it is operating at or near capacity, to an increase in demand will not be uniform for all industries. As just observed in the competitive industries, i.e., those where prices are set impersonally by the market, any increase in demand when supply can no longer be readily expanded will, predictably, raise prices. Similarly a reduction in demand will reduce prices. However, in the characteristic industrial market—those of oligopoly and administered prices—the increase in demand must be implemented by a specific decision by the firm to change its price. This decision may be delayed for a variety of reasons: inertia; the need to establish a consensus on the extent of the increase under circumstances where the antitrust laws forbid formal communication between firms; the fear of an adverse public reaction to the price advance; the fear that over a longer span of time the price increases will be damaging to the competitive position of the firm or industry; and the possibility of attracting the attention of the union and stimulating wage demands all may lead to delay. (It is worth repeating that this kind of price behavior can occur only in that part of the economy where producers are sufficiently few and are otherwise so situated as to have power over their own prices. Such behavior is not vouchsafed to the farmer or to the businessman who is one of many in the market.) For many of the same reasons price increases, when they occur, will not bring prices to the point where they maximize the short-run or current returns of the company. It is in the long-run that the corporation lives. It is the return over the fullness of time which is relevant to managerial calculation. If the prices that maximize profits at the moment will bring wage demands that will threaten the cost position of the company over time; or if there promises to be long-run damage to the competitive position of the company; or if the public reputation will be hurt, then short-run maximization of return does not accord with self-interest even when this is defined in the narrowest of pecuniary terms.[3] The firm will not proceed to maximize its current return unless something happens—an important point—to make this possible without damaging the longer-run interest.

Two things follow. In a period of high and rising demand, short-run possibilities for increasing prices are likely to run ahead of the long-run assessment of where prices should be. Therefore, firms in the typical industrial market are likely to have what amounts to a reserve of unliquidated gains from unmade price advances. Unlike the farmer or other competitive producer, who is effectively isolated from any such opportunity, firms in these markets could exact higher prices than they do. They will do so if circumstances so change as to make short-run maximization more nearly consistent with the firm's view of its long-run interest.

[3] It seems likely that many economists have been reluctant to concede the possibility of such "restraint" in pricing because it seemed to be in conflict with self-interest. In fact, no such forbearance need be involved.

As a result price increases in these industries are not tied tightly to capacity operations or, as in competitive industries, to rising demand. Demand in (say) the steel industry may fall to something less than capacity levels, but if there is an unliquidated gain, and something alters the relation between short- and long-run maximization so as to make the former more feasible, prices will still be increased. As just stated, this can happen when demand is falling. In the competitive industries, output being given, prices will never go up except by reason of an increase in demand. When demand falls, prices predictably will fall.[4]

While prices in the administered price industries may rise in face of some excess capacity and fall in the face of falling demand, the scope for such movements should not be exaggerated. Excess capacity, if it is considerable, will increase the danger that some firm will fail to go along or, at a later date, resort to surreptitious price-cutting. These dangers will act to enhance the doubts about the wisdom of raising prices to maximize short-run gains and increase the reluctance to do so. There will be similar and perhaps stronger fear of the longer-run consequences of such price increases when demand is falling. The action may have to be reversed. Perhaps meanwhile wages will have moved up partly because of the price increase. The important point is only that in industries characterized by oligopoly the relation between demand, capacity, and price has a degree of play. Prices are not restricted immediately demand is curbed or excess capacity appears.

V

In the inflation drama it remains only to introduce Hamlet. That, by common consent, is the union. It is the instigator presumptive of that most familiar of economic phenomena, the wage-price spiral.

The role of wages in relation to inflation has long been a troublesome matter for economists. Obviously wages have something to do with price increases. Yet it is plain that a

---

[4] These movements will be affected, also, by differential movements in demand and also differences in the rate at which different industries adapt their plant to changes in demand. To stress the role of unliquidated gains—in the absence of which one cannot satisfactorily explain the ability of industrial firms to respond as they do to wage increase—is not to exclude these commonplace effects. Cf. the article by Robert Solomon, "Galbraith on Market Structure and Economic Stabilization Policy," and my comment, *Review of Economics and Statistics*, 1958.

firm that advances its prices after a wage increase could have
done so before. At the previous lower costs and the higher
prices it would have made more money. The wage increase
did nothing to enable it to get the higher price. An advance
in steel wages adds only infinitesimally to the demand for
steel mill products and only after a time. In any event this is
not something which steel firms take into consideration in
their typically prompt response to a wage increase.[5]

The explanation lies in the existence of the margin of
unliquidated gain and in the further fact that the wage
advance, of itself, promptly increases the opportunity for
short-run maximization in relation to long-run maximization.
This is most obviously the case when the firm has been
unwilling to advance its prices because of fear that it would
attract the attention of the union which would press for wage
increases. Now the union's attention has manifestly been
attracted, and there need no longer be any reluctance on this
score. The danger of an adverse public reaction is also least
at such times. The public will ordinarily attribute the advance in prices to the union. In steel and other industries,
there is now a well-established policy of making the occasion
of a wage increase the opportunity for a rather larger increase
in prices and company revenues.

This is the core of the relation of wages to prices but not
quite all of it. It would be wrong to suggest that the initiative
to the whole movement lies with the wage demand of the
unions. Living costs rise, eroding the last wage gains and
stimulating efforts to recoup. And when demand and responding production are at capacity levels, profits will
ordinarily be good. These in turn act as the lodestone to
union demands. In the appropriate industries the unexploited
opportunity for price increases can now be seized. So it goes.
One cannot single out a particular spoke in a wheel, paint it
black (or red) and say that it shoves all the others. However,
its futility as a subject of social controversy notwithstanding,
nothing is more debated than the relative responsibility of
workers and employers for the price advances which comprise
inflation.

[5] It is, of course, a part of the progressive expansion of money incomes which sustains the inflationary movement. But it is still true that
the price increase precedes and does not follow the expansion in income.

VI

As stated, the wage, price, and profit spiral originates in the part of the economy where firms with a strong (or oligopolistic) market position bargain with strong unions. These price movements work themselves through the economy with a highly diverse effect on different groups. Where firms are strong in their markets and unions are effective, no one is much hurt, if at all, by inflation. Concern over the problem will be marked by the fortitude with which we all are able to contemplate the sorrows of others. Elsewhere the effect will be highly mixed. Those individuals and groups will suffer most who have least control over their prices or wages and hence the least capacity to protect themselves by increasing their own return. Or if such control, as in the case of agriculture, is slight, then the effect will depend on whether the income elasticity of the demand for the particular product —roughly the effect of increased incomes on the demand for the product—is small or great. And something will depend also on whether the particular producer's costs are affected promptly or belatedly by the increase in prices.

Thus, by way of illustration, farmers have little or no control over the prices at which they sell their products. Inflation reaches them by way of impersonal market movements. For the wheat or potato farmer the income elasticity is very low—as wage incomes rise individuals spend no more for bread or potatoes, and for potatoes there is indication that they spend less. Meanwhile the farmer's costs of fuel, fertilizer, and other factors from the oligopolistic sector of the economy, will have risen. For the beef cattle producer, by contrast, income elasticity is rather higher. He is the beneficiary of the well-known and statistically quite demonstrable tendency of people who have an increase in pay to celebrate with red meat. Other things equal, and in the cattle business they frequently are not, his position will be happier than that of the producer of bread grains or potatoes.

Such discrimination is pervasive. The individual or firm which, either in line of business or as the result of speculative acumen, holds large unhedged inventories, benefits from the increased demand for these and from the consequent increase in price.

At the other extreme are those who experience the rising costs but whose own prices remain largely unaffected because

they are fixed by law or custom or, at a minimum, by someone
else. This is the position, during inflation, of the teacher,
preacher, public servant, of (in general) the salaried professional and white-collar community, and of those who in
effect are reaping the reward of past services to society in
the form of pensions or other such payments. The result of
rising costs and comparatively fixed returns for all of these
groups is much too familiar to require exegesis. Those on
pensions suffer severely. Those who depend for their pay
on the public treasury are also especially likely to suffer
during inflation. Like all others they experience the increase
in prices. Their income for a variety of reasons is almost
certain to lag. This lag is of considerable consequence, and
it is something to which this essay will return.

Not all venders of professional services do suffer. Occasional groups have discretion over their prices and are able
to take prompt advantage of the general increase in money
wages and demand, to raise their own charges and revenues.
Lawyers and doctors normally fall in such a category. There
are others. In 1942 a grateful and very anxious citizenry
rewarded its soldiers, sailors, and airmen with a substantial
increase in pay. In the teeming city of Honolulu, in prompt
response to this advance in wage income, the prostitutes
raised the prices of their services. This was at a time when,
if anything, increased volume was causing a reduction in their
average unit costs. However, in this instance the high military
authorities, deeply angered by what they deemed improper,
immoral, and indecent profiteering, ordered a return to the
previous scale.

In a free market, in an age of endemic inflation, it is unquestionably more rewarding, in purely pecuniary terms, to be a
speculator or a prostitute than a teacher, preacher, or policeman. Such is what the conventional wisdom calls the structure of incentives.

VII

In basic outline the requirements for inflation control will
now be clear. When the economy is at or near capacity, firms
in the concentrated sector can advance their prices and will
have inducement from advancing wages to do so. Such
price increases, with their further effects, will be prevented
only if there is slack in the economy. Then various restraints

begin to operate on
ing wage advances, an
since firms may have un
rather less than capacity, th
measures may have to be cons
World War II, prices continued
olistic sector of the economy;
bargained with strong firms right
1949 and 1954. Prices as a whole
those in the more competitive mar
exceptional circumstances may interve   because
be wise to expect inflation whenever demand is strongly While
rising and unemployment is below, say, three or four million.

Were it possible to prevent wages from reacting on prices, and vice versa, then it would be possible to have price stability with production a good deal closer to current capacity and full employment. Wage movements would not then serve as a reason for raising prices and as a justification, or cover, for adding to profits. The derived effect of these increases on other sectors would be eliminated. It would thus be possible to have higher output and employment without inflation.

In the past there has been much argument whether, in the strategy of inflation control, one should seek to come to grips with the level of demand (in relation to the capacity of the economy and the labor force) or whether one should seek to deal with the wage-price spiral. Economists have generally emphasized the importance of the level of demand; to the layman the wage-price spiral has always seemed the phenomenon that most obviously required attention. The proper answer is that both are important. Inflation could be controlled by a sufficiently heavy reduction in the level of demand. It could be controlled with a less drastic reduction if something could be done to arrest the interaction of wages and prices or, to speak more precisely, of wages, profits, and prices.

The conflicts here will be evident. The introduction of slack, especially if it must be considerable, is in conflict with the imperatives of economic security. And the use of controls is in conflict with the ancient conviction that resources must be allocated efficiently between their various employments and that the free market is the most efficient and possibl even the only satisfactory instrument of such allocatio Setting the store that we do by the production of goods,

CHAPTER XVI

The Monetary Illusion

IN BRITAIN throughout the nineteenth century the Bank of England was able through the increase or decrease of the bank rate—in principle the rate of interest at which it stood ready to lend money to those who in turn were in the business of lending money—to have a measure of influence on the British banking and business life. The circumstances were undoubtedly favorable. The world was mostly at peace. There were no restraints on the international movement of capital funds; these were free to move anywhere in pursuit of a higher return. An increase in the rate would bring funds from abroad to take advantage of the higher earnings. A reduction would bring borrowers instead. Thus the volume of bank reserves could be influenced with some precision. The British economy of the last half of the century was exposed by free trade to the competition of the rest of the world. One can assume, as a result, that it was fairly sensitive to higher interest costs which meant higher carrying charges for new investment or to lower interest costs which bespoke a favorable opportunity for expansion. There is much room for debate on the extent of the effect of the Bank Rate on the British economy—how much investment was encouraged or discouraged and to what extent prices were inflated or deflated. Perhaps the bank rate was credited with much that would have happened anyway. Perhaps it derived prestige from its position as a Victorian conversation piece. But perhaps it was of consequence.

What is not in question is that the possibility of exercising such control came to have a compelling charm for all who were in any way identified with it. This was especially true of the banking community. For it meant that bankers, through the central bank, stood at the apex of economic influence. Their power, moreover, was not won by the crude, uncouth, and uncertain process of soliciting votes. It was the direct reward of financial achievement and wealth. Not only did monetary policy belong to the banking community, but specific steps were taken to safeguard the exercise of this authority from the intervention or intercession of politicians. The central bank was kept "independent" of the government and in degree above it. Such was the case for centuries with the Bank of England. It is still so, nominally, of the Federal Reserve System. This independence, though extensively celebrated in the conventional wisdom, would not long sustain determined opposition to the wishes of the Executive and the Congress. But it reflects, in at least vestigial form, the belief that monetary policy is the highly professional prerogative of the financial community. As such, it must be protected from the crude pressures of democratic government.

The management of the economy by monetary methods involved the exercise of subtle, as distinct from naked, power. No businessman, or indeed no citizen, was told what to do. Instead they were guided by forces of which they were themselves not wholly aware. If the economy must be given guidance, how gratifying that it be done in this discreet and seemly way.

Moreover, to most people money and credit, the way they are conceived and extinguished, and the fact that pieces of paper of little intrinsic worth can be so valuable, remain a great reservoir of mystery. Decisions on monetary policy have always been taken *in camera* and communicated to the public only by actions—movements in the interest rate or increases or decreases in central bank portfolios. A learned literature developed which was privy to the mystery and which speculated on the motives behind various moves. Its authors came to have a stake in the policy they interpreted. They belonged to a select few who understood. Outshining them, only, were those who were privy and really knew. Such was the charm of this policy that this affection was easily translated into claims for its effectiveness which, in fact, did invade the supernatural. Monetary policy was graced by effects not only mysterious but magical.

This has not invariably been so. In the nineteen-thirties the prestige of monetary policy was, for a time, very low. High interest rates had failed miserably to arrest the speculative boom of the late twenties; low rates were equally ineffective in dealing with the Great Depression. Bankers, in these years, as a result of error, unhappy accident, and the enthusiastic denigration of left-wing critics, had suffered a severe decline in popular esteem. Down with them went the faith in monetary policy. Keynes argued that the rate of interest was a roundabout way of influencing economic activity and of small practical utility.

From this nadir, in the years following World War II monetary policy had a great revival. Banks and bankers recovered their prestige and so did the instrument with which they were so intimately identified. Faith in monetary policy became a badge of resistance to the heresies of Keynes and proof that the individual had no part in the radicalism which sought to defame decent and respectable men because they were in the business of holding and lending money.

More important, something had to be done about inflation. The other measures for contending with this ineluctable phenomenon were under the handicap of being unpalatable, impractical, or un-American. This was the practical consequence of their being in conflict with other economic goals. Yet steps had to be taken. Monetary policy remained the only hope. To the affection which the policy elicited and the faith on which it was grounded was added a large element of wishful thinking. There was nothing else, so it had to work. Monetary policy became a form of economic escapism. Without it the realities would indeed be hard.

Unhappily, faith or urgent need is not an assurance of practical performance. Even if, as bankers have anciently suspected, doubts about monetary policy have on occasion been the invidious reflection of doubts about bankers, this still does not insure that monetary policy will work. As Chapter II has shown, the ultimate enemy of the conventional wisdom is circumstance. It is never in such peril as when enthusiastic exponents put it to a practical test. Monetary policy, despite its unparalleled position in the conventional wisdom, makes only secondary contact with the problem of inflation. And it has had the misfortune to be subject to extended experiment.

II

First of all, monetary policy suffers from the unfortunate absence of any occult effect. It has long been clear that economic management, especially in the United States, would be greatly facilitated if resort could occasionally be had to witchcraft. Monetary policy, by far the most promising possibility, involves none. This every good citizen must regret. More somberly, the policy makes no direct contact with the wage-price interaction. This not even its prophets suggest. Accordingly, it must work, if at all, by reducing the aggregate demand for goods. Its handle for accomplishing this is a higher interest rate and a diminished supply of funds for lending. By thus discouraging lending by banks and borrowing by consumers and producers, the policy is presumed to restrict or restrain what the latter have to spend. The reduction in this spending, if it occurs, will then have secondary (or multiplier) effects on the spending of others. The ultimate consequence is to reduce the demand for goods as a whole or to restrain the rate of increase in demand.[1] By thus keeping demand from pressing on capacity and on the labor force, prices are kept stable. Or such must be the hope.

That is the only avenue of effect.[2] An alternative form of exposition emphasizes the effect of this policy on the supply of money. But so far as this argument does not escape into mysticism, it comes to the same thing. The money supply increases or decreases as the result of increases or decreases in commercial bank lending. An increase in the money supply affects prices by way of the increased spending of borrowers from borrowed funds as well as through the multiplier by those from whom they buy. When one restricts the money supply, one restricts the spending associated with the lending and borrowing of funds. The measures are the same: the supply of funds available for lending is reduced, and the interest rate is raised to discourage borrowing. No matter how the cake is sliced the policy, if it is to work, must restrain borrowing. And thereby it becomes effective by reducing or restraining the total volume of spending. So far there is little disagreement between economists.

As just noted, direct spending from borrowed funds is of two kinds—by consumers for consumer goods and by busi-

[1] This will serve the same purposes as an absolute reduction if the plant capacity and labor force of the economy are also increasing. It is convenient in any discussion to speak in terms of absolute magnitudes—whether an increase in interest rates does or does not reduce total spending. But while this is a convenient simplification of language, and one that leads to no important error, the question in a growing economy will ordinarily be whether the rate of increase in demand is reduced relative to the rate of increase in capacity. The difference in these rates will be the source of the slack on which price stability depends.

[2] Theoretically the rise in the interest rate could encourage consumer saving from current income and by the same act reduce spending from current income. The possibility of such an effect, though once argued, is no longer seriously urged even by the most convinced supporters of monetary policy.

nessmen for investment. The advantage of looking at economic policy in the full context of economic attitudes and behavior will now be evident. To restrict consumer borrowing by increasing the interest cost on installment and other loans collides abruptly with the process of consumer demand creation. If consumer wants were independently determined, an increase in interest charges could, conceivably, operate through the consumer's demand schedule to reduce borrowing and spending. It seems unlikely that the elasticity of the response would be great, but the possibility exists. But as matters now stand, any step to discourage borrowing and buying will be automatically opposed by the machinery for consumer demand creation. A shrinkage in consumer borrowing will be merely a warning to those concerned with the synthesis of consumer demand to increase their efforts. Or they can take steps to annul the effect of the increased interest charge.

This is a matter of minimum difficulty. Consumer credit is ordinarily repaid in installments, and one of the mathematical tricks of this type of repayment is that a very large increase in interest rates brings a very small increase in the monthly payment. Thus a man who signs a note for $1800 on the purchase of a new car to be repaid over twenty-four months, and who agrees to an "add-on" of 6 per cent of this amount as interest, will have a total interest bill of $216 and monthly payments of $84. If the interest charge is increased by one-third to an add-on of 8 per cent, his total interest obligation becomes $288, but the increase in monthly payments in only $3. The one-third increase in interest brings but a one-thirtieth increase in the payment.[3] This increase can easily be offset by a lengthening of the term of repayment. In practice it is submerged by a variety of additional inspection, insurance, and other charges. Since the customer in contemplating the purchases is aware, not of the interest rate, but of the monthly charge, it will be seen how readily a very large increase in interest charges can, in practice, be offset. During the period of active monetary policy in the early fifties, increased finance charges were regularly followed by large increases in consumer loans. Want creation, and the process of financing it, was still acting to exaggerate rather than to restrain the inflationary effect of consumer spending.

There is no chance that monetary policy can have even a minimal effect on consumer spending while its conflict with

[3] *Consumer Instalment Credit,* pt. I, vol. 1, pp. 60-61.

the machinery of consumer want creation remains unresolved and, in degree, even unrecognized, and while we concede the paramount importance of the latter. And though the reasons have not been fully seen there is, in fact, considerable agreement that monetary policy does not make any effective contact with consumer borrowing and spending.

III

That the restriction of business investment by monetary policy involves a similar conflict with a prior goal will now be apparent to everyone. We set primary store by production. Monetary policy seeks to prevent price increases by cutting down on the investment by which productive growth is made possible and is sustained. It would be hard to imagine a more abrupt collision with the dominant position of production. Oddly enough, those who set the greatest store by monetary policy—bankers and businessmen—are often those who are most inclined to emphasize the importance of production and to view increases in output with most satisfaction.

In practice the conflict between monetary policy and production is not so severe. This is partly because of a surviving belief that monetary policy somehow makes contact with the price level without affecting the volume of investment. In the years between 1953 and 1957 the then Secretary of the Treasury, Mr. George Humphrey, regularly expressed his conviction that the economy required a high and rising volume of business investment and that incentives, including tax revision, were needed to encourage it. At the same time he strongly endorsed a policy of monetary restraint designed to prevent inflation. These remarkably contradictory positions can be reconciled only if there is faith that, by essentially occult means, monetary policy will stabilize prices without affecting the volume of producer borrowing, investment, and spending.

The conflict between production and a monetary policy designed to decrease business investment is also eased by our tendency, described in Chapter IX, to accept and even to applaud whatever rate of economic growth we are currently enjoying. Concern is rhetorical rather than real. Hence we are not notably disturbed by a policy which, by reducing the volume of new investment, seeks to lower the rate of economic growth so long as serious unemployment does not appear.

However, if individual firms were prevented by the policy from making the investment which seems to them wise and profitable, there would, of course, be objection. And this brings us to the final reason why the conflict rarely reaches the acute stage.

IV

In times of capacity or near-capacity production, the context in which inflation becomes a danger and its control indicated, profits and profits prospects are certain to be favorable. Because production is at or near capacity, investment in expansion will seem to the individual firm both advantageous and singularly logical from the point of view of the community. (The firm will be much more impressed by the visible service it renders in increasing the supply of its product than by the invisible effect of its investment in adding to total spending and thus to inflationary pressure.) For all of these reasons most investment will be extremely unresponsive to moderate increases in the interest rate which is the way in which monetary policy presents itself to the ordinary business firm.

If the policy is applied severely, some firms will be squeezed by the higher rates. And in practice, since interest rates are comparatively sticky, some rationing of credit will occur. Some firms which would like to borrow will be unable to do so. If the policy is pressed far enough, investment spending will doubtless be curtailed. In the end the slack required for price stability would appear. So would the conflict with our attitudes on the importance of production. There would be an equally urgent conflict between this policy and the economic security which is the counterpart of high production. But before this point is reached, another problem of even greater import arises. That is the effect of monetary policy on different kinds and sizes of firms.

As we have seen, when demand has been growing and the economy is at or near capacity, firms in the oligopolistic sector are likely to have a reserve of unliquidated gains. This enables them to pass higher interest charges along to the consumer. (If they can pass along wage increases, they can obviously do the same with interest.) And by raising prices and income they can resort to unliquidated gains for investment purposes. The need to price for returns sufficient to cover a considerable share of investment requirements has been a stock defense of industrial price increases for many years. Thus industries which have unliquidated gains are able, in effect, to contract out from under the effect of monetary policy. The attractiveness of the large firm as a bank customer and its ability to go directly to the market for funds also help exempt it from the effects of the policy.

Firms in competitive markets—those whose prices and costs are impersonally determined by the market for all— obviously cannot pass higher interest costs ahead to the customer. In the relevant short-run they cannot raise the prices that they do not control to get investment funds from their customers. As a rule, being small they cannot circumvent the rationing of bank credit by selling securities in the market. Hence for competitive industries—farmers, small builders, small retailers, service industries, dealers—monetary policy is effective. And it will be effective for these firms much before it affects the industries in which there is a greater measure of market control.

To recur again to the experience of the fifties, in these years and especially in 1955 and 1956 investment by agriculture, residential builders, and—although the evidence is less clear—by other small-scale industries did decline. At the same time investment by large firms, and in producer's durable goods where the role of the oligopolistic industries is dominant, was rising to record levels. Proof in economics is an evasive thing. But we do well to pay attention whenever experience affirms a theoretical probability.

It will be easy to see why monetary policy is regarded with equanimity and even approval by larger and stronger firms. Unless applied with severity over time it does not appreciably affect them. But for the same reason there must be grievous doubts about the workability of the policy. Before the large-volume investment spending of the larger and more powerful firms is affected, a severe squeeze will ordinarily be placed on the capital requirements of smaller scale firms. For such firms the conflict between monetary policy and productive growth will be highly visible and, indeed, very painful. This will set severe limits on the rigor with which the policy may be pursued. For apart from social aspects of a policy which denies growth to the numerous and small and favors the large and the powerful, farmers and small businessmen are not without political influence.

V

As noted, the most mercurial source of spending in the economy has long been recognized to be that for business investment. Spending by consumers and by governments have (consumer borrowing apart) substantial elements of reliability. They are related to income being received. They are grounded on customary patterns of behavior. In the case of government outlays they have a markedly greater constancy than the revenues which support them. Investment spending, by contrast, depends on an estimate of future returns. The singular feature of the future is that it cannot be known. Estimates as to what it holds will change. So accordingly will investment outlays. And the changes in these latter, by changing prospective earnings, change the future itself.

If monetary restraint is exercised over a period of time it may eventually affect the investment of larger firms. This may come about in a variety of ways but most obviously because the curtailment of the borrowing and investment of weaker firms and industries will, in the end, affect demand and investment prospects for the more concentrated sector of the economy. When this happens there will be a revision of investment plans, and this may be large.

Monetary policy thus operates on the most mercurial dimension of economic activity. This is the final source of inutility and it may, indeed, be a source of considerable danger. If, the conflict with production notwithstanding, it is applied with rigor and persistence to produce the requisite slack, there is danger that it will do too much. Or, to speak more precisely, there is unavoidable uncertainty as to just what it will do. It seeks to influence the most unpredictable element of aggregate demand. The result of this influence is, accordingly, unpredictable. There must always be danger that monetary policy, if pressed to the point where it will stabilize prices, will reduce investment to the point of causing a serious depression. Such a depression is not uncorrectible. But neither is it desirable. These matters are not, unhappily, entirely in the realm of analysis. This essay goes to press at a time when monetary policy, having been applied for several years without stabilizing prices, shows signs of precipitating an adventitiously large reduction in investment. The consequences, however temporary, could be unpleasant.

In the conventional wisdom, the faith in monetary policy is still strong. No other economic policy has ever shown such capacity to survive failure to be hailed as a success. It will be evident, however, that in relation to the problem of inflation—the endemic problem of the affluent society—it is dangerous to the degree that it is effective. Those whose love for monetary policy is great may occasionally wish to inquire of themselves whether the good name of the economic system might not deserve a prior claim to their affections.

CHAPTER XVII

Production versus Price Stability

IN THE POLITICAL SPECTRUM of modern economic policy, monetary measures are the instrument of conservatives. The weapon of liberals is fiscal policy. And among economists generally fiscal policy is regarded as the ultimate economic weapon. The friends of monetary policy aver its effectiveness, perhaps partly to allay their unconscious doubts. The effectiveness of fiscal policy is much more rarely debated. Moreover, it had the implicit blessing of Keynes. As the converse of the public spending which was the Keynesian remedy for unemployment, it has still a slight cachet of rational radicalism.

Fiscal policy is much simpler and more forthright in its operation than monetary policy. The mysticism has been exorcised, and the theoretical chain which links the original action and the ultimate effect, something always to be watched in economics, is far shorter and involves far fewer asseverations as to what *should* happen. The government taxes more than it spends. This difference is not spent. Hence it is a net reduction in the spending of the country as a whole. If this difference, which in the case of the United States government is the surplus in the cash consolidated budget,[1] is sufficiently increased, then total spending in the economy will no longer press on the capacity of the economy. The now famous slack will result. If this slack is large enough, firms will hesitate to raise prices—in terms of the present analysis short-run maximization will seem inconsistent with longer-run return—and wage demands will be resisted. Demand will not pull up prices in the competitive sector. Prices as a result will be

---

[1] These budget tables show all receipts as against all expenditures. They differ from the conventional budget totals, the one cited in the annual discussion of public profligacy, for the latter, as a matter of tradition, exclude some receipts and outlays, principally those on social security account.

stable unless, indeed, the process is pressed too far, in which case they will fall.

Business firms feel the impact of monetary policy initially in the form of a change in factor cost or availability—specifically in the cost or availability of credit for capital. Large firms and those with substantial market power are able, as we have seen, to pass this cost increase along to customers, and in case of a shortage of credit they can have recourse to another source of supply. Competitive and smaller firms have no similar escape. Fiscal policy works, in the main, by reducing demand. This reduction affects the demand for the products of all firms, large and small, strong and weak. No firm, in the technical idiom, can contract out of the movement in its demand curve. The effect of the policy will not be precisely the same, as between competitive and oligopolistic markets and as between large firms and small, but it is much more nearly equal.[2]

Yet in the years since World War II in the United States, fiscal policy has also revealed itself as a very poor defense against inflation. The reason was not that it failed to work but that not even its principal proponents argued for its vigorous use. It was favored in principle but not in practice. The explanation is not far to seek. Here is another unresolved conflict in economic goals. Once again the advantage of seeing things in full social context will be plain.

II

For reasons that will be explored in detail in the next chapter, government expenditures are likely at any given time to be near the minimum which the community regards as tolerable. Complaint about waste and inefficiency in performing these services, which is endemic in our political comment and rarely without foundation, should not be allowed to confuse the issue. Very important functions can be performed very wastefully and often are. And waste can rarely be eliminated by reducing expenditure. It is far easier to cut the function than the waste, and this is what occurs. In time of inflation, the economic context of which we are speaking, the situation of the public services is certain to be even more tenuous

---

[2] Where there are unliquidated gains, prices will fall less promptly and earnings will be less promptly reduced than in a competitive industry where there are no such gains.

because of the inevitable tendency for public pay scales and public budgets to lag behind the general increase in prices.

This means that a positive fiscal policy to counter inflation will almost always require an increase in taxes. The importance of cutting or postponing expenditures, however much it may be urged on the more vacuous margins of the conventional wisdom, may on occasion sustain hope. But the actual accomplishment will invariably be negligible. On this point experience is complete. Whenever inflation is a danger (and now and then when it is not) spokesmen urge the Administration and the Congress, and the latter urge upon themselves, sometimes with seeming seriousness, the importance of cutting expenditures. Nothing is ever accomplished of sufficient magnitude to affect appreciably the total spending of the economy. Quite often nothing is accomplished. And indeed the expectations of nonaccomplishment are such that the Congressional discussion of budget-cutting each winter has now assumed the innocent aspect of a folk rite. It begins as the budget time approaches. It reaches full pitch a few days after the budget is submitted. The gods are appeased by stern denunciations of public profligacy and inspired promises of vast economies. The ceremony is solemnly described to the people by press and radio. Thereafter the seemingly indispensable outlays are voted, and the result is more often to increase the budget than to reduce it.

To raise taxes to reduce demand encounters at the outset a problem of understanding. That, in the event of insufficient demand and depression, taxes should be cut and public outlays increased in order to increase aggregate demand and employment is now widely accepted. There is an inherent logic to the procedure. This is also true of cutting public expenditures to counter inflation—were this only possible. However, the logic of increasing taxes is by no means so evident. The first and obvious effect is to increase the consumer's living costs or reduce his income. This happens at a time when inflation is making it difficult for many people to maintain accustomed living standards. Other taxes add to the producer's costs. Thus to attack inflation by raising taxes seems at first glance a curiously backhanded procedure. It is strongly resisted by the very considerable number who insist, never without fervor and pride, that subtlety in economic relationships is an indication of error and that truth is revealed only to the uncomplicated mind.

III

The most serious problem of fiscal policy is the conflict with other economic goals.

It collides, first of all, with the tacit truce outlined in Chapter VII on income inequality. Taxes are the device by which governments have most nakedly sought to influence income distribution. As a result, they have a considerable practical and an even deeper symbolic importance in relation to this issue. Hence a proposal to increase taxes for fiscal reasons automatically provokes a debate on the question of inequality. Liberals, who hitherto had been abiding comfortably by the terms of the truce, are required by their faith to rally to the support of taxes which reduce inequality. Conservatives rally to oppose them. In wartime this debate can to some extent be evaded by invoking the doctrine of equality of sacrifice—the rich man can be told that his sufferings at the hands of the tax authorities are roughly the counterpart of those of the soldier under shellfire. Despite much concentrated thought, no entirely suitable reply has ever been devised by men of means. Thus in wartime it has been practical to employ the income tax to absorb excess purchasing power. In peacetime such use of taxation will at a minimum be complicated by a long argument over the essentially unrelated issue of equality.

Finally, there is the now classic conflict with production. Fiscal policy becomes effective only as the reduced demand brings output below the current capacity of plant and the labor force. Having persuaded ourselves that production is of paramount importance, we must now persuade ourselves to sacrifice it in return for price stability. Moreover, once again the sacrifice may have to be considerable. Where concerns are strongly organized in their markets and deal with strong unions, i.e., where the likelihood of unliquidated gains is great, the slack required, as already noted, may have to be quite large. Even though, in fact, the output is not of high urgency, the income to those whom the slack makes unemployed is of importance.

Unlike monetary policy, fiscal policy makes its initial contact with the economy not by reducing investment expenditure but by reducing (in the main) consumer expenditure. In not attacking investment it is thus, at first glance, less inimical to economic expansion or growth. However, too much should not be made of this distinction. Firms are encouraged to invest at least partly because production is pressing on capacity. When it ceases to do so—when there is slack—they can be expected to cut back on investment. Just as demand will have an acceleration effect on investment, to use the term familiar to economists, as production approaches capacity and the latter is enlarged, so it will have a decelerating effect as production drops away from capacity levels. So magnified, the movement in investment and therewith in total demand would appear offhand to reinforce the effect of fiscal policy. It gives a leverage to the change in spending that is brought about by government action. But it also means that once the economy ceases to be at capacity there is a substantial sacrifice in investment for growth. Or, to put the matter differently, growth will be at a maximum only when the economic system is under that pressure to use capacity which produces inflation.

Were the economy given to occasional bouts of stimulation with excessive investment and rising prices—the business cycle of the central economic tradition—then countercyclical repression of demand might involve no serious problem. Some who have seen no conflict between fiscal policy and growth have, without doubt, viewed it in such a context. But if full employment and full use of capacity is taken as the norm of economic policy, as in modern times it is, then the rate of investment associated with full use of capacity is also normal. A policy which holds production below capacity in the interest of price stability inescapably sacrifices economic growth.

However, the much more serious conflict is between fiscal policy and the unemployment which stability requires in modern markets. Insufficient production and growth can be tolerated but this unemployment cannot be. And to induce it deliberately is a politically unalluring policy. In addition, even though the unemployment necessary for price stability is not, as a national total, very great it will never be uniformly distributed. Those industries and communities that are stationary or in which demand is increasing more slowly will feel curtailment with especial severity. Here there will be pockets of unemployment and distress. The policy strikes with especial force not only on particular people but also on particular politicians.

Conservatives will always prefer inflation to its remedies. And faced with a choice between unemployment and price increases the liberal politician unhesitatingly condemns both.

The politics of an anti-inflationary fiscal policy could scarcely be less promising.

IV

Apart from monetary policy, fiscal policy is the only device for dealing with inflation that currently has standing in the conventional wisdom. But so long as its employment is in unresolved conflict with other and prior economic goals it will not be used with effective vigor, at least in peacetime.

This conflict and the resulting inutility of fiscal measures are not yet widely conceded by economists. The textbooks still elucidate the use of fiscal measures as a device for insuring price stability. They concede that we must settle for something less than completely full employment and that this will offer difficulties. But they assume that, given inflation, taxes can be increased. The only difficulty is that the policy never looks practical at any particular moment. Unfortunately, while the conflict with other goals persists, it never will.

One last possibility remains. That is to combine fiscal policy with control over prices and wages. As a result, prices and wages are unable to respond to the price-increasing influences that develop as production approaches capacity. The controls rather than the slack serve to prevent price increases at capacity operations. Thus they reconcile capacity output (and also related growth) with price stability. It would not be necessary to enforce any substantial amount of idle capacity and unemployment.

There is a general view that price and wage controls accomplish nothing of themselves—that they deal with symptoms rather than with causes. To use them is to juggle with the thermometer, not the furnace. If current demand is far in excess of the capacity of the economy, there is an important element of truth in this contention. The only recourse is to bring demand into balance with supply. Anything else is an escape. But if, by fiscal or other measures, the aggregate of demand is kept about equal to the current capacity of the economy, then any such view of wage and price controls is a gross oversimplification. Wages act on prices and prices on wages as capacity is approached. Controls prevent this interplay. In doing so they allow the economy to function closer to capacity without price increases.

A few economists have conceded this function explicitly;[3] rather more have concurred implicitly by agreeing that such controls are necessary in a wartime emergency; i.e., when there is no escape from the need to reconcile full use of capacity with the greatest possible degree of price stability. But on few things is the conventional wisdom so certain as the unwisdom of direct controls in peacetime. Nothing better establishes the good sense and soundness of an economist than a condemnation of such controls. Nothing more quickly brings into question his adequacy, even his motives, than the suspicion that he is soft on the subject of controls.

The objections to these controls are numerous, even comprehensive. To be effective it is assumed that they must apply comprehensively to all prices and all wages. This means that the administrative problems are indubitably grave and become more serious with passage of time. The specter of such control invokes the ancient resistance to the intrusions of government. This intrusion is indeed considerable, for the power to set prices is not insignificant in economic decision-making. To the extent that Social Darwinists and the utilitarian philosophers have successfully identified vitality and liberty with the free market, controls will be regarded as an even more far-reaching menace.

Finally, and perhaps most important, such controls are sharply in conflict with conventional attitudes toward production. As Chapter IX has shown, we set great store by the efficient allocation of resources as the device for maximizing production. That was the relevant instrument in the last century. Social nostalgia still accords it a central role. This allocation is accomplished in the capitalist society by the market—by the pull and push of market prices and market wages bringing labor, capital, and materials to the firms and industries of most efficient use. Obviously one cannot have both controls and a free market which performs this function.

None of this is certain. In the war years controls were consistent with a very large increase in output. That was because production was expanded along less stylized but far more effective dimensions than those related to improved resource allocation. Nor is it certain that the controls which would serve to arrest the wage-price spiral would have to be comprehensive. It is possible that very limited restraints

---

[3] Cf. for example Paul A. Samuelson, *Economics* (1st ed.; New York: McGraw-Hill, 1948), p. 435. Samuelson shares the doubts expressed here about reconciling this function with the current social ethos.

might serve to reconcile capacity output and price stability. This is an important point to which this essay will return. However, for the moment it is sufficient to note that price and wage control, as a way of reconciling price stability, maximum product, and minimum unemployment, is out of bounds. It too is in conflict, no less important if it is ostensible rather than real, with historic attitudes toward production.[4]

V

A word of summary is now in order. We are impelled by present attitudes and goals to seek to operate the economy at capacity where, we have seen, inflation must be regarded not as an abnormal but as a normal prospect. The same attitudes which lead us to set store by capacity use of plant and labor force largely deny us the use of measures for preventing inflation. Monetary policy collides with the process of consumer demand creation and, since it works on business investment, is in conflict with our emphasis on growth. It is also ineffectual, discriminatory and, possibly, dangerous. Fiscal policy is sharply at odds with the commitment to a level of output that insures full employment and the accompanying economic security. Direct controls, which in theory might reconcile high employment with price stability, are under a comprehensive ban. We assume that we must have them in unworkable mass or not at all. They are in ostensible conflict with the goal of efficient production, for that has anciently been identified with market allocation of resources.

These conflicts are partly obscured. The conservative disguises the conflict between monetary policy and production by his faith that his policy has occult or other transcendental effects not visible to the naked eye. The liberal, including the Keynesian economist, conceals the conflict between fiscal policy and production at full employment not so much by resort to mysticism as by a systematic refusal to face issues. This he accomplishes by keeping his advocacy of fiscal measures in general terms while being specifically critical of

---

[4] The hold of these ideas is sufficiently strong so that many would prefer the minor effect on output that would come from efficient resource allocation by the market in a context of price stability and some unemployment to the much greater effect on production which would come from (a) using the unemployed resources and (b) having the incentive to increased output which may be expected when demand presses on capacity.

unemployment and underuse of plant. He surrenders the opportunity for reconciling the conflict by agreeing that direct controls are unsound.

Thus the way is open to recurrent inflation. This, as Chapter XV has shown, has a highly discriminatory impact on different groups. And we shall see in the next chapter that there are deeper social consequences. Inflation strikes the economy at the point where it is most vulnerable to damage. We may put it down—after the process of consumer demand creation and its financing—as the second of the unsolved problems of the affluent society.

CHAPTER XVIII

The Theory of Social Balance

It is not till it is discovered that high individual incomes will not purchase the mass of mankind immunity from cholera, typhus, and ignorance, still less secure them the positive advantages of educational opportunity and economic security, that slowly and reluctantly, amid prophecies of moral degeneration and economic disaster, society begins to make collective provision for needs which no ordinary individual, even if he works overtime all his life, can provide himself.

—R. H. TAWNEY[1]

THE FINAL PROBLEM of the productive society is what it produces. This manifests itself in an implacable tendency to provide an opulent supply of some things and a niggardly yield of others. This disparity carries to the point where it is a cause of social discomfort and social unhealth. The line which divides our area of wealth from our area of poverty is roughly that which divides privately produced and marketed goods and services from publicly rendered services. Our wealth in the first is not only in startling contrast with the meagerness of the latter, but our wealth in privately produced goods is, to a marked degree, the cause of crisis in the supply of public services. For we have failed to see the importance, indeed the urgent need, of maintaining a balance between the two.

This disparity between our flow of private and public goods and services is no matter of subjective judgment. On the contrary, it is the source of the most extensive comment which only stops short of the direct contrast being made here. In the years following World War II, the papers of any major city—those of New York were an excellent example

[1] *Equality* (4th revised ed.), pp. 134-35.

—told daily of the shortages and shortcomings in the elementary municipal and metropolitan services. The schools were old and overcrowded. The police force was under strength and underpaid. The parks and playgrounds were insufficient. Streets and empty lots were filthy, and the sanitation staff was underequipped and in need of men. Access to the city by those who work there was uncertain and painful and becoming more so. Internal transportation was overcrowded, unhealthful, and dirty. So was the air. Parking on the streets had to be prohibited, and there was no space elsewhere. These deficiencies were not in new and novel services but in old and established ones. Cities have long swept their streets, helped their people move around, educated them, kept order, and provided horse rails for vehicles which sought to pause. That their residents should have a nontoxic supply of air suggests no revolutionary dalliance with socialism.

The discussion of this public poverty competed, on the whole successfully, with the stories of ever-increasing opulence in privately produced goods. The Gross National Product was rising. So were retail sales. So was personal income. Labor productivity had also advanced. The automobiles that could not be parked were being produced at an expanded rate. The children, though without schools, subject in the playgrounds to the affectionate interest of adults with odd tastes, and disposed to increasingly imaginative forms of delinquency, were admirably equipped with television sets. We had difficulty finding storage space for the great surpluses of food despite a national disposition to obesity. Food was grown and packaged under private auspices. The care and refreshment of the mind, in contrast with the stomach, was principally in the public domain. Our colleges and universities were severely overcrowded and underprovided, and the same was true of the mental hospitals.

The contrast was and remains evident not alone to those who read. The family which takes its mauve and cerise, air-conditioned, power-steered, and power-braked automobile out for a tour passes through cities that are badly paved, made hideous by litter, blighted buildings, billboards, and posts for wires that should long since have been put underground. They pass on into a countryside that has been rendered largely invisible by commercial art. (The goods which the latter advertise have an absolute priority in our value system. Such aesthetic considerations as a view of the countryside accordingly come second. On such matters we are consistent.) They picnic on exquisitely packaged food from a

portable icebox by a polluted stream and go on to spend the
night at a park which is a menace to public health and morals.
Just before dozing off on an air mattress, beneath a nylon
tent, amid the stench of decaying refuse, they may reflect
vaguely on the curious unevenness of their blessings. Is this,
indeed, the American genius?

II

In the production of goods within the private economy it
has long been recognized that a tolerably close relationship
must be maintained between the production of various kinds
of products. The output of steel and oil and machine tools is
related to the production of automobiles. Investment in transportation must keep abreast of the output of goods to be
transported. The supply of power must be abreast of the
growth of industries requiring it. The existence of these relationships—coefficients to the economist—has made possible
the construction of the input-output table which shows how
changes in the production in one industry will increase or
diminish the demands on other industries. To this table, and
more especially to its ingenious author, Professor Wassily
Leontief, the world is indebted for one of its most important
of modern insights into economic relationships. If expansion
in one part of the economy were not matched by the requisite
expansion in other parts—were the need for balance not
respected—then bottlenecks and shortages, speculative hoard-
ing of scarce supplies, and sharply increasing costs would
ensue. Fortunately in peacetime the market system operates
easily and effectively to maintain this balance, and this together with the existence of stocks and some flexibility in the
coefficients as a result of substitution, insures that no serious
difficulties will arise. We are reminded of the existence of the
problem only by noticing how serious it is for those countries
—Poland or, in a somewhat different form, India—which seek
to solve the problem by planned measures and with a much
smaller supply of resources.

Just as there must be balance in what a community produces, so there must also be balance in what the community
consumes. An increase in the use of one product creates,
ineluctably, a requirement for others. If we are to consume
more automobiles, we must have more gasoline. There must
be more insurance as well as more space on which to operate
them. Beyond a certain point more and better food appears

to mean increased need for medical services. This is the certain result of the increased consumption of tobacco and alcohol. More vacations require more hotels and more fishing rods. And so forth. With rare exceptions—shortages of doctors are an exception which suggests the rule—this balance is also maintained quite effortlessly so far as goods for private sale and consumption are concerned. The price system plus a rounded condition of opulence is again the agency.

However, the relationships we are here discussing are not confined to the private economy. They operate comprehensively over the whole span of private and public services. As surely as an increase in the output of automobiles puts new demands on the steel industry so, also, it places new demands on public services. Similarly, every increase in the consumption of private goods will normally mean some facilitating or protective step by the state. In all cases if these services are not forthcoming, the consequences will be in some degree ill. It will be convenient to have a term which suggests a satisfactory relationship between the supply of privately produced goods and services and those of the state, and we may call it social balance.

The problem of social balance is ubiquitous, and frequently it is obtrusive. As noted, an increase in the consumption of automobiles requires a facilitating supply of streets, highways, traffic control, and parking space. The protective services of the police and the highway patrols must also be available, as must those of the hospitals. Although the need for balance here is extraordinarily clear, our use of privately produced vehicles has, on occasion, got far out of line with the supply of the related public services. The result has been hideous road congestion, an annual massacre of impressive proportions, and chronic colitis in the cities. As on the ground, so also in the air. Planes collide with disquieting consequences for those within when the public provision for air traffic control fails to keep pace with private use of the airways.

But the auto and the airplane, versus the space to use them, are merely an exceptionally visible example of a requirement that is pervasive. The more goods people procure, the more packages they discard and the more trash that must be carried away. If the appropriate sanitation services are not provided, the counterpart of increasing opulence will be deepening filth. The greater the wealth the thicker will be the dirt. This indubitably describes a tendency of our time. As more goods are produced and owned, the greater are the opportunities for fraud and the more property that must be protected. If the provision of public law-enforcement services do not keep pace, the counterpart of increased well-being will, we may be certain, be increased crime.

The city of Los Angeles, in modern times, is a near-classic study in the problem of social balance. Magnificently efficient factories and oil refineries, a lavish supply of automobiles, a vast consumption of handsomely packaged products, coupled with the absence of a municipal trash collection service which forced the use of home incinerators, made the air nearly unbreathable for an appreciable part of each year. Air pollution could be controlled only by a complex and highly developed set of public services—by better knowledge stemming from more research, better policing, a municipal trash collection service, and possibly the assertion of the priority of clean air over the production of goods. These were long in coming. The agony of a city without usable air was the result.

The issue of social balance can be identified in many other current problems. Thus an aspect of increasing private production is the appearance of an extraordinary number of things which lay claim to the interest of the young. Motion pictures, television, automobiles, and the vast opportunities which go with the mobility, together with such less enchanting merchandise as narcotics, comic books, and pornographia, are all included in an advancing gross national product. The child of a less opulent as well as a technologically more primitive age had far fewer such diversions. The red schoolhouse is remembered mainly because it had a paramount position in the lives of those who attended it that no modern school can hope to attain.

In a well-run and well-regulated community, with a sound school system, good recreational opportunities, and a good police force—in short a community where public services have kept pace with private production—the diversionary forces operating on the modern juvenile may do no great damage. Television and the violent mores of Hollywood and Madison Avenue must contend with the intellectual discipline of the school. The social, athletic, dramatic, and like attractions of the school also claim the attention of the child. These, together with the other recreational opportunities of the community, minimize the tendency to delinquency. Experiments with violence and immorality are checked by an effective law-enforcement system before they become epidemic.

In a community where public services have failed to keep abreast of private consumption things are very different. Here, in an atmosphere of private opulence and public squalor, the private goods have full sway. Schools do not compete with television and the movies. The dubious heroes of the latter, not Miss Jones, become the idols of the young. The hot rod and the wild ride take the place of more sedentary sports for which there are inadequate facilities or provision. Comic books, alcohol, narcotics, and switch-blade knives are, as noted, part of the increased flow of goods, and there is nothing to dispute their enjoyment. There is an ample supply of private wealth to be appropriated and not much to be feared from the police. An austere community is free from temptation. It can be austere in its public services. Not so a rich one.

Moreover, in a society which sets large store by production, and which has highly effective machinery for synthesizing private wants, there are strong pressures to have as many wage earners in the family as possible. As always all social behavior is part of a piece. If both parents are engaged in private production, the burden on the public services is further increased. Children, in effect, become the charge of the community for an appreciable part of the time. If the services of the community do not keep pace, this will be another source of disorder.

Residential housing also illustrates the problem of the social balance, although in a somewhat complex form. Few would wish to contend that, in the lower or even the middle-income brackets, Americans are munificently supplied with housing. A great many families would like better located or merely more houseroom, and no advertising is necessary to persuade them of their wish. And the provision of housing is in the private domain. At first glance at least, the line we draw between private and public seems not to be preventing a satisfactory allocation of resources to housing.

On closer examination, however, the problem turns out to be not greatly different from that of education. It is improbable that the housing industry is greatly more incompetent or inefficient in the United States than in those countries—Scandinavia, Holland, or (for the most part) England—where slums have been largely eliminated and where *minimum* standards of cleanliness and comfort are well above our own. As the experience of these countries shows, and as we have also been learning, the housing industry functions well only in combination with a large, complex, and costly array of public services. These include land purchase and clearance for redevelopment; good neighborhood and city planning, and effective and well-enforced zoning; a variety of financing and other aids to the housebuilder and owner; publicly supported research and architectural services for an industry which, by its nature, is equipped to do little on its own; and a considerable amount of direct or assisted public construction for families in the lowest-income brackets. The quality of the housing depends not on the industry, which is given, but on what is invested in these supplements and supports.

III

The case for social balance has, so far, been put negatively. Failure to keep public services in minimal relation to private production and use of goods is a cause of social disorder or impairs economic performance. The matter may now be put affirmatively. By failing to exploit the opportunity to expand public production we are missing opportunities for enjoyment which otherwise we might have had. Presumably a community can be as well rewarded by buying better schools or better parks as by buying bigger automobiles. By concentrating on the latter rather than the former it is failing to maximize its satisfactions. As with schools in the community, so with public services over the country at large. It is scarcely sensible that we should satisfy our wants in private goods with reckless abundance, while in the case of public goods, on the evidence of the eye, we practice extreme self-denial. So, far from systematically exploiting the opportunities to derive use and pleasure from these services, we do not supply what would keep us out of trouble.

The conventional wisdom holds that the community, large or small, makes a decision as to how much it will devote to its public services. This decision is arrived at by democratic process. Subject to the imperfections and uncertainties of democracy, people decide how much of their private income and goods they will surrender in order to have public services of which they are in greater need. Thus there is a balance, however rough, in the enjoyments to be had from private goods and services and those rendered by public authority.

It will be obvious, however, that this view depends on the notion of independently determined consumer wants. In such a world one could with some reason defend the doctrine that the consumer, as a voter, makes an independent choice between public and private goods. But given the dependence effect—given that consumer wants are created by the process by which they are satisfied—the consumer makes no such choice. He is subject to the forces of advertising and emulation by which production creates its own demand. Advertising operates exclusively, and emulation mainly, on behalf of privately produced goods and services.[2] Since management and emulative effects operate on behalf of private production, public services will have an inherent tendency to lag behind. Automobile demand which is expensively synthesized will inevitably have a much larger claim on income than parks or public health or even roads where no such influence operates. The engines of mass communication, in their highest state of development, assail the eyes and ears of the community on behalf of more beer but not of more schools. Even in the conventional wisdom it will scarcely be contended that this leads to an equal choice between the two.

The competition is especially unequal for new products and services. Every corner of the public psyche is canvassed by some of the nation's most talented citizens to see if the desire for some merchantable product can be cultivated. No similar process operates on behalf of the nonmerchantable services of the state. Indeed, while we take the cultivation of new private wants for granted we would be measurably shocked to see it applied to public services. The scientist or engineer or advertising man who devotes himself to developing a new carburetor, cleanser, or depilatory for which the public recognizes no need and will feel none until an advertising campaign arouses it, is one of the valued members of our society. A politician or a public servant who dreams up a new public service is a wastrel. Few public offenses are more reprehensible.

So much for the influences which operate on the decision between public and private production. The calm decision between public and private consumption pictured by the conventional wisdom is, in fact, a remarkable example of the error which arises from viewing social behavior out of context. The inherent tendency will always be for public

[2] Emulation does operate between communities. A new school or a new highway in one community does exert pressure on others to remain abreast. However, as compared with the pervasive effects of emulation in extending the demand for privately produced consumer's goods there will be agreement, I think, that this intercommunity effect is probably small.

services to fall behind private production. We have here the first of the causes of social imbalance.

IV

Social balance is also the victim of two further features of our society—the truce on inequality and the tendency to inflation. Since these are now part of our context, their effect comes quickly into view.

With rare exceptions such as the post office, public services do not carry a price ticket to be paid for by the individual user. By their nature they must, ordinarily, be available to all. As a result, when they are improved or new services are initiated, there is the ancient and troublesome question of who is to pay. This, in turn, provokes to life the collateral but irrelevant debate over inequality. As with the use of taxation as an instrument of fiscal policy, the truce on inequality is broken. Liberals are obliged to argue that the services be paid for by progressive taxation which will reduce inequality. Committed as they are to the urgency of goods (and also, as we shall see in a later chapter, to a somewhat mechanical view of the way in which the level of output can be kept most secure) they must oppose sales and excise taxes. Conservatives rally to the defense of inequality—although without ever quite committing themselves in such uncouth terms— and oppose the use of income taxes. They, in effect, oppose the expenditure not on the merits of the service but on the demerits of the tax system. Since the debate over inequality cannot be resolved, the money is frequently not appropriated and the service not performed. It is a casualty of the economic goals of both liberals and conservatives for both of whom the questions of social balance are subordinate to those of production and, when it is evoked, of inequality.

In practice matters are better as well as worse than this statement of the basic forces suggests. Given the tax structure, the revenues of all levels of government grow with the growth of the economy. Services can be maintained and sometimes even improved out of this automatic accretion.

However, this effect is highly unequal. The revenues of the federal government, because of its heavy reliance on income taxes, increase more than proportionately with private economic growth. In addition, although the conventional wisdom greatly deplores the fact, federal appropriations have only an indirect bearing on taxation. Public services are considered and voted on in accordance with their seeming urgency. Initiation or improvement of a particular service is rarely, except for purposes of oratory, set against the specific effect on taxes. Tax policy, in turn, is decided on the basis of the level of economic activity, the resulting revenues, expediency, and other considerations. Among these the total of the thousands of individually considered appropriations is but one factor. In this process the ultimate tax consequence of any individual appropriation is *de minimus,* and the tendency to ignore it reflects the simple mathematics of the situation. Thus it is possible for the Congress to make decisions affecting the social balance without invoking the question of inequality.

Things are made worse, however, by the fact that a large proportion of the federal revenues are pre-empted by defense. The increase in defense costs has also tended to absorb a large share of the normal increase in tax revenues. The position of the federal government for improving the social balance has also been weakened since World War II by the strong, although receding, conviction that its taxes were at artificial wartime levels and that a tacit commitment exists to reduce taxes at the earliest opportunity.

In the states and localities the problem of social balance is much more severe. Here tax revenues—this is especially true of the General Property Tax—increase less than proportionately with increased private production. Budgeting too is far more closely circumscribed than in the case of the federal government—only the monetary authority enjoys the pleasant privilege of underwriting its own loans. Because of this, increased services for states and localities regularly pose the question of more revenues and more taxes. And here, with great regularity, the question of social balance is lost in the debate over equality and social equity.

Thus we currently find by far the most serious social imbalance in the services performed by local governments. The F.B.I. comes much more easily by funds than the city police force. The Department of Agriculture can more easily keep its pest control abreast of expanding agricultural output than the average city health service can keep up with the needs of an expanding industrial population. One consequence is that the federal government remains under constant pressure to use its superior revenue position to help redress the balance at the lower levels of government.

V

Finally, social imbalance is the natural offspring of persistent inflation. Inflation by its nature strikes different individuals and groups with highly discriminatory effect. The most nearly unrelieved victims, apart from those living on pensions or other fixed provision for personal security, are those who work for the state. In the private economy the firm which sells goods has, in general, an immediate accommodation to the inflationary movement. Its price increases are the inflation. The incomes of its owners and proprietors are automatically accommodated to the upward movement. To the extent that wage increases are part of the inflationary process, this is also true of organized industrial workers. Even unorganized white-collar workers are in a milieu where prices and incomes are moving up. The adaption of their incomes, if less rapid than that of the industrial workers, is still reasonably prompt.

The position of the public employee is at the other extreme. His pay scales are highly formalized, and traditionally they have been subject to revision only at lengthy intervals. In states and localities inflation does not automatically bring added revenues to pay higher salaries and incomes. Pay revision for all public workers is subject to the temptation to wait and see if the inflation isn't coming to an end. There will be some fear—this seems to have been more of a factor in England than in the United States—that advances in public wages will set a bad example for private employers and unions.

Inflation means that employment is pressing on the labor supply and that private wage and salary incomes are rising. Thus the opportunities for moving from public to private employment are especially favorable. Public employment, moreover, once had as a principal attraction a high measure of social security. Industrial workers were subject to the formidable threat of unemployment during depression. Public employees were comparatively secure, and this security was worth an adverse salary differential. But with improving economic security in general this advantage has diminished. Private employment thus has come to provide better protection against inflation and little worse protection against other hazards. Though the dedicated may stay in public posts, the alert go.

The deterioration of the public services in the years of inflation has not gone unremarked. However, there has been a strong tendency to regard it as an adventitious misfortune —something which, like a nasty shower at a picnic, happened to blight a generally good time. Salaries were allowed to lag, which was a pity. This is a very inadequate view. Discrimination against the public services is an organic feature of inflation. Nothing so weakens government as persistent inflation. The public administration of France for many years, of Italy until recent times, and of other European and numerous South American countries have been deeply sapped and eroded by the effects of long-continued inflation. Social imbalance reflects itself in inability to enforce laws, including significantly those which protect and advance basic social justice, and in failure to maintain and improve essential services. One outgrowth of the resulting imbalance has been frustration and pervasive discontent. Over much of the world there is a rough and not entirely accidental correlation between the strength of indigenous communist parties or the frequency of revolutions and the persistence of inflation.

VI

A feature of the years immediately following World War II was a remarkable attack on the notion of expanding and improving public services. During the depression years such services had been elaborated and improved partly in order to fill some small part of the vacuum left by the shrinkage of private production. During the war years the role of government was vastly expanded. After that came the reaction. Much of it, unquestionably, was motivated by a desire to rehabilitate the prestige of private production and therewith of producers. No doubt some who joined the attack hoped, at least tacitly, that it might be possible to sidestep the truce on taxation vis-à-vis equality by having less taxation of all kinds. For a time the notion that our public services had somehow become inflated and excessive was all but axiomatic. Even liberal politicians did not seriously protest. They found it necessary to aver that they were in favor of public economy too.

In this discussion a certain mystique was attributed to the satisfaction of privately supplied wants. A community decision to have a new school means that the individual surrenders the necessary amount, willy-nilly, in his taxes. But if he is left with that income, he is a free man. He can decide between a better car or a television set. This was advanced with some solemnity as an argument for the TV set. The difficulty is that this argument leaves the community with no way of preferring the school. All private wants, where the individual can choose, are inherently superior to all public desires which must be paid for by taxation and with an inevitable component of compulsion.

The cost of public services was also held to be a desolating burden on private production, although this was at a time when the private production was burgeoning. Urgent warnings were issued of the unfavorable effects of taxation on investment—"I don't know of a surer way of killing off the incentive to invest than by imposing taxes which are regarded by people as punitive."[3] This was at a time when the inflationary effect of a very high level of investment was causing concern. The same individuals who were warning about the inimical effects of taxes were strongly advocating a monetary policy designed to reduce investment. However, an understanding of our economic discourse requires an appreciation of one of its basic rules: men of high position are allowed, by a special act of grace, to accommodate their reasoning to the answer they need. Logic is only required in those of lesser rank.

Finally it was argued, with no little vigor, that expanding government posed a grave threat to individual liberties. "Where distinction and rank is achieved almost exclusively by becoming a civil servant of the state . . . it is too much to expect that many will long prefer freedom to security."[4]

With time this attack on public services has somewhat subsided. The disorder associated with social imbalance has become visible even if the need for balance between private and public services is still imperfectly appreciated.

Freedom also seemed to be surviving. Perhaps it was realized that all organized activity requires concessions by the individual to the group. This is true of the policeman who joins the police force, the teacher who gets a job at the high school, and the executive who makes his way up the hierarchy of Du Pont. If there are differences between public and private organization, they are of kind rather than of degree. As

[3] Arthur F. Burns, Chairman of the President's Council of Economic Advisers, *U. S. News & World Report*, May 6, 1955.
[4] F. A. Hayek, *The Road to Serfdom* (London: George Routledge & Sons, 1944), p. 98.

this is written the pendulum has in fact swung back. Our liberties are now menaced by the conformity exacted by the large corporation and its impulse to create, for its own purposes, the organization man. This danger we may also survive.

Nonetheless, the postwar onslaught on the public services left a lasting imprint. To suggest that we canvass our public wants to see where happiness can be improved by more and better services has a sharply radical tone. Even public services to avoid disorder must be defended. By contrast the man who devises a nostrum for a nonexistent need and then successfully promotes both remains one of nature's noblemen.

CHAPTER XIX

The Investment Balance

SOCIAL BALANCE relates to the goods and services we consume. There is an allied problem in the way we commit the resources that are available for investment in the economy. The same forces which bring us our plenitude of private goods and leave us poverty-stricken in our public services also act to distort the distribution of investment as between ordinary material capital and what we may denote as the personal capital of the country. This distortion has far-reaching effects. One of them is to impair the production of private goods themselves. The situation will be seen in sharpest focus if we pursue the latter point. It is not, however, the only or, indeed, the most important consequence.

Economic growth—the expansion of economic output—requires an increase in the quantity of the productive plant and equipment of the country or in its quality or, as in the usual case, in both. This is fully agreed. The increase in quantity is capital formation. The increase in quality is what we call technological advance.

In the earliest stages of economic development, from which so many of our economic attitudes are derived, the simple and sufficient way of getting more growth was to have more saving and therefore more material capital. Entrepreneurial talent was needed but, at least in western countries, it was almost invariably, if not invariably, forthcoming. To perform this function required some education. But, as the example of any number of great entrepreneurs from Commodore Vanderbilt to Henry Ford made clear, the education could be exiguous and often was. The existence of an educated and literate body of workers was desirable but by no means essential. Some of the greatest industrial enterprises in the United States in the past were manned principally by men who could speak no English. Most important of all, in all the earlier stages of development there was no close and predictable correlation between the supply of educated men and the nature of their training and the rate of technological innovation. Inventions were more often the result of brilliant flashes of insight than the product of long-prepared training and development. The Industrial Revolution in England was ushered in by the invention of the flying shuttle by John Kay, the spinning jenny by James Hargreaves, the spinning frame (presumptively) by Richard Arkwright and, of course, by James Watt's steam engine. These represented vast improvements in the capital which was being put to industrial use. But only in the case of Watt could the innovation be related to previous education and preparation. Kay and Hargreaves were simple weavers with a mechanical turn of mind. Arkwright had been apprenticed as a boy as a barber and a wigmaker and was barely literate.

However, with the development of a great and complex industrial plant, and even more with the development of a great and sophisticated body of basic science and of experience in its application, all this has been changed. In addition to the entrepreneurs (and perhaps one should add the accountants and clerks) who were more or less automatically forthcoming, modern economic activity now requires a great number of trained and qualified people. Investment in human beings is, *prima facie,* as important as investment in material capital. The one, in its modern complexity, depends on the other.

What is more important, the *improvement* in capital—technological advance—is now almost wholly dependent on investment in education, training, and scientific opportunity for individuals. One branch of the conventional wisdom clings nostalgically to the conviction that brilliant, isolated, and intuitive inventions are still a principal instrument of technological progress and can occur anywhere and to anyone.[1] Benjamin Franklin is the sacred archetype of the American genius and nothing may be done to disturb his position. But in the unromantic fact, innovation has become a highly organized enterprise. The extent of the result is predictably related to the quality and quantity of the resources being applied to it. These resources are men and women. Their quality and quantity depends on the extent of the investment in their education, training, and opportunity. They are the source of technological change. Without them investment in material capital will still bring growth,

[1] Cf. for example the article by G. Warren Nutter, *Monopoly, Bigness and Progress,* in *Journal of Political Economy,* December 1956.

but it will be the inefficient growth that is combined with technological stagnation.

II

We come now to the nub of the problem. Investment in material capital is distributed to the various claimant industries by the market. If earnings are high (at the margin) in the oil industry and low in the textile business, it is to the oil industry that capital will flow. This allocation by the market works, it would appear, with tolerable efficiency. Among the recognized crimes of economics, any interference with the "free flow" of capital has a very high standing.

But while this flow operates as between different material claimants on investment funds, it operates only with manifest uncertainty and inefficiency as between material and personal capital. Nearly all of the investment in individuals is in the public domain. And virtually all of it is outside the market system. It is the state which, through primary and secondary schools, and through the colleges and universities, makes the largest investment in individuals. And where, as in the case of private colleges and universities, the state is not directly involved, the amount of the investment is not directly related to the eventual pay-out in production. Investment in refineries being higher than in textile mills, the refineries will draw investment funds. But engineers to design the refineries may be even more important—in effect yield a higher return. And the highest return of all may come from the scientist who makes a marked improvement in the refining process. These are not imaginative possibilities but common probabilities. Yet the high return to scientific and technical training does not cause the funds to move from material capital to such investment. There is no likely flow from the building of the refineries to the education of the scientists. Here, at the most critical point in the vaunted process of investment resource allocation, is an impediment of towering importance. Characteristically, however, it has received little comment. It is not, like the tariff or monopoly, one of the classic barriers to capital movement. Hence it did not get a foothold in economics in the last century and, accordingly, under the intellectual grandfather clause which has such sway in the science it has no real standing now.

There can be no question of the importance of the impediment. Investment in individuals is in the public domain; this investment has become increasingly essential with the advance of science and technology; and there is no machinery for automatically allocating resources as between material and human investment. But this is not all. As we have seen in earlier chapters, there is active discrimination against the investment in the public domain and hence in any part of it. The investment in the refinery is an unmitigated good. It adds to our stock of wealth. It is a categorical achievement. But the training of the scientists and engineers who will run the refinery, improve its economic efficiency, and possibly in the end replace it with something better is not a categorical good. The money so invested is not regarded with approval. On the contrary, it is widely regarded as a burden. Many will judge the magnitude of the achievement in this area by the smallness of the investment. Others will hold this investment in abeyance while arguing the ancient issue of equality. So incredible is the provision for such investment that a considerable part will have to be begged. Even the prestige of the word investment itself is not regularly accorded to these outlays. A century ago, when educational outlays were not intimately related to production, men sensibly confined the word investment to the increases in capital which brought a later increase in product. Education was a consumer outlay. The popular usage has never been revised.[2]

Could it be legally arranged that youngsters were sorted out at an early age, possibly by their test score in mathematics, and the promising then be indentured for life to a particular corporation, the flow of investment into human development might soon be placed on a rough parity with that into material capital. Firms would perceive the need for investing in their scientific and engineering stock much as major-league baseball clubs have learned the wisdom of investing in their farm teams. Under ideal arrangements any surplus talent could be marketed. The cost of unsuccessfully trying to educate the inevitable errors of selection would be either written off or partially retrieved by using the individuals as salesmen. Under such a system, which as noted would unfortunately involve the elimination of the liberty of the individuals in question, it is fairly certain that investment in human beings would rise and at a rapid rate.

[2] Since this was written and under the impact of Soviet scientific achievements there has been considerable discussion of our lag in *investment* in scientific education. However, this is being treated as a kind of aberration, and not as a fundamental flaw in our machinery of resource allocation.

But so long as free choice remains, such investment must remain largely a public function. The individual, since he is only at the beginning of earning power, cannot himself make any appreciable part of the investment. Whether his parents can and will be willing to do so is a highly accidental matter. His future employer can hardly be expected to invest in an asset that may materialize in the plant of a competitor or another industry. At most he will, as now, distribute scholarships and fellowships in the hope of ultimately influencing the choice of those in whom the investment is nearly complete. This has no appreciable effect on the total of the investment in peop!e. It is a scalping operation. It does, however, suggest the store which is set by the resulting assets.

III

Human development, in other words, is what economists have long termed an external economy. Its benefits accrue to all firms; it is not sufficiently specific to any one to be bought and paid for by it.

What is true of human development is also true of one of its principal fruits. That is scientific research. A society which sets for itself the goal of increasing its supply of goods will tend, inevitably, to identify all innovation with additions to, changes in, or increases in its stock of goods. It will assume, accordingly, that most research will be induced and rewarded by the market.

Much will be. Under the proper circumstances—firms must be of adequate size in the industry, and certain other conditions must be met[3]—we may expect our economy to do a superior job of inventing, developing, and redesigning consumers' goods and improving their process of manufacture. Nor is there reason to doubt that similar attention will be given, under equally favorable circumstances, to the capital goods industries which support this consumers' goods consumption. Much of this achievement will impress us only so long as we do not inquire how the demand for the products so developed is contrived and sustained. If we do we are bound to observe that much of the research effort—as in the automobile industry—is devoted to discovering changes that can be advertised. The research program will be built around the need to devise "selling points" and "advertising pegs" or to accelerate "planned obsolescence." All this suggests that

[3] Cf. *American Capitalism*, pp. 84-94 (2d ed.).

the incentive will be to allocate research resources to what, in some sense, are the least important things. The quantity is more impressive than the way it is allocated. Still one would not wish to suggest that the American economy is delinquent in the attention it devotes to change and improvement in consumers' goods. Clearly it is not.

These incentives, however, operate over but a small part of total scientific and research activity and, indeed, over but a small part that is potentially applicable to the production of goods. Thus a very large amount of highly useful research cannot be specialized to or be sustained by any marketable product. This is most obviously true of much so-called basic research. But it is also true of a large amount of applied effort. The modern air transport is the stepchild of the military airplane. It would never have sustained the underlying research and development endeavor on its own. The same is true in even greater degree of the nonmilitary uses of nuclear energy. There are numerous other cases.

It is because military considerations have induced a large allocation of resources to research that this problem is, on the whole, less striking than that of investment in personal resources. Although the research must be in the public domain, military urgency has helped to offset this blight. There is little comfort for man in the circumstances which have induced this allocation of resources or from the resulting weapons. But it has catalyzed a great deal of important scientific innovation and development. Far more significant research lies back of the effort to exceed the speed of sound than lies back of even the best new soap. It may well be more significant for industry itself. In any event the rate of technical progress in American industry in recent decades would have been markedly slower had it not been for militarily inspired and for this reason publicly-supported research.

IV

As noted, one must where possible deal with the conventional wisdom on its own terms. The conventional wisdom stresses the paramount urgency of increased production of goods. To show that even for this purpose its allocation of investment is irrational—that it is tolerable for research only as a byproduct of military claims and that for investment in individuals it can make no claim at all to rationality—is impressive. However, it would be barbarous to suggest that the only claim to be made on behalf of education is the increased production of goods. It has its independent and, one must suppose, its higher justification. A horse almost certainly appreciates a comfortable stable, a secure supply of oats, a measure of recreation, and conceivably the pleasure of being esteemed at least as highly as any other horse in the stable. The nontheological quality which most distinguishes men from horses is the desire, in addition to these attributes of material and psychic well-being, to know, understand, and reason. One may hope that investment in the things that differentiate man from his animals requires no further justification. If, however, this investment is less than would be justified even for the production of goods, one wonders how very much less than the ideal it must be for the purposes of human satisfaction and fulfillment.

V

A final and rather more speculative issue remains, which is the joint legacy of the problem of social balance in consumption and of balanced investment in material and personal capital.

As Chapter XIV has argued, the process by which wants are now synthesized is a potential source of economic instability. Production and therewith employment and social security are dependent on an inherently unstable process of consumer debt creation. This may one day falter. And a decay in emulative compulsions or in the ability to synthesize demand could bring a fall in consumption, an increase in unemployment, and a difficult problem of readjustment.

However great or small these dangers, they will be lessened if our consumption is widely distributed—if productive energies serve uniformly the whole span of man's wants. Since public wants are not contrived, they are not subject to a failure of contrivance. Since they are not sold on the installment plan, they are not subject to curtailment by any of the factors which may make people unwilling or unable to incur debt. Thus the better the social balance the more immune the economy to fluctuations in private demand.

One is tempted to press the matter further. Simple minds, presumably, are the easiest to manage. Better education, one product of improved social balance, might well be expected to lessen the effectiveness of synthesis and emulation in the manufacture of new wants. At first glance, therefore, it could be regarded as inimical to the process by which demand is now sustained. But there can also be little doubt that education has a marked influence in widening the span of the individual's wants. Synthesis and emulation are most persuasive in creating desire for simple physical objects of consumption or simple modes of enjoyment which require no previous conditioning of the consumer. Houses; automobiles; the uncomplicated forms of alcohol, food, and sex; sports; and movies require little prior preparation of the subject for the highest enjoyment. A mass appeal is thus successful, and hence it is on these things that we find concentrated the main weight of modern want creation. By contrast, more esoteric desires—music and fine arts, literary and scientific interests, and to some extent travel—can normally be synthesized, if at all, only on the basis of a good deal of prior education. Thus the effect of education and *pro tanto* of social balance is to increase the range of wants to be satisfied and to lessen the dependence on those which must be contrived. Or, more accurately, this is a plausible hypothesis. For so stern have been the forces channeling our thoughts in the past that there is little to go on in these fertile valleys of the imagination.

CHAPTER XX

The Transition

IN ONE SENSE the main task of this essay has been accomplished. Its concern has been with the thralldom of a myth —the myth that production, by its overpowering importance and its ineluctable difficulty, is the central problem of our lives. We have now seen the sources of this myth. And we have seen some of the consequences—the tenuous and maybe dangerous process of consumer demand creation, recurrent inflation, social imbalance—to which the myth commits us. Emancipation of the mind is a no less worthy enterprise than emancipation of the body. The bondsman, given his freedom and persuaded of its virtues, is ordinarily left to enjoy it. Nor is his emancipator blamed for failing to give him a list of things to do.

And a concern for new goals, once the old ones become suspect, is not only the next order of philosophical business but the inevitable one. Social philosophy, far more than nature, abhors a vacuum. Men must see a purpose in their efforts. This purpose can be nonsensical and, as we have seen, if it is elaborately nonsensical that is all to the good. Men can labor to make sense out of single steps toward the goal without ever pausing to reflect that the goal itself is ludicrous. But they must not question the goal. For to do so is to initiate a search for one that serves better. Thus it is that an essay such as this is far more important for what it destroys—or to speak more accurately, for the destruction which it crystallizes, since the ultimate enemy of myth is circumstance—than for what it creates.

This is sharply at odds with the conventional wisdom. The latter sets great store by what it calls constructive criticism. And it reserves its scorn for what it is likely to term a purely destructive or negative position. In this, as so often, it manifests a sound instinct for self-preservation.[1] The attack on the conventional or accepted thought is dismissed as an inferior and, indeed, a wanton activity and, as such, not something that should be taken seriously. At the same time "constructive alternatives" are invited. These are a much lower order of danger. The threat to the conventional wisdom is always its own irrelevance, not the appeal of a relevant alternative. In postwar West Germany, in contrast with the Weimar regime, governments have displayed notable stability of tenure. Considerable credit goes to the constitutional provision for the so-called "constructive veto." This, in effect, requires the parliament to decide on a new administration before it votes out the old one. To settle in advance on such an alternative is difficult or impossible. Thus parliaments have had no choice but to maintain the status quo. The conventional wisdom finds similar strength in asserting the moral superiority of constructive criticism.

However, as always, it is sound strategy to deal with the conventional wisdom on its own terms. If it inquires how we escape the present preoccupation with production; or how we escape the race to manufacture more wants for more goods and then yet more wants for yet more goods; or what is to fill the seemingly vast vacuum which abandoning this race would leave in our lives; or what are to be the symbols of happiness if goods cease to be so regarded, then it is well that there be answers. The defenses of the conventional wisdom are formidable. One should not concede it any points. What replaces the profound preoccupation with production?

II

In the world of minor lunacy the behavior of both the utterly rational and the totally insane seems equally odd. The notion that ours, inevitably, is a world of deep poverty in which production is of supreme urgency is an old one. So is the corresponding behavior. The discovery that production is no longer of such urgency—that it is something of which we

[1] The same instinct has caused the conventional wisdom to turn vigorously on the debunker of public reputations. Obviously the man who, because of psychological, commercial, or other motivation, concerns himself with trying to separate truth from fiction in assessing human accomplishments is a grave threat to the man of conventional wisdom. This threat has been greatly abated in modern times by reducing the debunker, even when he is unqualifiedly concerned with the truth, to the level of a literary pariah.

are reasonably assured and which, paradoxically, is most
threatened by our failure to see it in proper perspective[2]—
involves a major wrench in our attitudes. What was sound
economic behavior before cannot be sound economic behavior
now. What were the goals of individuals, organizations and,
perhaps more especially, of government before may not be
so now. Many who will find it possible to believe that production has lost its pristine urgency will still find the changes
in behavior and policy that this suggests rather difficult to
swallow. This behavior and these policies will have an air
of fecklessness, even of danger. And this, needless to say,
will be exploited vigorously by the conventional wisdom.

It was ever so. In the depression years many could agree
that the clear and immediate cause of difficulty was a shortage
of demand for goods. That the private economy might find
its equilibrium not with a demand sufficient to insure full
employment but at a level where substantial millions were left
unemployed seemed plausible enough. Yet, having conceded
all this, it was still not easy to agree that the government
should supplement the deficient private demand by public
borrowing and spending. This seemed vastly reckless. The
Keynesian diagnosis was one thing, but the Keynesian remedy
was another.

Again in the thirties the diminishing urgency of the problem of production began to manifest itself in increasing
surpluses of agricultural products. For a time it was possible,
and not without reason, to attribute these surpluses to the
Great Depression. But in the forties it became clear that
increasing productivity in agriculture was outdistancing consumer needs even when demand was at full employment
levels. It was clearly greater than the farm industry's capacity
for adjustment. Many came to accept this diagnosis in one
form or another. But two of the more obvious remedies—to
control production or to give away the surplus to people
who could eat it—continued to be regarded with horror. In
the early years of the New Deal the slaughter of little pigs,
a primitive form of production control, created a mild form
of political trauma. Ever after, statesmen advocated control,
though it was an obvious and indeed inescapable remedy, only
after much hesitation and many elaborate manifestations of
dismay designed to appease the gods and placate the conventional wisdom. Wherever possible euphemisms were em-

---

[2] Committing us, to repeat, to the tenuous process of private want
creation, causing social imbalance, contributing to economic instability,
and threatening, among other things, the supply of trained manpower.

ployed—as this is written, instead of taking acres out of production they are being put into a soil bank.

Similarly, when the other obvious remedy, that of giving away food, was first broached it was soundly denounced. To wish to give milk to Hottentots became, for a time, a symbol of advanced economic irresponsibility. Ultimately the necessities of the case triumphed. Under the guidance of an impeccably conservative Secretary of Agriculture, Mr. Ezra Taft Benson, world-wide gifts of food in large quantity became an established policy. If the Hottentots have not yet acquired dried skim milk, it is only because they have not sufficiently pressed their request. But again elaborate disguise was essential. The receiving countries "bought" the products with their own currency, which meant that they supplied money that cost them nothing and which the United States agreed not to use in appreciable amount. Men would rarely have been poor in this world had they been able to satisfy their desires by purchases made with money of their own manufacture and which their well-supplied venders agreed to accept without question.

Life and certainly the language would be simpler were we to accept change, and the consequent policies, at their face value. But it would also destroy an engaging, almost Oriental, quality of our political life which leads us to drape the urgencies of the present in the symbols of the past. Though production has receded in importance, we shall doubtless continue to pretend that it isn't so.

III

For the number of questions which we agree to resolve in accordance with whether production is aided or retarded—made more or less important—is enormous. If something seems to contribute to increased production, it is good. If it fails to do so, it is useless. If it damages production, it is evil. If it can be shown that a tax is damaging to incentives and thus to production, it is *per se* a bad tax; and even if this result cannot be shown, it is still worth alleging. Our oldest and in some ways our most beloved topic of controversy is the tariff. Its enemies have always argued that the industries it nurtures are inefficient—that resources would be used more efficiently elsewhere. They have never doubted that efficiency was the decisive consideration. And their opponents, while challenging the defense of the higher efficiency of free trade in various ways, never challenged that criterion as such.

Similarly, the debate over the large corporation has been concerned almost exclusively with its efficiency. Its defenders have justified it by its competence as a producer. Its critics wondered if it might have exceeded the optimally efficient size. The corporation is a creature of no small cultural and political importance. Until very recently these aspects of its existence have been uniformly dismissed as of small account. As with the corporation so with the trade union. It is defended or condemned in accordance with its effect on the productivity of its members. That it has made work more tolerable; has enhanced the dignity of its members; and through seniority rules accorded its members what seem to be the natural rights of advancing age are not decisive. The decisive thing is the effect these have had on productivity.

If a locality is declining—if power, transportation, raw material supplies, consumer taste, or the tax laws have given other areas or countries an advantage—then one should encourage the people to leave. Mobility means efficiency. It is true that the ties of family, friends, pastor and priest, countryside and mere inertia may make this a Draconian and even cruel prescription. But it is the efficient course. Until relatively recent times a large amount of industrial and occupational disease could be justified on the grounds that considerations of cost did not permit of its elimination. Such a contention is no longer acceptable in the conventional wisdom. The latter would not hesitate, however, to point out that the concessions won over the years by the coal miners has speeded the relative decline of this industry. Given the importance of production, this was most unfortunate.

But if the things produced are not of great urgency, it follows that the efficiency of the process by which they are produced ceases to be an overriding consideration. New and usually much more difficult tests must be applied. It is not unlikely, indeed, that these will already be found playing a considerable but surreptitious role and this now becomes obtrusive.

Thus the argument over the progressive income tax has long been concerned with its effect on efficiency. Some have argued that it impairs incentives to increased efficiency. Others have argued that it does not. But if efficiency is not decisive, then the debate must go forward on other grounds. These may well include the simple and uncouth question of who is to pay how much. However, it is with this question that many who now talk about efficiency are really concerned.

Moreover, if efficiency is no longer a prime criterion, tariff policy will have to be resolved on the basis of how far we should go in making trade the handmaiden of larger national policy or what part compassion should play in easing the problems of distressed industries or areas. But, in fact, trade policy is already partly subordinate to both international comity and local charity. Efficiency has already partly surrendered to these other and more urgent considerations.

If the modern corporation must manufacture not only goods but the desire for the goods it manufactures, the efficiency of the first part of this activity ceases to be decisive. One could indeed argue that human happiness would be as effectively advanced by inefficiency in want creation as efficiency in production. Under these circumstances, the relation of the modern corporation to the people who comprise it—their chance for dignity, individuality, and full development of personality—may be at least as important as its efficiency. These may be worth having even at higher cost of production. Evidently the unions, in seeking to make life tolerable on the job, were being governed by a sound instinct. Why should life be intolerable to make things of small urgency?

Attitudes toward the declining community may need to be revised. The happiness and contentment of the people of Lawrence and Lowell and their preference, remarkable as it may seem, for life in these ancient towns, now becomes a consideration to set against the efficiency with which they are employed. The rational and compassionate society may seek to avoid the heartbreaks of an industrial Diaspora. If the goods have ceased to be urgent, can we sternly command men to leave their homes to produce them with maximum efficiency?

Coal has numerous substitutes. The marginal urgency of its present employments is low. The workers who made their life more livable at the expense of the most efficient production of coal may well have had reason on their side. In any case the substitutes—oil, water power, and atomic energy—are cleaner and more pleasant to work with.

The Benthamite test of public policy was "what serves the greatest happiness of the greatest number," and happiness was more or less implicitly identified with productivity. This is still the official test. In modern times the test has not been very rigorously applied. We have sensed though we have not recognized the declining importance of goods. Yet even in its deteriorated form we cling to this criterion. It is so much simpler than to substitute the other tests—compassion, individual happiness and well-being, the minimization of community or other social tensions—which now become relevant.

IV

Much more than decisions on economic policy are involved. A system of morality is at stake. For what we regard as the Puritan inheritance was soundly grounded on economic circumstance. In a country that was being carved from the wilderness, thrift and labor were the obligations of everyone, for they conserved and enlarged the supply of goods which sustained life itself. And the central or classical tradition of economics was more than an analysis of economic behavior and a set of rules for economic polity. It also had a moral code. The world owed no man a living. Unless he worked he did not eat. The obligation thus imposed required him to labor on his own behalf and therewith on behalf of others. Failure to work, even when it could be afforded, was offensive to what came to be called the Victorian, but could as well have been named the economic, morality. "To live in idleness, even if you have the means, is not only injurious to yourself, but a species of fraud upon the community."[3]

But if the goods have ceased to be urgent, where is the fraud? Can the North Dakota farmer be indicted for failure to labor hard and long to produce the wheat that his government wishes passionately it did not have to buy? Are we desperately dependent on the diligence of the worker who applies maroon and pink enamel to the functionless bulge of a modern motorcar? The idle man may still be an enemy of himself. But it is hard to say that the loss of his effort is damaging to society. Yet it is such damage which causes us to condemn idleness.

Again, the fact that a man was damaging society by his failure to produce has been, in the last analysis, the basis for a fair amount of highly convenient indifference and even cruelty in our behavior. The churches have long featured the virtue of loving one's neighbor. But the practical churchman has also recognized the need to reconcile this with basic economic necessities. A good deal of practical heartlessness

[3] William A. Alcott (a New England moralist and schoolmaster of the last century) quoted by Irving G. Wyllie in *The Self-Made Man in America* (New Brunswick: Rutgers University Press, 1954), p. 41.

was what served the social good. Many people have always found it painful to work. To show them compassion might be to damage production. The heartbreaks of migration in pursuit of jobs might be considerable, but how much worse the inefficiency of producing in the wrong place. No tears should be wasted on the farmers who go bankrupt. This is the path to more efficient farm production. In the United States, as in other western countries, we have for long had a respected secular priesthood whose function it has been to rise above questions of religious ethics, kindness, and compassion and show how these might have to be sacrificed on the altar of the larger good. That larger good, invariably, was more efficient production. The sacrifice obviously loses some of its point if it is on behalf of the more efficient production of goods for the satisfaction of wants of which people are not yet aware. It is even more tenuous, in its philosophical foundations, if it is to permit the more efficient contriving of wants of which people are not aware. And this latter is no insignificant industry in our time.

At this point even the most calloused of readers will regard with sympathy the tragic implications for established ideas which the rejection of scarcity and the acceptance of affluence involves. The almost incredibly elaborate efforts of the conventional economic wisdom to protect the present myth become understandable. One has a sense of disloyalty, almost of treachery, in destroying it.

Yet the escape from the thralldom of productive efficiency and unremitting labor is not without its opportunities. However, one final bridge must be built between the world of scarcity and that of affluence. For in the world of scarcity the need for goods was, as just noticed, powerfully reinforced by the compulsion to work. The individual who did not work, unless rarely favored by circumstance, was penalized by a total loss of income. That penalty still widely persists even though it now enforces the production of relatively unimportant goods. And the need to provide jobs requires us to face the unhappy choice either of having the economy constantly under inflationary strain or consigning some part of the working force to joblessness and inferior income. Obviously we shall not reap the rewards of affluence until we solve this problem.

CHAPTER XXI

The Divorce of Production from Security

WE HAVE SEEN that while our productive energies are used to make things of no great urgency—things for which demand must be synthesized at elaborate cost or they might not be wanted at all—the process of production continues to be of nearly undiminished urgency as a source of income. The income men derive from producing things of slight consequence is of great consequence. The production reflects the low marginal utility of the goods to society. The income reflects the high total utility of a livelihood to a person. For this reason, although there is conventional effort to deny it, income and employment rather than the goods have become our basic economic concern. This is revealed in the almost uncontrollable tendency to think of depressions not in terms of lost output but in terms of unemployment and of the equally powerful tendency to identify good times with full employment rather than with high production.

Moreover, the urgency of offering employment to all who seek it is probably increasing. This is a not unnatural consequence of affluence. When the income of the employed worker is high, it is not easy to defend a situation in which a small minority of workers have no employment income at all. Such discrimination seems altogether too flagrant. With increasing opulence we are thus more firmly committed to finding jobs for everyone. Our situation is that of a factory which must be operated at top speed for three shifts and seven days a week even at some risk of eventual breakdown, not because the product is in demand—on the contrary, much ingenuity is required to clear the shipping platform—but because any lower rate of operation will leave some of the people in town without a livelihood. If that misfortune is the alternative, then the factory may have to be so operated. But the question of freeing the community from such dangerous dependence will unquestionably arise.

In the real world, apart from the danger of breakdown,[1] there is also the problem of inflation. So long as we are committed by the imperatives of employment and income to operate at the capacity of plant and labor force, we shall have the threat of rising prices. Persistent inflation is not a happy prospect. It is also the long-run enemy of social balance.

The solution, or at least one part of it, is to have a reasonably satisfactory substitute for production as a source of income. This and this alone would break the present nexus between production and income and enable us to take a more relaxed and rational view of output without subjecting individual members of the society to hardship.

II

An obvious device for breaking the nexus between production and income security is at hand—that is the system of unemployment compensation. It provides income apart from production. To serve, however, it must be cast in a new and radically different role. In the past, unemployment compensation has served two principal purposes. It has eased the hardship of the worker who was making a routine change of jobs such as might be the result of a declining demand for one product and an increasing demand for another. And it has protected the worker from short-run changes in the level of aggregate demand which, on occasion, reduced the requirement for workers below the presently available labor force. Unemployment compensation did not protect him from a continuing failure to employ the full labor force, for the duration of the payments was strictly limited and useful, though they might be as a stopgap they were far from being a substitute for wage income. In 1956 payments in different states averaged from $18 to $36 weekly. In the same year average wages in manufacturing establishments were just under $80 weekly.

The meagerness of the payments is related to attitudes toward production. If production is all-important, then there should be no source of income that is a close substitute. People should be required to work and produce—or else. And in fact nothing has so haunted the discussion of social security legislation as the specter of the worker who lives

[1] See pp. 161 ff.

amiably off his unemployment compensation check and contributes nothing to society in return. So payments have been kept at levels relevant to survival rather than to comfort. And although the most painful prospect facing the worker under modern capitalism is not the short-term unemployment that is insured but the unemployment associated with depression and continuing deficiency in demand—the kind of unemployment that was experienced by so many through the decade of the thirties—this greater risk has remained essentially uncovered. Satisfactory insurance against such long-term unemployment would also provide the opportunity for long-term malingering. The lazy worker needed to be faced with the fact that sooner or later his eligibility would be exhausted and he would have to find a job. And to be satisfactory, the benefits would have to be larger.

Were unemployment compensation to approach the level of the weekly wage, we should in fact be prepared for some increase in deliberate idleness—in malingering as a way of life. So long as production was accorded priority, any increase in voluntary idleness was *pro tanto* intolerable although, in keeping with the refined illogic with which the conventional wisdom regarded production, involuntary unemployment in depression, and the consequent loss of output, was never especially reprehensible. But in a world where production is no longer urgent we can obviously view an increase in voluntary idleness with some equanimity. Yet even if the unemployment compensation were close to the wage, it is not certain that the malingering would be great. Fears in this matter have always been extraordinarily exaggerated. In the thirties it was widely assumed that unemployment compensation, even as a badly paid alternative to toil, would be seized upon by a large number of people. In fact, the proportion of the active labor force exercising this option has always been negligible. The aversion to idleness is remarkably strong both in those who view with misgivings those who work and in those who work. The tendency to think of idleness as "a species of fraud upon the community" is not peculiar to the upper-income classes. One problem in winning a measure of release from our present commitment to full employment is the stigma which for a long time will continue to attach to any kind of unemployment. It will continue to be disreputable.

If unemployment is a disaster for individuals, we have no choice but always to produce at or near the capacity of the labor force. The continuing result will be the tensions and the dangers associated with the need to fabricate demand for increasingly unimportant goods and the persistent inflation which follows from the instability of the economy at full employment. To many even the escape or partial escape from these troubles will not seem to justify a reduction in the incentive to work or a possible subsidy to idleness. Even with the support of logic and necessity one can go only so far in breaking the icons.

However, there are ways of avoiding any important effect on incentives. At the same time the system can be so designed as to keep it from adding to inflation and to make it an important and even vital reinforcement to other fiscal policy as a protection against depression. Since depressions remain a major threat to economic security this latter is a consideration of central importance.

III

If the level of unemployment compensation is very close to the employed wage, this will be a cause of upward pressure on wages as the economy approaches full employment. If unemployment is a financially attractive alternative to employment, the bargaining position, both of individual workers and of unions, will be increased. And if some workers must be bid out of well-compensated unemployment by employers, this will add to the upward pressure on wages. We have seen that as capacity of plant and labor force are approached, there are now strong forces causing wages to act on prices and prices on wages. The effect of unemployment compensation that is close to the weekly wage would add to inflationary pressures. It would make unemployment tolerable, but it would make the approach to full employment even more inflationary than now.

But at full employment the level of unemployment compensation need not be high. At this point comparatively little hardship is caused if it is low in comparison with the employed wage. Workers are not relying on such compensation to tide them over long-term unemployment, for there is none. The traditional purpose of such compensation, as noted, is to help the individual during routine job transfers. When employment is high and job opportunities are numerous, these transfers will be quickly made. An alternative to relying on unemployment compensation is at hand. That is to find a job. One reason for the large gap that appeared between the level of unemployment compensation and the level of wages in the years following World War II was that these were years of virtually full employment. As a result the level of compensation, for the great majority of workers, was a matter of small consequence and secondary political interest.

When there is some general unemployment—when the economy is not operating at the full capacity of the labor force—conditions are almost exactly reversed. Then opportunities are few; the time in transition between jobs will be greater; there is now no certain escape from unemployment into a job. The chance for re-employment does not depend on the individual's own efforts. Such efforts will be unavailing as long as there is an insufficiency in aggregate demand. It is on this that the unemployment depends. This being so, high compensation rates do not interfere with re-employment. And since the capacity of the economy and the labor force are not being fully used, high compensation rates do not add to inflationary pressures. They do add to income and consumer demand. This they do automatically. As a man loses his wage he gains alternative income of the same order of magnitude. Thus such payments act far more effectively than any deliberate fiscal policy—spending on public enterprises, for example—to arrest deflation and enhance macroeconomic security.

The clear answer, therefore, is that unemployment compensation should be increased as unemployment increases and should be diminished as full employment is approached. It will be convenient to have a name for such a system, and we may call it Cyclically Graduated Compensation[2] or more conveniently by the initials CGC. It would not be difficult to design, and it represents an essential advance over the present static system. Indeed it is hard to think of a single measure of economic reform that would have more satisfactory effect. Apart from breaking the connection between output and economic security, of the importance of which more will be said presently, it would largely eliminate the hazard of depression unemployment for the worker. By stabilizing demand it would go far to mitigate the threat of depression. At the same time there would be no addition to the inflationary pressures at full employment and no interference, at such times, with the search for jobs. To the extent that malingering is induced by high rates of unemployment

---

[2] The reference to the business cycle here is not to the ancient rhythmic movement but rather to changes in the level of demand and employment of whatever nature and however induced.

compensation this problem disappears. When jobs are plentiful, there would be no incentive to such idleness, for compensation would be relatively low. When jobs are unavailable, no useful distinction can be made between those who are voluntarily and those who are involuntarily unemployed. Neither can find work.

IV

The administration of the present system of unemployment compensation by the individual states, together with its commitment to the principle of insurance and reserves and the use of merit ratings, has made it notably inflexible. Changes in the level and duration of compensation come slowly as the result of action by the individual state legislatures. To get CGC by state action would be quite hopeless.

Fortunately this is not necessary or desirable. The present system, administered by the states and with the present differentials between states, should continue to provide the basic payment.[3] CGC should be a purely federal enterprise. Economic policy relating to the level of economic output is now a recognized federal responsibility. The federal government is accountable. *Pro tanto,* the unemployment associated with changes in output is a federal responsibility. Since such unemployment has no conceivable actuarial aspect, it should be a current budgetary charge. When seasonally adjusted unemployment remains above the level which represents the amount necessarily associated with full employment for a specified period of time, the federal supplement would become payable. This would take the form of a specified fraction of the difference between the worker's weekly earnings over a period in his last employment and his entitlement under established unemployment compensation. By way of illustration, if it is assumed that 2.0 million is the maximum amount of unemployment associated with full employment— i.e., the maximum amount attributable to seasonal idleness, those engaged in changing jobs and the others for whom unemployment is a short-term affair—CGC would be paid in the amount of say half the difference between standard unemployment compensation and the individual's last wage. When unemployment passed 3.0 million, the CGC payment would rise to two-thirds and perhaps at 4 million to a top of four-

[3] However more satisfactory federal standards would be required. They are needed in any case.

fifths of the difference. At this point the worker who earned the average 1956 weekly wage of $80, and who was entitled to a regular (and comparatively generous) payment in that year of $36, would have a total weekly income of $71.20. Of this $35.20 would be from CGC. (The surviving difference represents the continuing concession to the Puritan principle that leisure should be less amply rewarded than work.) Moreover although under CGC the unemployment and the employed wage can come very close together, and this is a central virtue of the device, the differential in favor of the employed wage cannot be entirely eliminated. The normal if surprising preference of people for work ought, no doubt, to be reinforced by a pecuniary incentive so that if a job is available a man can be depended upon to take it.

The present limitation on the number of weeks for which compensation may be paid is based on the belief that the individual can, given time and effort, find a new job. This is true of short-term unemployment—the unemployment that is incidental to changing demand for workers under conditions of full employment and ample job opportunities. It is not the case of unemployment which is caused by shifts in the level of output that are beyond the power of the individual worker, by his own effort, to correct. Therefore the worker should be entitled to compensation for this type of unemployment for as long as it lasts. In other words, as long as unemployment continues above the specified levels, the total of the CGC and the regular payments should continue. The extra cost, beyond the normal period of eligibility, is also logically a federal responsibility.

When aggregate demand in the economy falls below the level that employs the entire labor force, the resulting unemployment does not distribute itself uniformly across the country. Depending on their industries some areas and communities are seriously affected; in others the impact is slight. To the worker who lives in a town where 50 per cent of the working force is unemployed, it is not entirely reassuring to know that over the country as a whole the average unemployment is comparatively low. The question will arise as to whether CGC might have a regional or local adjustment. Might it not be declared in effect in an area or community of high unemployment even though the national unemployment is below the minimum? And might it not be suspended in areas where unemployment is low even though total unemployment is above the minimum? The advantage of cautious steps in this direction will be evident. It would make CGC more effective in the areas afflicted by unemployment; it would minimize its competition with jobs in those areas that are not. The danger is that it will interfere with interregional migration in search of employment. But this, we have seen, is no longer subject to the imperatives of a poor society. A system of regional or local adjustments would be a logical development.

There will be objection that once the rates are advanced to the level associated with a higher volume of unemployment, the pressure of unions and voters generally will be against their reduction even as unemployment declines. This may be so. It is unhappily impossible in a democratic society to think of a single measure for the improvement of social well-being which is not subject to subversion by ill-conceived minority or even majority pressures. The post office, not precisely a novelty among institutions of civilized government, continues to be subject to the efforts of citizens to have it carry their mail if not for nothing at least for a minor fraction of the cost. But the principles of CGC are well within the range of popular understanding which is rarely as low as ordinarily assumed. Compensation can be high when unemployment is substantial only because it is low when unemployment is low. Then it does not keep people from taking jobs. Nor does it put pressure on wage rates by forcing employers to bid against high compensation levels. These are not matters that are difficult to grasp. Those who believe so almost certainly underrate the intelligence and responsibility of union leaders, the rank and file, and of workers generally.

V

As matters now stand there is but one point at which the American economy can function. That is the level at which virtually the full labor force is employed. This, we have seen, is a point of considerable tension. The synthesis of consumer wants must proceed at a high and what could be a breakneck rate. At full employment the economy is patently unstable. Prices move relentlessly upward. But if production is much below the full employment level, a drastic reduction in income is visited on those who are unable to find jobs. This is taken as a serious indication of economic failure, and is.

With CGC we widen the band within which the economy can function. This we do by insuring that no particular group of people is singled out for misfortune when demand falls

below full employment levels. The manifest unfairness of
doing so now excludes unemployment as a policy. Or, to put
the matter differently, we are seeking to insure that there is
a range of output over which the economy can function which
accords with the imperfect and awkward instruments available to regulate the level of output. At present the problem of
keeping the economy at full employment levels and avoiding
inflation is roughly equivalent to asking a reluctant surgeon
to do a lobotomy with a spade. In addition, CGC helps insure
that mild unemployment will not become serious unemployment. It adds to purchasing power and demand as unemployment increases and to the labor force as unemployment
declines.

Those who are appalled by a measure which seems to give
sanction to unemployment should bear several facts in mind.
The unemployment here being tolerated is at the margin.
The total civilian labor force in 1956 was 67.5 millions.
Subject to considerations to be mentioned in a moment, economic management requires an operating margin of possible
unemployment of up to perhaps four million. There are no
longer grounds for contending that the goods produced by
these workers are of urgent importance. Given the stigmata
anciently associated with idleness, the effect of this unemployment on those affected may be a more serious matter.

However, as usual in economic affairs, the goal is not per-
fection but the best that can be managed. CGC represents a
marked improvement over the present situation. It offers the
prospect of a sufficient operating margin for price stability.
It compensates the unemployment associated with this margin,
whereas such unemployment may now occur anyway and
without effective compensation. By adding a new and important automatic stabilizer, it helps to insure that the unemployment associated with stability will not become the more
serious unemployment associated with depression. This requires a special word.

Through increased public outlays and through the reduction or remission of taxes, we have at hand measures for
dealing with a deficiency in aggregate demand and thus with
depression. The use of these measures is not in conflict with
other social goals and for this reason depression, in contrast
with inflation, is not an intractable problem of the affluent
society. Nonetheless, it remains the major threat to economic
security. In particular, private spending can fall away more
rapidly than fiscal measures can provide a substitute. Hence
there is always danger of painful unemployment while cor-

rective action is getting under way of overtaking a deflationary spiral. This is made more probable because of the inevitability of debate over whether the time has arrived for deliberate fiscal action—for spending or tax reduction—and the omnipresent hope that if things are left alone recovery will come anyway. We have also seen that the danger of the downward spiral has been enhanced by the modern process of consumer demand and debt creation.

CGC is not a substitute for other fiscal measures. But it does insure comparative stability in wage income. This is a large sector of total income. It is also the one which is most threatened by the large commitment to consumer debt, i.e., it is here that in the event of deflation there is danger of a large cut in current spending as people seek to maintain their debt service. Most important, CGC elides the danger, indeed the near certainty, of delay that is implicit in deliberate fiscal action.

Our need is for a measure which enables us to escape the tensions that are inevitable in the present imperative to produce at capacity, and the hazards in trying to do so, while improving our defenses against more serious unemployment. All of this is accomplished by lifting the level of compensation as employment recedes and as unemployment changes its basic character from an incident in job transfer, to a source of requisite slack for price stability, to a basic threat to economic security.

To repeat, all this implies a lessened pressure on the labor force. It implies that a small amount of unemployment will, in a degree, be considered normal.

In recent years there has been the beginning of a discussion of the four-day week. In 1956 it was formally advanced as a prospect by the Republican candidate for the Vice-presidency, Mr. Richard M. Nixon. This discussion tacitly accepts the fact that we do not urgently need the goods that are produced on the other two or three. Perhaps the problem of adjusting to three days' leisure a week are not greatly less serious than those of adjusting to rather longer periods— properly paid, it is again to be recalled—at intervals during a lifetime.

VI

Since inflation is the implacable enemy of social balance, we cannot have it in a society where the redress of such balance is a central goal. The effect of CGC is to make tolerable the unemployment which is associated with price stability. To minimize this unemployment, even though it has been rendered at least partially painless, will still be thought by many a desirable goal of policy. It will also have the probable effect of increasing the rate of economic growth.

If such a maximum employment policy is pursued, and if inflation is to be avoided, the only possible course is to have more controls. Given full employment or any close approach to it, wages and prices are subject to large discretionary movements. The only preventative is some public restraint on this discretion.

This might not be so very difficult to arrange. In the conventional wisdom the only possible system of control is one that controls all prices and all wages. This is then, and perhaps rightly, dismissed as unworkable, at least in ordinary times. But more limited action might restrain the interaction of prices and wages and allow the economy to approach more closely to full employment without sacrifice of price stability. It need not cover all industries. No problem exists where there are no unions and where employers obviously have no discretionary power over prices. There are other industries —like the service trades—which could probably be dismissed as derivative rather than pace-setting in their role. Where, on the basis of past behavior, prices and wages do interact to bring persistent price advances, wage increases that are held to require a price increase might be subject to ratification by a public tribunal or one on which representatives of management, labor, and the public participated. It is not inappropriate that the public should intervene when it is the public that pays. Wage increases not alleged to require price increases would not be subject to such ratification. Wage advances so granted and those found to be within the capacity of the industry to absorb could not thereafter, without showing of cause, be offset by price increases. There is no reason why such or—since this suggestion is illustrative—similar arrangements could not be highly decentralized and characterized by comparative informality.

In one branch of the conventional wisdom—given patience, faith, and prayer—unemployment, inflation, and controls can all be avoided. The real menace in this view lies with those who persist in suggesting that we cannot reconcile irreconcilables. At a minimum they are inconvenient; at the worst they are subversive. In light of existing attitudes a limited system of controls might well provide the most satisfactory reconciliation. But a divorce of production from the imperatives of employment and individual economic security is also a possibility. So is a combination of the two. A rich country, like a rich man, has the luxury of choice. The only thing it lacks, much as we might wish for it, is the privilege of avoiding choice.

Those who find intolerable the designs here offered may wish to reflect, at least momentarily, on whether it is because they are asserting this privilege.

CHAPTER XXII

The Redress of Balance

OUR NEXT TASK is to find a way of obtaining and then of maintaining a balance in the great flow of goods and services with which our wealth each year rewards us. In particular, we must find a way to remedy the poverty which afflicts us in public services and which is in such increasingly bizarre contrast with our affluence in private goods. This is necessary to temper and, more hopefully, to eliminate the social disorders which are the counterpart of the present imbalance. It is necessary in the long run for promoting the growth of private output itself. Such balance is a matter of elementary common sense in a country in which need is becoming so exiguous that it must be cherished where it exists and nurtured where it does not. To create the demand for new automobiles we must contrive elaborate and functionless changes each year and then subject the consumer to ruthless psychological pressures to persuade him of their importance. Were this process to falter or break down, the consequences would be disturbing. In the meantime there are large ready-made needs for schools, hospitals, slum clearance and urban redevelopment, sanitation, parks, playgrounds, police, and a thousand other things. Of these needs almost no one must be persuaded. They are unavailable only because, as public officials of all kinds and ranks explain each day with practiced skill, the money to provide them is unavailable. So it has come about that we get growth and increased employment along the dimension of private goods only at the price of increasingly frantic persuasion. We exploit but poorly the opportunity along the dimension of public services. The economy is geared to the least urgent set of human wants. It would be far more secure if it were based on the whole range of need.

II

The problem will not be settled by a resolve to spend more for schools and streets and other services and to tax accordingly. Such decisions are made every day, and they do not come to grips with the causes of the imbalance. These lie much deeper. The most important difference between private and public goods and services is a technical one. The first lend themselves to being sold to individuals. The second do not. As noted above,[1] in the evolution of economic enterprise, the things which could be produced and sold for a price were taken over by private producers. Those that could not, but which were in the end no less urgent for that reason, remained with the state. Bread and steel went naturally to private enterprise, for they could readily be produced and marketed by individuals to individuals. Police protection, sanitation, and sewer systems remained with public authority for, on the whole, they could not. Once the decision was taken to make education universal and compulsory, it ceased to be a marketable commodity. With the rise of the national state so did national defense. The line between public and private activity, as we view it at any given moment, is the product of many forces—tradition, ideological preference, and social urgency all play some part. But to a far greater degree than is commonly supposed, functions accrue to the state because, as a purely technical matter, there is no alternative to public management.

The goods and services which are marketable at a price have a position of elementary strategic advantage in the economy. Their price provides the income which commands labor, capital, and raw materials for production. This is inherent in the productive process. In the absence of social intervention, private production will monopolize all resources. Only as something is done about it will resources become available for public services. In Anglo-Saxon constitutional history, the requirement of an affirmative act to divert resources from private to public use was the key weapon of parliament in contending for power with the sovereign. The king had no—or, more precisely, but few—recurring revenues. Hence all taxes for public purposes had to be specifically voted. Gradually it became settled that there must be redress of grievances before supply. Apart from the use of the power of the purse as the protector of popular liberty, there was much else to be said for the practice. In poor and ill-governed societies private goods meant comfort and life itself. Food, clothing, and shelter, all technically subject to private purchase and sale, had an urgency greater than any public

[1] Pp. 109 to 112.

service with the possible exception of the provision of law and order. The burden of proof was on any step that diverted resources from the satisfaction of these simple biological requirements to the almost invariably spendthrift services of the state.

Recurring revenues are now commonplace. The control of the purse is still an element in the distribution of power between the legislative and executive authority. But it is only one element in a complex relationship and, unlike England under the Stuarts, the approval of expenditures, not the voting of taxes, is the linchpin of the legislature's power. Yet a good deal remains unchanged. We still seek to synthesize, on behalf of private goods, an urgency that was once provided not by Madison Avenue but by the even more effective importunities of hunger and cold. And for a very large part of our public activity, revenues are relatively static. Although aggregate income increases, many tax systems return a comparatively fixed dollar amount. Hence new public needs, or even the increase in the requirements for old ones incident on increasing population, require affirmative steps to transfer resources to public use. There must first be a finding of need. The burden of proof lies with those who propose the expenditure. Resources do not automatically accrue to public authority for a decision as to how they may best be distributed to schools, roads, police, public housing, and other claimant ends. We are startled by the thought. It would lead to waste.

But with increasing income, resources do so accrue to the private individual. Nor when he buys a new automobile out of increased income is he required to prove need. We may assume that many fewer automobiles would be purchased than at present were it necessary to make a positive case for their purchase. Such a case must be made for schools.

III

The solution is a system of taxation which automatically makes a pro rata share of increasing income available to public authority for public purposes. The task of public authority, like that of private individuals, will be to distribute this increase in accordance with relative need. Schools and roads will then no longer be at a disadvantage as compared with automobiles and television sets in having to prove absolute justification.

The practical solution would be much eased were the revenues of the federal government available for the service of social balance. These, to the extent of about four-fifths of the total, come from personal and corporation income taxes. Subject to some variations, these taxes rise rather more than proportionately with increases in private income. Unhappily they are presently pre-empted in large measure by the requirements of national defense and the competition of arms. In the mid-fifties defense expenditures were rather more than half of all the expenditures of the federal government and rather more than the total expenditures of states and localities combined. Were this sum to become available in any considerable part for the civilian services of governments in the years ahead, social balance could be quickly restored. And present income taxes would admirably keep the balance and without formally upsetting the present compromise on the question of equality. The word "formally" should perhaps be stressed, for in one articulate and influential branch of the conventional wisdom high tax rates are justifiable for military purposes but immoral and confiscatory if used for civilian purposes.

Perhaps the time will come when federal revenues and the normal annual increase will not be pre-empted so extensively for military purposes. Conventional attitudes hold otherwise; on all prospects of mankind there is hope for betterment save those having to do with an eventual end, without war, to the arms race. Here the hard cold voice of realism warns there is no hope. Perhaps things are not so utterly hopeless.

But meanwhile the problem of social balance must be faced. So far as the federal government is concerned, it must be accomplished while relying primarily on the personal and corporate income taxes. As we shall see presently, there are other taxes with a high claim to consideration, but there are other units of government with higher claim to their use. As usual, the solution is implicit in the alternatives. The test is not that high military costs make reductions in other public outlays necessary. Rather it is whether, given these military outlays, we are more in need of the services that improve social balance or the additional private goods with which we are more affluently supplied than ever before. When the issue is so presented and faced, there can be but one conclusion.[2]

[2] This discussion assumes a satisfactory level of employment. Taxes and expenditures may be respectively lowered and increased to correct an insufficiency in demand. When social imbalance is great it will be clear that there is a strong case for correcting a shortage of demand by increased spending for needed public services rather than by a tax reduction which allows of increased spending for less needed private goods.

However, even though the higher urgency of the services for social balance are conceded, there is still the problem of providing the revenue. And since it is income taxes that must be used, the question of social balance can easily be lost sight of in the reopened argument over equality. The truce will be broken and liberals and conservatives will join battle on this issue and forget about the poverty in the public services that awaits correction and, as we shall see presently, the poverty of people which can only be corrected at increased public cost. All this—schools, hospitals, even the scientific research on which increased production depends—must wait while we debate the ancient and unresolvable question of whether the rich are too rich.

The only hope—and in the nature of things it rests primarily with liberals—is to separate the issue of equality from that of social balance. The second is by far the more important question. The fact that a tacit truce exists on the issue of inequality is proof of its comparative lack of social urgency. In the past the liberal politician has countered the conservative proposal for reduction in top-bracket income taxes with the proposal that relief be confined to the lower brackets. And he has insisted that any necessary tax increase be carried more than proportionately by the higher-income brackets. The result has been to make him a co-conspirator with the conservative in reducing taxes, whatever the cost in social balance; and his insistence on making taxes an instrument of greater equality has made it difficult or impossible to increase them. Meanwhile, the individual with whom he sympathizes and whom he seeks to favor are no longer the tax-ridden poor of Bengal or the first Empire but people who, by all historical standards, are themselves comparatively opulent citizens. In any case, they would be among the first beneficiaries of the better education, health, housing, and other services which would be the fruits of improved social balance, and they would be the long-run beneficiaries of more nearly adequate investment in people.

The rational liberal, in the future, will resist tax reduction, even that which ostensibly favors the poor, if it is at the price of social balance. And, for the same reason, he will not hesitate to accept increases that are neutral as regards the distribution of income. His classical commitment to greater equality can far better be kept by attacking as a separate issue the more egregious of the loopholes in the present tax laws. These loopholes—preferential treatment of capital gains and the special depletion allowances for mineral, including in particular oil, recovery—are strongly in conflict with traditional liberal attitudes, for this is inequality sanctioned by the state. There is work enough here for any egalitarian crusader.

IV

While there is much that the federal government must do by way of redressing balance, as Chapter XVIII has suggested, it is in state and local services that the imbalance is most striking. Here, however, the solution—although it involves another wrench in liberal attitudes—is most clear. It involves much expanded use of the sales tax.

So long as social balance is imperfect there should be no hesitation in urging high rates. Coverage should be general on consumer products and services. In the affluent society no useful distinction can be made between luxuries and necessaries. Food and clothing are as difficult as ever to do without. But they can be and frequently are among the most opulent of expenditures.

The relation of the sales tax to the problem of social balance is admirably direct. The community is affluent in privately produced goods. It is poor in public services. The obvious solution is to tax the former to provide the latter— by making private goods more expensive, public goods are made more abundant. Motion pictures, electronic entertainment, and cigarettes are made more costly so that schools can be more handsomely supported. We pay more for soap, detergents, and vacuum cleaners in order that we may have cleaner cities and less occasion to use them. We have more expensive cars and gasoline so that we may have highways and streets on which to drive them. Food being comparatively cheap and abundant, we tax it in order to have better medical services and better health in which to enjoy it. This forthright solution has the further advantage that sales taxation can be employed with fair efficiency by states and even by cities. It is in the services rendered by these governments that the problem of social balance is especially severe. The yield of the sales tax increases with increasing production. As wants are contrived for private goods more revenues are provided for public use. The general property tax, the principal alternative to the sales tax, is rigid and inflexible. Since its rates must ordinarily be raised for additional services, including those that are associated with increasing income and product, the burden of proving need is especially heavy. This tax is a poor servant of social balance.

During the present century the use of sales taxation by states and cities has been growing. Liberals have ordinarily resisted its use. At a minimum they have viewed it with grave misgiving. This has again made the liberal the effective enemy of social balance. The reasons for this opposition provide an interesting example of how ideas, as they remain stereotyped in face of change, can force those who hold them into roles inconsistent with their own professions. The American liberal has been, all things considered, the opponent of better schools, better communities, better urban communications, and indeed even of greater economic stability.

The effect of a sales tax varies greatly as between a poor and an affluent country, and the difference is one not of degree but of kind. Under the *ancien régime* in France the tax on salt achieved an enduring reputation for its oppressiveness which it retains in parts of modern India to this day. In the United States a tax on salt, even one that doubled or trebled its price, would work no perceptible hardship. It is not that salt is more dispensable now than in the day of the *gabelle*. But where it was then a major object of expenditure it is now an insignificant one. And where the price of salt once affected visibly and directly what remained for other use, it is now too small to have a noticeable effect.

As with salt so with other things. In a family which can buy only bread and cloth, a tax on bread and clothing means that children will be hungrier and less well clad. In a family which can buy many things the adjustment comes at the margin in spending for gasoline, installment payments, the races, or the quality of the ceremonial steak.

Thus does affluence alter the case against sales taxation. It will be argued that some people are still very poor. The sales tax, unlike the income tax, weighs heavily on the small consumption of such individuals. But if the income tax is unavailable or in service of other ends, the only alternative is to sacrifice social balance. A poor society rightly adjusts its policy to the poor. An affluent society may properly inquire whether, instead, it shouldn't remove the poverty. As we shall see in the next chapter, moreover, improved social balance is one of the first requisites for the elimination of poverty. The modern liberal rallies to protect the poor from the taxes which in the next generation, as the result of a higher investment in their children, would eliminate poverty.

V

There is another objection to greatly multiplied use of the sales tax which is that, unlike the personal and corporation income taxes, it makes no positive contribution to economic stability. The latter do so in two respects. Falling on the corporations and the well-to-do, they weigh most heavily on income that is on its way to be saved rather than on income that is on its way to be spent for consumers' goods. The investment of saved income has long been considered the most mercurial and hence the least certain link between the receipt of income and its return to the spending stream. The income tax thus taps and insures spending where this is intrinsically the least certain. Income taxes and especially the personal income tax have, in addition, their role as built-in stabilizers of the economy. As incomes fall the personal tax, through the mechanism of the progressive rates, automatically reduces itself. As a result, and not without reason, it has come to be regarded as central to the strategy of economic management.

However, it is of the essence of the present argument that other goals share in urgency with protection and maximization of total output. One is the social balance that is served by sales taxation. Moreover, the principal purpose of the measures outlined in the last chapter was to make possible the escape from the commitment to maximum production without doing damage to individual economic security.

But social balance also adds to the stability and security of production along another dimension, for we have seen that exploitation of the solid needs of the public sector of the economy, as distinct from the tenuous and expensively synthesized wants for private goods, will almost certainly contribute to stability and orderly economic growth. Production will then be based on the whole range of human wants, not a part. As such it will be more secure.

Finally, with better social balance, investment in human resources will be kept more nearly abreast of that in material capital. This, we have seen, is the touchstone for technological advance. As such it is a most important and possibly the most important factor in economic growth. Such are the paradoxes of economic policy.

The much increased use of the sales tax, as here suggested, is obviously not intended as a substitute for the income tax. This has long been the fond dream of conservatives. The present intention, which is to break the deadlock imposed by the extraneous relation of the income tax to equality and divert a much increased share of resources to public need, accords with the conventional wisdom of neither conservatives nor liberals.

Nonetheless, it is the latter who will be most reluctant. Apart from the ancient commitment to equality, the Keynesian system is, pre-eminently, the conventional wisdom of liberals. And here support for the income tax is categorical. Keynes did not foresee that the rapid expansion in output which was implicit in his ideas would soon bring us to the time when not total output but its composition would become the critical matter. Had he survived, he would no doubt have been perturbed by the tendency of his followers to concentrate their policy on the single goal of increased output. He did not lack discrimination. But his followers or some of them will almost certainly continue to protect the Keynesian system, with its concentration on aggregate demand and output, from ideas which Keynes might have been disposed to urge. Such is the fate of anyone who becomes a part of the conventional wisdom.

VI

Given a sufficiency of demand, the responding production of goods in the modern economy is almost completely reliable. We have seen in the early chapters of this essay why men once had reason to regard the economic system as a meager and perilous thing. And we have seen how these ideas have persisted after the problem of production was conquered. There will be some who will still suggest that to divert more resources to public use will be to imperil private production. There is not the slightest ground for this suggestion; and we have seen, in fact, that the risk lies in another direction—that our reliance on private goods is by methods that threaten the stability of demand, and that social imbalance imperils the prospect for long-run economic growth. Still the fear will be expressed.

Here is the last advantage of sales taxation as a technique for diverting resources to public use. This tax has been recommended for years by the most impeccable of conservatives. Such august audiences as the National Association of Manufacturers have repeatedly heard and applauded speeches reciting its virtues. It has been made clear that it does not damage incentives or interfere with production. It is true that the sales tax has been given these credentials as an alternative to other taxes. But it has received this blessing from those who speak with the prestige of producers. As a political point this is not negligible.

One final observation may be made. There will be question as to what is the test of balance—at what point may we conclude that balance has been achieved in the satisfaction of private and public needs. The answer is that no test can be applied, for none exists. The traditional formulation is that the satisfaction returned to the community from a marginal increment of resources devoted to public purposes should be equal to the satisfaction of the same increment in private employment. These are incommensurate, partly because different people are involved, and partly because it makes the cardinal error of comparing satisfaction of wants that are synthesized with those that are not.

But a precise equilibrium is not very important. For another mark of an affluent society is the opportunity for the existence of a considerable margin for error on such matters. The present imbalance is clear, as are the forces and ideas which give the priority to private as compared with public goods. This being so, the direction in which we move to correct matters is utterly plain. We can also assume, given the power of the forces that have operated to accord a priority to private goods, that the distance to be traversed is considerable. When we arrive, the opulence of our private consumption will no longer be in contrast with the poverty of our schools, the unloveliness and congestion of our cities, our inability to get to work without struggle, and the social disorder that is associated with imbalance. But the precise point of balance will never be defined. This will be of comfort only to those who believe that any failure of definition can be made to score decisively against a larger idea.

CHAPTER XXIII

The New Position of Poverty

"THE STUDY OF THE CAUSES of poverty," Alfred Marshall observed at the turn of the century, "is the study of the causes of the degradation of a large part of mankind." He spoke of contemporary England as well as of the world beyond. A vast number of people both in town and country, he noted, had insufficient food, clothing, and houseroom; they were: "Overworked and undertaught, weary and careworn, without quiet and without leisure." The chance of their succor, he concluded, gave to economic studies "their chief and their highest interest."[1]

No contemporary economist would be likely to make such an observation about the United States. Conventional economic discourse does make occasional obeisance to the continued existence of some poverty. "We must remember that we still have a great many poor people." This usefully allays uneasiness about the relevance of conventional economic goals and especially of economic efficiency. For some people wants must be synthesized. Hence the importance of the goods is not *per se* very high. But others are far closer to need. And hence we must not be cavalier about the urgency of providing them with the most for the least. The sales tax may have merit for the opulent, but it still bears heavily on the poor. Thus poverty survives in economic discourse partly as a buttress to the conventional economic wisdom. Still, in a world of a weekly industrial wage of eighty dollars and a $3960 median family income, it can no longer be presented as a universal or massive affliction. It is more nearly an afterthought.

The privation of which Marshall spoke was, a half century ago, the common lot at least of all who worked without special skill. As a general affliction, it was ended by increased

[1] *Principles of Economics* (8th ed.), pp. 2-4.

output which, however imperfectly it may have been distributed, nevertheless accrued in substantial amount to those who worked for a living. The result was to reduce poverty from the problem of a majority to that of a minority. It ceased to be a general case and became a special case. It is this which has put the problem of poverty into its peculiar modern form.

II

For poverty does survive. There is no firm definition of this phenomenon and again, save as a tactic for countering the intellectual obstructionist, no precise definition is needed. In part it is a physical matter; those afflicted have such limited and insufficient food, such poor clothing, such crowded, cold and dirty shelter that life is painful as well as comparatively brief. But just as it is far too tempting to say that, in matters of living standards, everything is relative, so it is wrong to rest everything on absolutes. People are poverty-stricken when their income, even if adequate for survival, falls markedly behind that of the community. Then they cannot have what the larger community regards as the minimum necessary for decency; and they cannot wholly escape, therefore, the judgment of the larger community that they are indecent. They are degraded for, in the literal sense, they live outside the grades or categories which the community regards as acceptable. In the mid-fifties, by acceptable estimate, one family in thirteen in the United States had a cash income from all sources of less than a thousand dollars. In addition a very large number of individuals, not members of families, were in this income class. To some extent family life is itself a luxury of an adequate income. The hard core of the very poor was declining but not with great rapidity.[2]

A substantial share of these low incomes are in agriculture —in 1964, 27.4 per cent of all farm families had cash incomes of less than a thousand dollars as compared with 4.9 per cent of urban families who were below this level. These rural families had further incomes in the form of shelter and farm-grown food which causes the estimate of cash income

[2] *Statistical Abstract, 1957,* p. 312. In 1955, 7.7 per cent of families were estimated to have had incomes of less than $1000 as compared with 8.8 in 1954, 8.6 in 1953 and 8.5 in 1952. These figures reflected a reduction from 11.5 per cent in 1950 when, however, prices were considerably lower.

to understate their position. However, there is probably
more danger of exaggerating than of minimizing the contribution of the unpainted shacks, the reluctant animals, and
the barren garden patches by which the rural poor eke out
their income.

This agricultural poverty has a tendency to be concentrated in specific areas. The Appalachian plateau and its
valleys, parts of the southern coastal plain and the Piedmont
plateau, the country of low hills between the Appalachians
and the Mississippi, the cutover lands of the Lake States, the
Ozark plateau, all provide examples. In 1950 in such areas
nearly a million farm families had *gross* receipts of less than
$1200 and about a quarter of a million had less than $250. In
the southern Appalachians the average net income of *all* full-
time farmers in 1949 was less than $500. In the southern
Piedmont the average was only slightly higher. In 1950 a
million and a half farm families, principally in the above-
mentioned areas, had net cash incomes from all sources of
less than a thousand dollars.[3] The modern locus of poverty
is even more the rural than the urban slum.

III

One can think of modern poverty as falling into two broad
categories. First there is what may be called *case* poverty.
This one encounters in every community, rural or urban,
however prosperous that community or the times. Case
poverty is the poor farm family with the junk-filled yard
and the dirty children playing in the bare dirt. Or it is the
grey-black hovel beside the railroad tracks. Or it is the base-
ment dwelling in the alley.

Case poverty is commonly and properly related to some
characteristic of the individuals so afflicted. Nearly everyone
else has mastered his environment; this proves that it is not
intractable. But some quality peculiar to the individual or
family involved—mental deficiency, bad health, inability to
adapt to the discipline of modern economic life, excessive
procreation, alcohol, insufficient education, or perhaps a
combination of several of these handicaps—have kept these
individuals from participating in the general well-being.

[3] *Development of Agriculture's Human Resources,* A Report on Problems of Low Income Farmers (United States Department of Agriculture, 1955). Figures showing gross receipts exclude farmers over
sixty-five years of age.

Second, there is what may be called *insular* poverty—that which manifests itself as an "island" of poverty. In the island everyone or nearly everyone is poor. Here, evidently, it is not so easy to explain matters by individual inadequacy. We may mark individuals down as intrinsically deficient; it is not proper or even wise so to characterize an entire community. For some reason the people of the island have been frustrated by their environment.

This is not the place to explore in detail the causes of insular poverty. They are complex and many of the commonly assigned causes are either excessively simple or wrong. The resource endowment or the fertility of the land, the commonplace explanations, have little to do with it. Connecticut, a state of high incomes, has few resources and a remarkably stony soil. West Virginia is richly endowed. Connecticut has long been rich and West Virginia poor.

Insular poverty has something to do with the desire of a comparatively large number of people to spend their lives at or near the place of their birth. This homing instinct causes them to bar the solution, always open as an individual remedy in a country without barriers to emigration, to escape the island of poverty in which they were born. And so long as they remain they are committed to a pattern of agricultural land use or of mining, industrial, or other employment which is unproductive, episodic, or otherwise unremunerative.[4] Meanwhile the poverty of the community insures that educational opportunities will be limited, that health services will be poor, and that subsequent generations will be ill prepared either for mastering the environment into which they are born or for migration to areas of higher income outside. It is a reasonable presumption, too, that the homing instinct operates most powerfully among the poorly educated.

In some circumstances escape may not be possible. Especially in the urban slum, race or poverty may confine individuals to an area of intrinsically limited opportunity. And once again the environment perpetuates its handicaps through

[4] Thus in the Appalachian plateau, settlement occurred along the valleys on farms which were of the small scale appropriate to a largely self-sufficient agriculture. Time has rendered such agriculture obsolete. Other areas produce the same crops far more efficiently; changing standards have made what once seemed a tolerable standard of living exceedingly primitive. Yet the massive reorganization of land use that would be required—far larger farms or conceivably highly capitalized forest enterprises—are far beyond the capacities, both educational and financial, of the people involved. Meanwhile the homing instinct causes them—or at least a large number—to persist in the area.

poor schools, evil neighborhood influences, and bad preparation for life.

The most certain thing about modern poverty is that it is
not efficiently remedied by a general and tolerably well-
distributed advance in income. Case poverty is not remedied
because the specific individual inadequacy precludes employment and participation in the general advance. Insular poverty
is not directly alleviated because the advance does not
necessarily remove the specific frustrations of environment to
which the people of these islands are subject. This is not to
say that it has no effect. Secure job opportunities elsewhere,
a concomitant of industrial advance, work against the homing
instinct. And so even more directly does the spread of in-
dustrialization. The appearance of industry in parts of the
Tennessee Valley area has had a strong remedial effect on the
insular poverty of those areas. But it remains that advance
cannot improve the position of those who, by virtue of self
or environment, cannot participate or are not reached.

IV

These circumstances have caused a profoundly interesting
although little recognized change in what may be termed the
political economy of poverty. With the transition of the very
poor from a majority to a comparative minority position,
they ceased to be automatically an object of interest to the
politician. Political identification with those of the lowest
estate has anciently brought the reproaches of the well-to-do,
but it has had the compensating advantage of alignment with
a large majority. Now any politician who speaks for the very
poor is speaking for a small and also inarticulate minority. As
a result the modern liberal politician aligns himself not with
the poverty-ridden members of the community but with the
far more numerous people who enjoy the far more affluent
income of (say) the modern trade union member. Ambrose
Bierce, in *The Devil's Dictionary*, called poverty "a file
provided for the teeth of the rats of reform." It is so no
longer. Reform now concerns itself with people who are
relatively well-to-do—whether the comparison be with their
own past or with those who are really at the bottom of the
income ladder.

The poverty-stricken are further forgotten because it is
assumed that with increasing output poverty must disappear.
Increased output eliminated the general poverty of all who

worked. Accordingly it must, sooner or later, eliminate the special poverty that still remains. As we have just seen, this is not to be expected or, in any case, it will be an infinitely time-consuming and unreliable remedy. Yet just as the arithmetic of modern politics makes it tempting to overlook the very poor, so the supposition that increasing output will remedy their case has made it easy to do so too.

To put the matter another way, the concern for inequality had vitality only so long as the many suffered privation while a few had much. It did not survive as a burning issue in a time when the many had much even though others had much more. It is our misfortune that when inequality declined as an issue, the slate was not left clean. A residual and in some ways rather more hopeless problem remained.

V

An affluent society, that is also both compassionate and rational, would, no doubt, secure to all who needed it the minimum income essential for decency and comfort. The corrupting effect on the human spirit of a small amount of unearned revenue has unquestionably been exaggerated as, indeed, have the character-building values of hunger and privation. To secure to each family a minimum standard, as a normal function of the society, would help insure that the misfortunes of parents, deserved or otherwise, were not visited on their children. It would help insure that poverty was not self-perpetuating. Most of the reaction, which no doubt would be almost universally adverse, is based on obsolete attitudes. When poverty was a majority phenomenon, such action could not be afforded. A poor society, as this essay has previously shown, had to enforce the rule that the person who did not work could not eat. And possibly it was justified in the added cruelty of applying the rule to those who could not work or whose efficiency was far below par. An affluent society has no similar excuse for such rigor. It can use the forthright remedy of providing for those in want. Nothing requires it to be compassionate. But it has no high philosophical justification for callousness.

Nonetheless any such forthright remedy for poverty is beyond reasonable hope. Also, as in the limiting case of the alcoholic or the mental incompetent, it involves difficulties. To spend income requires a minimum of character and intelligence even as to produce it. By far the best hope for the elimination, or in any case the minimization, of poverty lies in less direct but, conceivably, almost equally effective means.

The first and strategic step in an attack on poverty is to see that it is no longer self-perpetuating. This means insuring that the investment in children from families presently afflicted be as little below normal as possible. If the children of poor families have first-rate schools and school attendance is properly enforced; if the children, though badly fed at home, are well nourished at school; if the community has sound health services, and the physical well-being of the children is vigilantly watched; if there is opportunity for advanced education for those who qualify regardless of means; and if, especially in the case of urban communities, law and order are well enforced and recreation is adequate—then there is a very good chance that the children of the very poor will come to maturity without grave disadvantage. In the case of insular poverty this remedy requires that the services of the community be assisted from outside. Poverty is self-perpetuating because the poorest communities are poorest in the services which would eliminate it. To eliminate poverty efficiently we should invest more than proportionately in the children of the poor community. It is there that high-quality schools, strong health services, special provision for nutrition and recreation are most needed to compensate for the very low investment which families are able to make in their own offspring.

The effect of education and related investment in individuals is to enable them either to contend more effectively with their environment, or to escape it and take up life elsewhere on more or less equal terms with others. The role of education as an antidote to the homing instinct which crowds people into the areas of inadequate opportunity and frustration is also clear. However, in the strategy of the attack on insular poverty a place remains for an attack on the frustrations of the environment itself. This is particularly clear in the case of the slum. Slum clearance and expansion of low and middle-income housing removes a comprehensive set of frustrations and greatly widens opportunity. There is a roughly parallel opportunity in the rural slum. By identifying a land use which is consistent with a satisfactory standard of living, and by assisting with the necessary reorganization of land and capital, public authority can help individuals to surmount frustrations to which they are now subject. The process promises to be expensive and also time-consuming. But the question is less one of feasibility than of will.[5]

Nor is case poverty in the contemporary generation wholly intransigent. Much can be done to treat those characteristics which cause people to reject or be rejected by the modern industrial society. Educational deficiencies can be overcome. Mental deficiencies can be treated. Physical handicaps can be remedied. The limiting factor is not knowledge of what can be done. Overwhelmingly it is our failure to invest in people.

VI

It will be clear that to a remarkable extent the requirements for the elimination of poverty are the same as for social balance. (Indeed a good deal of case poverty can be attributed to the failure to maintain social balance.) The myopic preoccupation with production and material investment has diverted our attention from the more urgent questions of how we are employing our resources and, in particular, from the greater need and opportunity for investing in persons.

Here is a paradox. When we begin to consider the needs of those who are now excluded from the economic system by accident, inadequacy, or misfortune—we find that the normal remedy is to make them or their children productive citizens. This means that they add to the total output of goods. We see once again that even by its *own terms* the present preoccupation with material as opposed to human investment is inefficient. The parallel with investment in the supply of trained and educated manpower discussed above[6] will be apparent.

But increased output of goods is not the main point. Even to the most intellectually reluctant reader it will now be evident that enhanced productive efficiency is not the *motif* of this volume. The very fact that increased output offers itself as a by-product of the effort to eliminate poverty is one of the reasons. No one would be called upon to write at such length on a problem so easily solved as that of increasing

[5] The problem of the rural slum, and its reorganization, is one on which one must say either very little or very much. I have had to follow the first course here. I have treated the problem at more length in "Inequality in Agriculture—Problem and Program," J. J. Morrison Memorial Lecture, Ontario Agricultural College, Guelph, Canada, 1956.
[6] Chapter XIX.

production. The main point lies elsewhere. Poverty—grim, degrading, and ineluctable—is not remarkable in India. For few the fate is otherwise. But in the United States the survival of poverty is remarkable. We ignore it because we share with all societies at all times the capacity for not seeing what we do not wish to see. Anciently this has enabled the nobleman to enjoy his dinner while remaining oblivious to the beggars around his door. In our own day it enables us to travel in comfort through south Chicago and the South. But while our failure to notice can be explained, it cannot be excused. "Poverty," Pitt exclaimed, "is no disgrace but it is damned annoying." In the contemporary United States it is not annoying but it is a disgrace.

CHAPTER XXIV

Labor, Leisure, and the New Class

IN A SOCIETY of high and increasing affluence there are three plausible tendencies as regards toil. As the production of goods comes to seem less urgent, and as individuals are less urgently in need of income for the purchase of goods, they will work fewer hours or days in the week. Or they will work less hard. Or, as a final possibility, it may be that fewer people will work all the time.

In the last century a drastic decline has occurred in the work week. In 1850 it is estimated to have averaged just under seventy hours, the equivalent of seven ten-hour days a week or roughly six at from six in the morning to six at night. A hundred years later the average was 40.0 hours or five eight-hour days.[1]

This decline reflects a tacit but unmistakable acceptance of the declining marginal urgency of goods. There is no other explanation. However, such is the hold of production on our minds that this explanation is rarely offered. The importance and rewards of leisure are urged, almost never the unimportance of goods. Or, since production per hour has been increasing as the work week has declined, it is said that we are able to reduce the work because more is produced in less time. No mention is made of the fact that even more would be produced in more time. Or, finally, the decline is related to the feeling that steps must be taken to share the available work as productivity per worker rises. This also implies that the marginal urgency of production is low or negligible, but again the point remains unmade.

A reduction in the work week is an exceedingly plausible reaction to the declining marginal urgency of product. Over

[1] J. Frederic Dewhurst and Associates, *America's Needs and Resources,* A New Survey, p. 1053. These figures are the weighted average of agricultural and nonagricultural workers. The average work week in nonagricultural enterprise in 1950 was estimated to be 38.8 hours.

the span of man's history, although a phenomenal amount of education, persuasion, indoctrination, and incantation have been devoted to the effort, ordinary people have never been quite persuaded that toil is as agreeable as its alternatives. Thus to take increased well-being partly in the form of more goods and partly in the form of more leisure is unquestionably rational. In addition, the institution of overtime enables the worker to go far to adjust work and income to his own taste and requirements. It breaks with the barbarous uniformity of the weekly wage with its assumption that all families have the same tastes, needs, and requirements. Few things enlarge the liberty of the individual more substantially than to grant him a measure of control over the amount of his income.

Unfortunately in the conventional wisdom the reduction in hours has emerged as the only legitimate response to increasing affluence. This is at least partly because the issue has never been faced in terms of the increasing unimportance of goods. Accordingly, though we have attributed value to leisure, a ban still lies on other courses which seem to be more directly in conflict with established attitudes on productive efficiency. In a society rationally concerned with its own happiness these alternatives have a strong claim to consideration.

II

The first of these is that work can be made easier and more pleasant.

The present-day industrial establishment is a great distance removed from that of the last century or even of twenty-five years ago. This improvement has been the result of a variety of forces—government standards and factory inspection; general technological and architectural advance; the fact that productivity could be often increased by substituting machine power for heavy or repetitive manual labor; the need to compete for a labor force; and union intervention to improve working conditions in addition to wages and hours.

However, except where the improvement contributed to increased productivity, the effort to make work more pleasant has had to support a large burden of proof. It was permissible to seek the elimination of hazardous, unsanitary, unhealthful, or otherwise objectionable conditions of work. The speed-up might be resisted—to a point. But the test was not what was agreeable but what was unhealthful or, at a minimum, excessively fatiguing. The trend toward increased leisure is not reprehensible, but we resist vigorously the notion that a man should work less hard while on the job. Here older attitudes are involved. We are gravely suspicious of any tendency to expend less than the maximum effort, for this has long been a prime economic virtue.

In strict logic there is as much to be said for making work pleasant and agreeable as for shortening hours. On the whole it is probably as important for a wage earner to have pleasant working conditions as a pleasant home. To a degree, he can escape the latter but not the former—though no doubt the line between an agreeable tempo and what is flagrant feather-bedding is difficult to draw. Moreover, it is a commonplace of the industrial scene that the dreariest and most burdensome tasks, requiring as they do a minimum of thought and skill, frequently have the largest numbers of takers. The solution to this problem lies, as we shall see presently, in drying up the supply of crude manpower at the bottom of the ladder. Nonetheless the basic point remains: the case for more leisure is not stronger on purely *prima facie* grounds than the case for making labor-time itself more agreeable. The test, it is worth repeating, is not the effect on productivity. It is not seriously argued that the shorter work week increases productivity—that men produce more in fewer hours than they would in more. Rather it is whether fewer hours are always to be preferred to more but more pleasant ones.

III

The third of the obvious possibilities with increasing affluence is for fewer people to work. This tendency has also been operating for many years although in a remarkably diverse form. Since 1890, when one boy in four and one girl in ten between the ages of ten and fifteen were gainfully employed, large numbers of juveniles have been retired from the labor force and their number now is negligible. At the same time a large number of women have been added. In 1890 19.5 per cent of the female population ten years and over was in the labor force and by 1953 this proportion had risen to 29.7 per cent.[2] However, this change reflects in considerable measure the shift of tasks—food preparation, clothing manu-

[2] *Ibid.*, pp. 726-27.

facture, even child-rearing—out of the home. Women who previously performed them have gone along to other work. The woman who takes charge of a day nursery has joined the labor force, as have the women whose children she cares for.

For seventy-five years the proportion of the male population in the labor force has been constant at around seventy-five per cent of those over ten years of age. There are a smaller percentage of the very young and of those over sixty-five, but this has been offset by the increase in population in the ages between twenty and sixty-five where the proportion of workers to the total is very high.[3]

With diminishing marginal urgency of goods it is logical that the first to be spared should be old and young. We have yet, however, to view this tendency consistently and comprehensively. We are able to dispense with the labor of those who have reached retiring age because the goods they add are a low order of urgency, whereas a poor society must extract the last ounce of labor effort from all. But we have ordinarily subjected those who retire to a drastic reduction in income and living standards. Obviously, if the retirement can be afforded because the product is no longer urgent, a satisfactory—meaning for most purposes the customary—living standard can be accorded to the retired employee for the same reason. Similarly we have excluded youngsters from the labor market, partly on the ground that labor at too early an age is unduly painful and injurious to health, and partly to make way for educational opportunity. But while we have felt it possible to dispense with the goods that the youngsters produce, we have yet to provide them, at least in full and satisfactory measure, with the education that their exemption from labor was designed to make possible. If we are affluent enough to dispense with the product of juvenile labor, it again follows that we are affluent enough to provide the education that takes its place.

In addition to releasing the old and young, it may be that we need not use all of the labor force at all times. This possibility was explored in Chapter XVII. If the marginal urgency of goods is low, then so is the urgency of employing the last man or the last million men in the labor force. By allowing ourselves such slack, in turn, we reduce the standards of economic performance to a level more nearly consonant with the controls available for its management. And in so widening the band of what is deemed tolerable performance lies our

[3] *Ibid.*, pp. 725-26.

best hope of minimizing the threat of inflation with its further and persistent threat to social balance.

Such a step requires much more adequate provision than now for those who are temporarily unemployed. We have seen, however, that such measures are possible and, indeed, have a vital stabilizing effect. And again such compensation accords with the logic of the situation. If our need for production is of such a low order of urgency that we can afford some unemployment in the interest of stability—a proposition, incidentally, of impeccably conservative antecedents—then we can afford to give those who are unemployed the goods that enable them to sustain their accustomed standard of living. If we don't need what the unemployed do not make, we can obviously afford them what they customarily eat and wear.

IV

However, the greatest prospect that we face—indeed what must now be counted one of the central economic goals of our society—is to eliminate toil as a required economic institution. This is not a utopian vision. We are already well on the way. Only an extraordinarily elaborate exercise in social camouflage has kept us from seeing what has been happening.

Nearly all societies at nearly all times have had a leisure class—a class of persons who were exempt from toil. In modern times and especially in the United States the leisure class, at least in any identifiable phenomenon, has disappeared. To be idle is no longer considered rewarding or even entirely respectable.

But we have barely noticed that the leisure class has been replaced by another and much larger class to which work has none of the older connotation of pain, fatigue, or other mental or physical discomfort. We have failed to appreciate the emergence of this New Class, as it may be simply called, largely as the result of one of the oldest and most effective obfuscations in the field of social science. This is the effort to assert that all work—physical, mental, artistic, or managerial—is essentially the same.

This effort to proclaim the grand homogeneity of work has commanded, for different reasons, the support of remarkably numerous and diverse groups. To economists it has seemed a harmless and, indeed, an indispensable simplification. It has enabled them to deal homogeneously with all of the different kinds of productive effort and to elaborate a general theory of wages applying to all who receive an income for services. Doubts have arisen from time to time, but they have been suppressed or considered to concern special cases.[4] The identity of all classes of labor is one thing on which capitalist and Communist doctrine wholly agree. The president of the corporation is pleased to think that his handsomely appointed office is the scene of the same kind of toil as the assembly line and that only the greater demands in talent and intensity justify his wage differential. The Communist officeholder cannot afford to have it supposed that his labor differs in any significant respect from that of the comrade at the lathe or on the collective farm with whom he is ideologically one. In both societies it serves the democratic conscience of the more favored groups to identify themselves with those who do hard physical labor. A lurking sense of guilt over a more pleasant, agreeable, and remunerative life can often be assuaged by the observation "I am a worker too" or, more audaciously, by the statement that "mental labor is far more taxing than physical labor." Since the man who does physical labor is intellectually disqualified from comparing his toil with that of the brainworker, the proposition is uniquely unassailable.

In fact the differences in what labor means to different people could not be greater. For some, and probably a majority, it remains a stint to be performed. It may be preferable, especially in the context of social attitudes toward production, to doing nothing. Nevertheless it is fatiguing or monotonous or, at a minimum, a source of no particular pleasure. The reward rests not in the task but in the pay.

For others work, as it continues to be called, is an entirely different matter. It is taken for granted that it will be enjoyable. If it is not, this is a source of deep dissatisfaction or frustration. No one regards it as remarkable that the advertising man, tycoon, poet, or professor who suddenly finds his work unrewarding should seek the counsel of a psychiatrist. One insults the business executive or the scientist by suggesting that his principal motivation in life is the pay he receives.

---

[4] Marshall defined labor as "any exertion of mind or body undergone partly or wholly with a view to some good other than the pleasure derived directly from the work." (*Principles of Economics*, p. 65.) This definition obviously recognizes a category of individuals for whom work is a reward in itself. However, this group, having been introduced, plays little or no further part in Marshall's analysis. It has played almost no formal role in economic theory since.

Pay is not unimportant. Among other things it is a prime index of prestige. Prestige—the respect, regard, and esteem of others—is in turn one of the more important sources of satisfaction associated with this kind of work. But, in general, those who do this kind of work expect to contribute their best regardless of compensation. They would be disturbed by any suggestion to the contrary.[5]

Such is the labor of the New Class. No aristocrat ever contemplated the loss of feudal privileges with more sorrow than a member of this class would regard his descent into ordinary labor where the reward was only the pay. In the years following World War II a certain number of grade schoolteachers left their posts for substantially higher paid factory work. The action made headlines because it represented an unprecedented desertion of an occupation which was assumed to confer the dignity of the New Class. The college professor, who is more securely a member of the New Class than the schoolteacher, would never contemplate such a change even as an exercise in eccentricity and no matter how inadequate he might consider his income.

In keeping with all past class behavior, the New Class seeks energetically to perpetuate itself. Offspring are not expected to plan their lives in order to make a large amount of money. (Those who go into business are something of an exception at least partly because income, in business, is uniquely an index of prestige.) But from their earliest years the children are carefully indoctrinated in the importance of finding an occupation from which they will derive satisfaction—one which will involve not toil but enjoyment. One of the principal sources of sorrow and frustration in the New Class is the son who fails to make the grade—who drops down into some tedious and unrewarding occupation. The individual who meets with this misfortune—the son of the surgeon who becomes a garage hand—is regarded by the community with pity not unmixed with horror. But the New Class has con-

[5] We have here an important reason why the income tax, despite high marginal rates and frequent warnings of the damage these may do in impairing incentives, has so far had no visibly deleterious effect. The surtax rates fall almost entirely on members of the New Class. These are people who, by their own claim except when they are talking about the effect of income taxes, are not primarily motivated by money. Hence the tax, which also does not disturb the prestige structure—people are rated by before-tax income—touches no vital incentive. Were high marginal rates to be placed on (say) the overtime income of automobile workers, we would expect a substantial withdrawal of effort. Here pay, as an incentive, remains important.

siderable protective powers. The son of the surgeon rarely does become a garage hand. However inadequate, he can usually manage to survive, perhaps somewhat exiguously, on the edge of his caste. And even if, as a salesman or an investment counselor, he finds little pleasure in his work, he will be expected to assert the contrary in order to affirm his membership in the New Class.

V

The New Class is not exclusive. While virtually no one leaves it, thousands join it every year. Overwhelmingly the qualification is education.[6] Any individual whose adolescent situation is such that sufficient time and money is invested in his preparation, and who has at least the talents to carry him through the formal academic routine, can be a member. There is a hierarchy within the class. The son of the factory worker who becomes an electrical engineer is on the lower edge; his son who does graduate work and becomes a university physicist moves to the higher echelons; but opportunity for education is, in either case, the open sesame.

There can be little question that in the last hundred years, and even in the last few decades, the New Class has increased enormously in size. In early nineteenth-century England or the United States, excluding the leisure class and considering the New Class as a group that lived on what it has carefully called earned income, it consisted only of a handful of educators and clerics, with, in addition, a trifling number of writers, journalists, and artists. In the United States of the eighteen-fifties it could not have numbered more than a few thousand individuals. Now the number whose primary identi-

[6] Political capacity is another qualification, and it is of especial importance to those who seek to make their escape after reaching their adult years. The intensity of the campaigns for local political offices— city councilors, school committeemen, sheriffs, and county supervisors —is to be explained by this fact as also is the enduring interest in appointive political office. Those who are already members of the New Class often fail to see how such posts are valued as an *entrée*. They look askance at the competition for such posts between the less well educated members of the community. They fail to realize that such posts provide the greatest opportunity for such individuals and that it is upon such people that we depend for much good (as well as some bad) civic enterprise. The union is another important opportunity for the individual of political capacity. Cf. the interesting sketches by Harvey Swados in *On the Line* (Boston: Atlantic-Little, Brown, 1957).

fication is with their job, rather than the income it returns, is undoubtedly in the millions.

Some of the attractiveness of membership in the New Class, to be sure, derives from a vicarious feeling of superiority—another manifestation of class attitudes. However, membership in the class unquestionably has other and more important rewards. Exemption from manual toil; escape from boredom and confining and severe routine; the chance to spend one's life in clean and physically comfortable surroundings; and some opportunity for applying one's thoughts to the day's work, are regarded as unimportant only by those who take them completely for granted. For these reasons it has been possible to expand the New Class greatly without visibly reducing its attractiveness.

This being so, there is every reason to conclude that the further and rapid expansion of this class should be a major and perhaps next to peaceful survival itself, *the* major social goal of the society. Since education is the operative factor in expanding the class, investment in education, assessed qualitatively as well as quantitatively, becomes very close to being the basic index of social progress. It enables people to realize a dominant aspiration. It is an internally consistent course of development.

Recent experience has shown that the demand for individuals in the occupations generally identified with the New Class increases much more proportionately with increased income and well-being. Were the expansion of the New Class a deliberate objective of the society this, with its emphasis on education and its ultimate effect on intellectual, literary, cultural, and artistic demands, would greatly broaden the opportunities for membership. At the same time the shrinking in the number of those who engage in work *qua* work is something to be regarded not alone with equanimity but with positive approval. For one of the inevitable outlets for the intellectual energies and inventiveness of the New Class will be in finding substitutes for routine and repetitive manual labor. To the extent that such labor is made scarce and more expensive, this tendency will, of course, be accelerated. To minimize the number of people doing such work is the counterpart of the goal of expanding the New Class.

It is a measure of how little we need worry about the danger from reducing the number of people engaged in work *qua* work that, as matters now stand, our concern is not that we will have too few available for toil but too many. We worry lest such technical advances as automation, an already realized dividend of the expansion of the New Class, will proceed so rapidly as to leave a surplus of those who still work. This, indeed, could be the greater danger.

VI

I venture to suggest that the unprofessional reader will find rather reasonable and rational the ideas here offered. Why should men struggle to maximize income when the price is many dull and dark hours of labor? Why especially should they do so as goods become more plentiful and less urgent? Why should they not seek instead to maximize the rewards of all the hours of their days? And since this is the plain and obvious aspiration of a great and growing number of the most perceptive people, why should it not be the central goal of the society? And now to complete the case, we have a design for progress. It is education or, more broadly, investment in human as distinct from material capital.

But in the more sophisticated levels of the conventional wisdom, including, regrettably, some professional economists, any such goal will seem exceedingly undesirable. The production of material goods, urgent or otherwise, is the accepted measure of our progress. Investment in material capital is our basic engine of progress. Both this product and the means for increasing it are measurable and tangible. What is measurable is better. To talk of transferring increasing numbers of people from lives spent mostly in classical toil to lives which, for the most part, are spent pleasantly has less quantitative precision. Since investment in individuals, unlike investment in a blast furnace, provides a product that can be neither seen nor valued, it is inferior. And here the conventional wisdom unleashes its epithet of last resort. Since these achievements are not easily measured, as a goal they are "fuzzy." This is widely deemed to be a fatal condemnation. The precise, to be sure, is usually the old and familiar. Because it is old and familiar it has been defined and measured. Thus does insistence on precision become another of the tautological devices by which the conventional wisdom protects itself. Nor should one doubt its power.

Yet anyone who finds this analysis and these proposals sensible should not be entirely discouraged. We are here in one of the contexts where circumstance has marched far beyond the conventional wisdom. We have seen how general are the efforts to join the New Class and how rapid is its expansion. We are not here establishing a new economic and social goal but identifying one that is already widely if but tacitly accepted. In this situation the conventional wisdom cannot resist indefinitely. The economist of impeccable credentials in the conventional wisdom, who believes that there is no goal in life of comparable urgency with the maximization of total and individual real income, would never think of applying such a standard to himself. In his own life he is an exponent of all the aspirations of the New Class. He educates and indoctrinates his children with but one thing in mind. It is not that they should maximize their income. This is abhorrent. He wants above all that they will have an occupation that is interesting and rewarding. On this he hopes, indeed, that they will take their learned parent as their model.

CHAPTER XXV

On Security and Survival

IN OUR SOCIETY the increased production of goods—privately produced goods—is, as we have seen, a basic measure of social achievement. This is partly the result of the great continuity of ideas which links the present with a world in which production indeed meant life. Partly it is a matter of vested interest. Partly it is a product of the elaborate obscurantism of the modern theory of consumer need. Partly it reflects an erroneous view of the problem of national security. And partly, we have seen, the preoccupation with production is forced quite genuinely upon us by tight nexus between production and economic security. However, it is a reasonable assumption that most people pressed to explain our concern for production—a pressure that is not often exerted—would be content to suggest that it serves the happiness of most men and women. That is sufficient.

The pursuit of happiness is admirable as a social goal. But the notion of happiness lacks philosophical exactitude; there is agreement neither on its substance nor its source. We know that it is "a profound instinctive union with the stream of life,"[1] but we do not know what is united. As just noted, precision in scholarly discourse not only serves as an aid in the communication of ideas, but it acts to eliminate unwelcome currents of thought, for these can almost invariably be dismissed as imprecise. To have argued simply that our present preoccupation with production of goods does not best aid the pursuit of happiness would have got nowhere. The concepts to which one would have been committed would have been far too vague.

Any direct onslaught on the identification of goods with happiness would have had another drawback. Scholarly discourse, like bullfighting and the classical ballet, has its rules

[1] Bertrand Russell, *The Conquest of Happiness* (London: Allen & Unwin, 1930), p. 248.

and they must be respected. In this arena nothing counts so heavily against a man as to be found attacking the values of the public at large and seeking to substitute his own. Technically his crime is arrogance. Actually it is ignorance of the rules. In any case he is automatically removed from the game. In the past this has been a common error of those who have speculated on the sanctity of present economic goals—those who have sought to score against materialism and Philistinism. They have advanced their own view of what adds to human happiness. For this they could easily be accused of substituting for the crude economic goals of the people at large the more sensitive and refined but irrelevant goals of their own. The accusation is fatal.

The reader will now appreciate the care with which the defenses against such an attack have been prepared. The question of happiness and what adds to it has been evaded, for indeed only mathematicians and participants on radio quiz programs are required to solve problems that can as sensibly be sidestepped. Instead, the present argument has been directed to seeing how extensively our present preoccupations, most of all that with the production of goods, are compelled by tradition and by myth. Released from these compulsions we become free for the first time to survey our other opportunities. These at least have a plausible relation to happiness. But it will remain with the reader, and ultimately one hopes with the democratic process, to reconcile these opportunities with his own sense of what makes life better.

II

A society has one higher task than to consider its goals, to reflect on its pursuit of happiness and harmony and its success in expelling pain, tension, sorrow, and the ubiquitous curse of ignorance. It must also, so far as this may be possible, insure its own survival.

The ideas with which this essay is concerned bear heavily on this considerable goal. The survival of a society rests on the same factors which make its survival worth while, for the simple but compelling reason that illusion is the enemy of both.

The point is not difficult to make. Nor, as compared perhaps with other things in the book, will persuasion be too difficult. This is another area where circumstance—in this instance at almost terrifying speed—had been undermining the conventional wisdom.

More specifically, as this is written (at the end of 1957) it is nearly two years since Chapter XII on the economics, so-called, of national security was first drafted. At that time it seemed hard to believe that people might soon be persuaded that crude increases of production had little to do with national defense and that the attitude that stressed such calculations was positively damaging.

Since then the Soviet Union has revealed a breath-taking series of scientific and technical advances. No one or at least not many have suggested that she was handicapped in doing so by too small a Gross National Product. Those who once talked so resonantly of production have been silent, at least on this subject. It has become evident that our failure to match this achievement was the result of the failure to concentrate the requisite resources on the desired ends. Some have even pointed out that in the same week the Russians launched the first earth satellite we launched a magnificent selection of automobile models including the uniquely elegant new Edsel. The lesson was not completely learned. Too much was attributed to fortuitous factors—unwise budget cuts, the perverse personality of the Secretary of Defense, interservice conflict, and generally poor administration. We have not yet seen that the causes were far deeper—that our economy, and the economic theory that explains and rationalizes its behavior, immobilizes all but a minor fraction of the product in private and, from the standpoint of national security, irrelevant production. We have not seen that the problem is far more than one of a bigger budget—that it is one of our attitude toward the goals of the society itself. A society which sets as its highest goal the production of private consumer goods will continue to reflect such attitudes in all its public decisions. It will entrust public decisions to men who regard any other goal as incredible—or radical. We have yet to see that not the total of resources but their studied and rational use is the key to achievement.

There would seem to me even a likelihood that one branch of the conventional wisdom will react to arguments such as those here advanced by saying that they are inappropriate in a world of tension. Production, it will be said, is still our problem—and how much more so in the cold war. It will be said, in effect, that we must continue to avoid any reflection on what we are producing. The urgency of our situation requires that we remain blind. To contemplate what might better our happiness would be a diversion. We must continue to expend our energies on what does not. To reflect on the relation of our resource use to security and survival would take our minds away from producing what we do not urgently need.

III

The nature of the deployment of the resources that would best serve our survival is beyond the scope of this essay. For myself I have little faith in the safety or security which derives from a never-ending arms race—from a competition to elaborate ever more agonizing weapons and to counter those of the enemy. If the possibility exists, the risks of negotiation and settlement, however great these may be, would still seem to provide a better prospect for survival than reliance on weapons which we can only hope are too terrible to use.

But whatever the paths to survival, the problem is the same. Were the Russians to disappear from the world, or become overnight as tractable as church mice, there would remain vast millions of hungry and discontented people in the world. Without the promise of relief from that hunger and privation, disorder would still be inevitable. The promise of such relief requires that we have available or usable resources. The requirement is, of course, much more urgent in a world in which differing economic and political systems are in competition.

Even when the arms race ends, as it must, the scientific and technological frontier will remain. Either as an aspect of international competition, or in pursuit of the esteem and satisfaction which go with discovery, we shall want to seek to cross it and be in on the crossing. In the field of consumer satisfaction, as we should by now agree, there is little on which one can fault the American performance. But this is not all and, as we should now, hopefully, also agree, an economy that is preoccupied however brilliantly with the production of private consumer products is supremely ill fitted for many of these frontier tasks. Under the best of circumstances its research will be related to these products rather than to knowledge. The conventional wisdom will provide impressive arguments to the contrary. No one should be fooled.

And not only does a great part of modern scientific work

lie outside the scope of the market and private enterprise but so does a large area of application and development. Private enterprise did not get us atomic energy. It has shown relatively slight interest in its development for power for the reason that it could not clearly be fitted into commercial patterns of cost and profit. Though no one doubts the vigor with which it addresses itself to travel within the United States, General Motors has little interest in travel through space.

As matters now stand, we have almost no institutions that are by central design and purpose directed to participation in modern scientific and technological progress and its large-scale application. We have no organization capable, for example, of taking on the large-scale development of atomic power generators or radically new departures in passenger-carrying aircraft in advance of knowledge that these will be commercially feasible. Much has been accomplished by research and development, not immediately subject to commercial criteria, under the inspiration of military need. This has done more to save us from the partial technological stagnation that is inherent in a consumers' goods economy than we imagine. But it is also a narrow and perilous prop, and it has the further effect of associating great and exciting scientific advances with an atmosphere of fear and even terror.

IV

Nor is this all. The day will not soon come when the problems of either the world or our own polity are solved. Since we do not know the shape of the problems we do not know the requirements for solution. But one thing is tolerably certain. Whether the problem be that of a burgeoning population and of space in which to live with peace and grace, or whether it be the depletion of the materials which nature has stocked in the earth's crust and which have been drawn upon more heavily in this century than in all previous time together, or whether it be that of occupying minds no longer committed to the stockpiling of consumer goods, the basic demand on America will be on its resources of ability, intelligence, and education. The test will be less the effectiveness of our material investment than the effectiveness of our investment in men. We live in a day of grandiose generalization. This one can be made with confidence.

Education, no less than national defense or foreign assistance, is in the public domain. It is subject to the impediments to resource allocation between private and public use. So, once again, our hope for survival, security, and contentment returns us to the problem of guiding resources to the most urgent ends.

To furnish a barren room is one thing. To continue to crowd in furniture until the foundation buckles is quite another. To have failed to solve the problem of producing goods would have been to continue man in his oldest and most grievous misfortune. But to fail to see that we have solved it and to fail to proceed thence to the next task would be fully as tragic.

INDEX

INDEX

AAF, 133

Abramovitz, Moses, 104 n.

Affluence, and economic preoccupations, 68; economic security, 92; employment, 228; in Europe, 13-14, 37; ideas, 13-15, 117; inflation, 188, 197; problems of, 227, 255; in United States, 13-14, 37, 57; want creation, 128, 197. *See also* Wealth

Affluent society, and depression, 237; income, 255; sales tax, 245-6; social balance, 202-3, 249; work, 259-61

AFL, 18

Agriculture, in Appalachians, 253 n; in Canada, 95; farm income, 251-2; and Keynes, 151, poverty of, 251-2; prices in depression, 45, 94; and pure competition, 170; research in, 105-6; support prices, 88-9, 93, 95, 98; surpluses, 222; in United States, 95, 119; universal risk insurance, 95. *See also* Farmers

Agriculture, Department of, 207

Alcott, William A., 226 n.

Aldrich, Winthrop, 80

American Assembly, 26

American Farm Economic Association, 94 n.

American Revolution, 31 n.

Americans for Democratic Action, 101, 154; *ADA World*, 152 n.

Antitrust laws, 82, 109, 172

Appalachians, 252-3, 253 n.

Arkwright, Richard, 213

Asia, 37

Assassins, 77

Australia, 37

Automobile installment credit 1955-6, 162

Bank of England, 179-80

Bank rate, 179; in Britain, 179-80

Batten, Barton, Durstine & Osborn, 128

Beckerman, W., 114

Beecher, Henry Ward, 55

Bellamy, Edward, 50

Bengal, 244

Benson, Ezra Taft, 223

Bentham, Jeremy, 225

Beveridge, William (Lord), 15

Bierce, Ambrose, 254

Brandt, Karl, 94-5

Bricker, John W., 149

Brown, E. H. Phelps, 27 n.

Browning, Robert, 154

Budget, balanced, 23-5, 152; cutting, 191; deficit, 61; in depressions, 23-6; surplus, 189-90

Built-in stabilizers, 98

Burns, Arthur F., 210 n.

Business, borrowing, 163, 182, 184, 185; in depression, 94; economic security, 85-6, 91, 92-3; inflation, 175-6, 208; monetary policy, 185-6, 190; New Class, 265-7; research, 105-6; Veblen, 51. *See also* Investment

Business cycle, 44-6, 61 n, 89, 151, 193, 232

Business Week, 155

Businessman, and conventional

wisdom, 20, 21; in depressions, 45; as economic force, 18, 81; vs. economists, 82; and equality, 73; European vs. American, 95; hostility to government, 148; and intellectuals, 148-50, 155-6; in modern corporation, 76-7; and prestige, 154-5; and prices, 172; and production, 102, 146-50, 155, 156, 157; and public officials, 156; and social security, 84, 88; and taxes, 71, 155; in Washington, 138-9, 142

Cairnes, J. F., 29 n.
California, real estate speculation in, 49
Canada, 92, 95
Cannes, 79
Capital, free flow of, 214; material, 212, 213-14, 218, 268-9; personal, 212, 213-16, 218, 247, 268-9
Capital formation, 70, 71, 113; defined, 212; in England, 71, 107; Norway, 71; as index of economic growth, 106-7
Capital gains, 74, 244
Capitalism, 95; Marx's views of, 60, 62, 65
Carey, Henry Charles, 47-9, 59 n, 52
Carlyle, Thomas, 31
Carnegie, Andrew, 40, 155
Carnegie Corporation, ix
Carney, Stephen J., 147-8
Cartels, 86
CGC, 232, 238
Chevallier, Gabriel, 156
Chicago, 102, 255
China, 81
Churchill, Sir Winston, 67 n, 153
CIO, 18
Civil War, 27, 40, 44
Clark, John Bates, 118
Class conflict, 63, 64
Clemence, Richard V., 45 n.
Clochemerle, 156
Coefficients, 200
Commager, Henry Steele, 52 n.

Commons, John R., 50 n.
Communism, 25-6, 70, 134, 264
Communist party, 101; and inflation, 209
Competition, 41-3, 168, 170, 172-3, 190; in Britain, 179; insecurity of competitive model, 69, 84, 86-90; pure, 169; Social Darwinism, 56-7
Congress, 26, 165, 180, 191-2, 207
Connecticut, 253
Conservatives, and balanced budget, 152; full employment, 153; and government, 152; inequality, 206, 244; inflation, 167, 168, 191; monetary policy, 189, 197; production, 83, 196; security, 84, 89; taxes, 72, 192, 206, 244, 248-9
Consumer borrowing, 183, 184
Consumer credit, 161-3, 164-5; in United Kingdom, 165; in United States, 165
Consumer debt, and CGC, 237; creation of, 159-60, 162-3, 219; dangers of, 160-3, 164; increase in, 159-60, 164; view of, 159
Consumer demand, 122; and debt, 158, 164; interest rate, 183; production, 124-7; theory of, 117-18, 129, 146, 155, 157; unsolved problem, 197
Consumer need, theory of, 270
Consumer saving, 161, 182 n.
Consumer spending, 163, 187; and fiscal policy, 192; and inflation, 183; in Korean war, 141; and monetary policy, 184
Consumer want creation. *See* Dependence effect, Want creation
Controlled Materials Plan, 138
Conventional wisdom, 18, 25-6, 130, 227; balanced budget, 23-5, 152; and business executive, 20, 21; civilian morale, 139; constructive criticism, 220; and consumer borrowing, 161; consumer demand, 124-5, 127; and controls, 238-9; depressions, 168; and

events, 21-5, 25, 26, 181; federal appropriations 207; Federal Reserve, 180; and fiscal policy, 193; and inequality, 72, 73, 83; inflation, 167; international affairs 133-4; and Keynes, 122, 153-5; of liberals and conservatives, 19; of Marxists, 66; and military policy, 133-6, 139-41, 144; and monetary policy, 181, 188; and production, 83, 95-7, 102, 105, 110, 114, 135, 139-40, 221-2, 230, 272, 273; and the public official, 21; public services, 112, 205-6; and research, 218; scholarship, 19-21; security, 84-6, 93-6, 98, 159; and stable prices, 167; structure of incentives, 176; and survival, 271, 273; taxes, 243, 248; technological advance, 213; work, 259, 268

Corporation, 56, 64, 94, 97, 108, 170-1, 224, 225; business executive in, 147, 156; and depression, 157; monetary policy, 185-6; and organization man, 210-11; prices, 88-9, 172-3, 185; regulation of, 151; and research, 105

Countervailing power, 42 n., 170 n.

Croffut, W. A., 78 n.

Cyclically Graduated Compensation. *See* CGC

Darwin, Charles, 53
Deauville, 79
Defense, Department of, 141
Delmonico's, 55
Demand, and CGC, 232; controls, 194; fiscal policy, 190, 192-4; inflation control, 177; private goods, 248-9
Democrats, 101, 154
Dependence effect, 136-7, 139; definition of, 129; and production, 130; public services, 204-5
Depew, Chauncey, 55
Depletion allowance, 74, 244
Depression, 23-4, 43-6, 48-9,

51, 60-1, 64, 66, 68, 89-90, 91, 108, 113, 151, 169, 208, 222, 228, 229-31, 232; and CGC, 236; economic security, 93-4, 107, 157; inefficiency of, 97-9, 106; and monetary policy, 188; public services, 209; as self-correcting, 165; and taxes, 191. *See also* Great Depression

Destutt de Tracy, A., 60
Dewhurst, J. Frederic, 96 n., 259 n., 261 n.
Diaspora, 225
Direct controls, 195-7. *See also* Prices, Wages
Douglas, Lewis W., 24
Duesenberry, James S., 125-6
Du Pont (E. I. du Pont de Nemours and Company), 210

East India Company, 32
Economic security, and consumer credit, 165; inflation, 169, 177; monetary policy, 185; preoccupation with, 93-4; production, 94-7, 99, 154, 157-9; in thirties, 89
Economic stabilization, 173; as public policy, 89
Economics, American tradition in, 47; central tradition, 29, 35-6, 38, 40, 43, 44, 46, 47, 64-5, 67-8, 69-70, 85; current problems, 116-17, 122, 250; defense of production, 114-16; "Dismal Science," 31; formation of ideas, 28-9; history of, 29-67; interpretation of behavior, 17-18, obsolescence of central ideas, 15; preoccupation with productivity, inequality, and insecurity, 68; wealth of national communities, 27
Eden, Sir Anthony, 153
Edsel, 272
Education, 274; investment in, 267. *See also* Social Balance
Eisenhower, Dwight David, 73
Eisenhower Administration, 148, 153

Employment, as basic economic concern, 228; level of, 243. *See also* Full employment, Unemployment

England, economic conditions, 27, 29, 30, 35, 78; economic discussion, 37; housing, 203; Industrial Revolution, 213; of Marshall, 250; and New Class, 267; public wages, 208; rate of capital formation, 71; Ricardo, 118; Social Darwinism, 53; social legislation, 54; Stuarts, 242

Excise tax, 206

Factory Acts, 22

Fair Trade laws, 88

Farmers, aid to, 151, 164; in competitive market, 172, 186; income in fifties, 76; and inflation, 175; monetary policy, 186; production, 226; security, 87, 88-9, 90-1, 93-6, 157. *See also* Agriculture

F.B.I., 207

Federal government, and defense, 243; inflation, 207-8; social balance, 207-8, 243, 245; taxes, 207-8, 243-4

Federal Reserve System, Board of Governors of, 74 n., 164; relation to government, 180

Feudalism, 34, 106, 264

Fiscal policy, 189, 196; consumer spending, 193; income inequality, 192; inflation, 190-1, 197; investment, 192-3; market structure, 190; politics, 193-4; prices, 189, 193-4; production, 192-4; unemployment, 193; wages, 189

Florida, 97

Ford, Henry, 91, 155, 212

Ford Motor Company, 91

Forsytes, 92

France, 209, 246; French army, 133

Franklin, Benjamin, 213

Free market, controls, 195-6; inflation, 169, 176-7

Free trade, in Britain, 179

Full employment, 152-3, 194, 196, 222, 228, 230-4, 235-6, 238; definition of, 170; as norm, 193; price stability, 177

Galbraith, Catherine A. ix

Galbraith, John Kenneth, 42 n., 170 n., 173 n., 257 n.

General Electric Company, 57, 88

General Motors Corporation, 21, 57, 88, 142, 274

General Property Tax, 207, 245

Genghis Khan, 28

George, Henry, 48-50

Germany, 28, 131-3, 134 n., 221; social insurance in, 92

Goering, Hermann, 131

Goldsmith, Selma, 75

Gorer, Geoffrey, 102 n.

Gould, Jay, 78

Gray, Alexander, 32 n.

Great Britain, and bank rate, 179-80; liberalism, 150; production 19th century, 108; social insurance, 92; unemployment, 99; war production, 132 n. *See also* England

Great Depression, 44-6, 52, 64, 151; and agriculture, 222; balanced budget, 23-4; government intervention, 168-9; monetary policy, 180; security, 92-3; in United States and Canada, 92

Gross National Product, 97, 101, 109-10, 133, 135, 140, 199, 272

Guggenheim Foundation, John Simon Guggenheim Memorial Foundation, ix

Haileybury College, 32

Hamburg, 131-2, 136, 139

Hamilton, Alexander, 22

Hamlet, 173

Harberger, Arnold C., 107 n.

Hargreaves, James, 213

Harriman, Averell, 80

Harriman, E. H., 76

Harris, Seymour E., ix, 110 n.

Harvard University, ix, 39

Hayek, F. A., 210 n.

Haynes Foundation, California Institute of Technology, ix

Hearst, William Randolph, 76

Henry of Champagne, 77

Hill, James J., 76

Hiroshima, 131

Hitler, Adolf, 131

Hofstadter, Richard, 55 n., 56 n.

Holland, 27, 203

Hollywood, 156, 202

Holmes, Justice Oliver Wendell, 54

Honolulu, 176

Hoover, Herbert, 24, 150

Hopkins, Sheila V., 27 n.

Hottentots, 223

Housing, and social balance, 203-4

Human development, external economy of, 216. *See also* Investment, New Class

Humphrey, George M., 62 n., 142, 184

Imperialism, Marxian view, 63-4

Income, in affluent society, 255; agricultural, 76, 252-3; as basic economic concern, 228; and CGC, 237; in fifties, 77, 160-1, 251-2; in inflation, 207-9; and liberty, 260; and New Class, 265, 267, 268; for 1928 to 1950, 74-5; from private goods, 241-2; and production, 228-9; and public activity, 241-3; redistribution of, 69, 81-2, 150; and Ricardo, 32-3; rise in vs. inequality, 76, 78; and tax policy, 72-3; in 20th century, 82 n.

Income tax, 70, 73, 82, 151, 164, 192, 206-7, 224, 243-5, 246-8

India, 79, 81, 91, 200, 246, 258

Industrial Revolution, 28, 92, 213

Industry, conversion to war, 133; in United States, 212; in World War I, 134 n.

Inequality, 68-9, 244, 255; case for, 70-1; as economic issue, 72, 75, 147, 206; in economic tradition, 69-70; and income tax, 70, 74, 206, 243; pre-occupation with, 68; and social balance, 206-7

Inflation, 220; consequences of, 175-6; control of, 176-7, 181-2, 196, 238; and countervailing power, 170 n.; dangers, 196-7, 229; and expenditures, 191; farmers, 175; fiscal policy, 190-2, 196; and income, 174 n., 207-9; investment, 185; Korean war, 141; monetary policy, 169, 181-2, 184-6, 196; and production, 158, 169-71, 185; public employment, 208-9; public services, 190; remedies for, 167-9, 171, 176, 196; responsibility for, 174; and social balance, 206, 207-8, 229, 237; taxes, 191-2, 194; unemployment compensation, 231; and unions, 174-5, 177; in United States, 167; and wages, 172-4, 176-7

Inland Steel Company, 95 n.

Input-output, 200

Interest rate, 179, 180, 182-4, 185-7

International trade, 44

Investment, by business, 163, 102, 104-8, 192, in education, 267-8; funds, 214; in individuals, 214-18, 247, 256-8, 268-9, 274; in material capital, 268-9, 274; in public domain, 214-15; rate of, 163

Iowa, 91

Iron law of wages, 30-1, 33-4, 37, 60

Italy, 209

Jaszi, George, 75 n.

Jevons, William Stanley, 118

Johnson, Dr. Samuel, 67

Joint Committee on the Economic Report, 97 n.

Josephson, Matthew, 78 n.

Juvenile delinquency, 202-3

Kaitz, Hyman, 75 n.
Kay, John, 213
Kaysen, Carl, ix, 110 n.
Kendrick, John W., 104 n.
Kent, James, 22
Kentucky, 91
Keynes, John Maynard (Lord), 25, 26, 27 n., 24 n., 89, 123, 125, 151-3, 154, 168 181, 189, 196, 222
Korean war, 141

Labor, 170; limiting production in American economy, 106; natural price of, 33; Veblen, 51
Labor force, 170, 182, 229, 232, 234-6, 237, 261-3
Labor productivity, 199; data on, 95-6
Labour party, in Britain, 153
La Follette, Robert, 23
Lake States, 252
Lawrence, 225
Lehman, Herbert, 80
Lend Lease, 137 n.
Leontief, Wassily, 200
Liberalism, in Britain and United States, 152-3; concept of liberal state, 22-3, 29-30; conventional wisdom, 18, 22; liberal economic society, 35, 111-12
Liberals, and economic security, 90; employment, 152-3, 194; expanding economy as goal, 82; fiscal policy, 189, 192, 193, 196; inequality, 71-2; inflation, 167-8, 193; poverty, 255; production, 149-54, 196; program in America, 150-1; public services, 209; social balance, 206, 244; social security in U.S., 85; taxes, 73, 206, 244-6, 248
Liebenberg, Maurice, 75 n.
Lloyd, Henry Demarest, 50
Lloyd George, David, 23
Lochner v. New York, 54 n.
Los Angeles, 102, 120, 139, 202
Lowell, 225
Ludendorff, Erich, 134 n.
Lynes, Russell, 156

Macmillan, Harold, 153
M. A. Hanna Company, 142
Madison Avenue, 202, 242
Maginot Line, 133
Malthus, Thomas Robert, 31-4, 37, 44, 53, 90, 108
Marginal cost, 170 n.
Marginal productivity theory, 38, 40, 67
Marginal utility, 120, doctrine of diminishing, 118-19, 122
Market behavior, theory of, 93
Marshall, Alfred, 38, 47, 120, 250-1, 264 n.
Martin, Bradley, 55
Marx, Karl, 30, 36, 43, 45, 48, 59-68, 95, 111
Marxians (Marxists), 30, 61-2, 64-6, 68, 72, 74, 95
Materialism, 63-4,
Maytag, Fred II, 71, 73 n.
Mazur, Paul, 161n.
Menger, Karl, 118
Mercantilism, 34
Miami Beach, 79
Middle East, 81; display of wealth, 79; economic life, 28-9; rate of capital formation, 71
Mill, John Stuart, 29, 35, 38, 47 n.
Mills, C. Wright, 79 n.
Mises, Ludwig von, 149 n.
Mississippi River, 252
Mitchell, Wesley C., 45, 50 n.
Mohammed, 59
Monetary policy, 178; agriculture, 186; bank borrowing, 183; of bankers, 180-2; business investment, 184-6, 196, 210; competitive market, 186, 190; consequences of, 186-8; consumer borrowing and spending, 182-4; definition of, 169; economic security, 185, 188; Great Depression, 180; inflation, 181-2, 185, 197; interest rate, 182-4, 185-6; large and small firms, 185-7, 190; mystery of, 180; prices, 184, 186, 187; production, 184-6; revival of, 180-1; supply of money, 182-3; wage-price interaction, 182
Money supply, 182-3

Monopoly, 41, 43, 50, 86, 107
Morgan, J. Pierpont, 76-7, 155
Muñoz-Marin, Governor Luis, x

Napoleon, time of, 134
The Nation, 52
National Association of Manufacturers, 56, 66, 71 n., 102, 248
National Bureau of Economic Research, 75 n., 104 n.
National defense, 274; and production, 154, 157, 272; taxes, 243
New Class, 263, 266, 269
New Deal, 52, 79, 89, 138, 222
The New Republic, 52
New York City, 55, 147, 198
New York state, labor legislation, 54
New Zealand, 38
Newport, Rhode Island, 55
Nice, 79
Nixon, Richard M., 237
North Dakota, 226
Norway, capital formation in, 71
Nutter, G. Warren, 213 n.

Old-age and survivors insurance, 99
Olds, R. E., 155
Oligopoly, 170 n., 173, 175, 177, 185, 186, 190
Ozarks, 252

Palais des Nations, ix
Palm Beach, 79
Pampas, 37
Pangloss, Dr., 65
Panic of 1907, 44
Parker, Cola G., 56
Parks, Ruth M., ix
Parliament, 241; acts of, 30
Patten, Simon N., 50 n.
Philistinism, 271
Pitt, William, 258
Poland, 200
Poor Laws, 53

Population, theory of; Malthus, 32-3, 37-8; Ricardo, 33-4
Poverty, in Asia, 32; elimination of, 256-7; inequality, 49-51, 67; man's normal lot, 13-14; in Marshall's day, 250; minimum income, 255; political economy of, 254; production, 83, 221, 251, 254-5, 257-8; in public services, 198; root of economic attitudes, 14, 16; Social Darwinism, 55-6; today, 251-3, 258; in West, 16
Poverty, case, 252, 254, 257
Poverty, insular, 253-4
Price control, 86, 88, 141, 177, 194-6, 238
Prices, 93, 201; administered, 172, 173; bank rate, 179; business cycle, 89; CGC, 236, 237; in competitive industries, 171-3, 189 n.; in competitive market, 177, 186, 187; determination, 117; discrimination, 89; farmer's, 45, 88-9, 93, 94, 95, 99; fiscal policy, 190, 192-4; interest rate, 182 n.; monetary policy, 181, 184, 185, 188; money supply, 182; monopoly, 107; in 19th century, 168; oligopoly, 171, 173, 177, 185; in peacetime, 168; setting by business, 85-7, 88, 170-1; steel industry, 174-5; wages, 174-5, 176-7, 194-5, 232; since World War II, 167. *See also* Inflation
Privately produced goods, balance in, 200-3, 240; vs. public services, 110-13, 143, 165-6, 198-9, 210-11, 212, 241-2; sales tax, 245-6; wealth of, 198-9
Production, 67, 198, 220-1, 227-8, 239, 247, 258, 260, 263, 264, 270, 272, 273; balance in, 200-2, 205; business executive, 146-8, 150; conservatives, 83, 157; consumer debt, 161, 165, 218-19; consumer wants, 125-9, 136; controls, 195-6; dependence effect, 129, 136; diminishing marginal utility, 118-21; economic growth, 212; economic secur-

ity, 95-6, 99-100, 107, 157-8, 232; economic theory, 114-15, 129; education, 218; excess, 103; fiscal policy, 192-4; in Hamburg, 131-3; happiness, 270; importance of, 102, 125, 156; income, 81, 82, 114, 228-9, 241; inequality, 70; inflation, 169-72, 177-8; interrelation of products, 199-200; Keynes, 151; labor force, 104, 106, 108-9, 158, 170; liberals, 150-5, 159; loss of, 97-9, 106-7, 108, 113, 150; military power, 140-4, 157; monetary policy, 184-5; national security, 154, 157, 272; in peace, 109, 113, 136, 138; politics, 152, 158; poverty, 257-8; preoccupation with, 99-100, 103, 107-8, 113-14, 154; prestige of goods, 155, 157-8, 199; private goods and public services, 110-13, 143, 165-6, 198-205, 210; research, 105, 216-18; sales tax, 248; social balance, 203, 205-6, 218, 257; social security, 161; unemployment, 99, 158, 230-1; in war, 108, 136-8, 141-2, 152; ways to increase, 103-4, 109 113, 150. *See also* Gross National Product

Profit, and price regulation, 86-7; rate of, 65-6; Ricardo, 33

Proust, Marcel, 155

Public services, and advertising, 205, 211; attack on, 210-11; consumer debt, 165-6; cost of, 210; federal appropriations for, 206; housing, 204; inflation, 191, 208-9; poverty in, 198-9, 240; private goods, 98-9, 201-2, 210, 241-2; production, 165; prosperity, 204-5, 249; social balance, 201, 202, 205, 210-11, 240, 244-5; taxes, 210

Public spending, 61, 162, 164, 190; and fiscal policy, 189-90; Keynes, 151; socialism, 112; unemployment, 189

Public welfare payments, 98

Public worker, and inflation, 208-9

Public works, 61

Pure competition, 170

Puritan ethos, 226, 234; modern merchandising, 159

Radio Corporation of America, 21

RAF Bomber Command, 131, 132

Randall, Clarence B., 21 n., 95 n.

Recession, 45

Rembrandt, 78

Republicans, 101, 237

Resources, 274; human, 213-18, 244, 247; for public use, 248

Ricardo, David, 30-7, 39-40, 46, 50, 51, 53, 58-9, 62, 69-70, 81, 90, 100, 102, 118, 130, 156

Robinson, Joan, 61 n., 66 n.

Robinson-Patman Act, 88

Rockefeller, John D., 40, 56

Rolling readjustment, 45

Roosevelt, Franklin Delano, 23, 24, 52, 151, 152 n.

Roosevelt Administration and balanced budget, 24; New Deal, 52, 79, 89, 138, 222

Ruskin, John, 59

Russell, Bertrand, 270

Russia, 117, 134, 273; technological advance in, 107, 141 n., 215, 272

Sales tax, 206, 245-9, 250

Salter, Sir Arthur, 64

Samuelson, Paul A., 122 n., 195 n.

Sarasota, 102

Scandinavia, housing, 203; social insurance, 92

Schlesinger, Arthur M. Jr., ix, 24 n.

Schumpeter, Joseph A., 45 n., 61 n., 63 n., 65 n.

Scientific research, 216, 273. *See also* Technological advance

Secretary of Defense, 272
Sée, Henri, 22n.
Sismondi, Léonard, 66
Smith, Adam, 22, 29-31, 32, 34, 38, 47, 48, 60, 65, 118
Social balance, 201-5, 212, 240, 249; and Congress, 207; in consumption, 218-19; definition of, 201; dependence effect, 204; education, 218-19, 244; federal government, 207-8, 210, 243; housing industry, 203-4; inequality, 206; inflation, 206, 208, 229; investment in people, 257; local governments, 207, 245; Los Angeles, 202; production, 203, 205-6; prosperity, 246, 249; taxes, 206-7, 243-7
Social Darwinism, 53-9, 68, 195
Social insurance, 22; old age, 84, 88, 99; unemployment, 84, 88
Social security, 85, 88, 151, 164, 190 n., 218, 229
Socialism, 55, 59, 112, 155, 161
Soil bank, 223
Solomon, Robert, 173 n.
South America, 79, 81, 209
Soviet Union. *See* Russia
Spencer, Herbert, 53-6
Sraffa, Piero, 33 n.
Standard Oil Company, 40, 56
Stigler, G. J., 40 n.
Stock market, 44, 86
Strachey, John, 64
Stuarts, 242
Subsidies, 108
Sumner, William Graham, 54, 56-7
Supreme Court, 54
Survival, 271-5
Sutton, Francis X., 110 n., 148 n.
Swados, Harvey, 266 n.
Sweezy, Alan, ix
Swigert, Ernest L., 71 n.
Switzerland, 134

Tariffs, 82, 86, 107
Taussig, Frank W., 39
Tawney, R. H., 70, 102, 198
Taxes, 72-4, 189, 206-7, 210, 223, 241-2, 245-6; capital gains, 74, 244; consumer debt, 164; depletion allowance, 74, 244; distribution of income, 72, 74, 192; equality, 72, 74, 192; by federal government, 207-8; by government spending, 151; inflation, 191, 194; production, 114; public services, 209, 242; salt tax, 246-7; social balance, 206, 207, 244-5; in states and locally, 207, 245-6. *See also* General Property tax, Income tax, Sales tax
Technological advance, 113, 150, 212, 273; investment in, 104-5, 213, 247, 274; in modern industry, 213-14; 19th century, 213; in peace, 109; in war, 108
Tennessee, 91
Tennessee Valley, 254
Third Reich, 132
Thirty Years' War, 28, 131
Tobin, James, 110 n.
Trade associations, 88
Trade unions, 18, 22, 38, 43, 51, 54, 76, 82, 87, 88, 94, 97, 107, 115, 151, 170 n., 172, 193, 224, 225, 231, 235, 238, 254, 266 n.; and inflation, 174-5; wage increases, 174, 176
Treasury, Department of the, 142

Unemployment, 98, 161, 196, 236-7; automobile industry, 162; CGC, 232-7; federal responsibility, 233, 234; fiscal policy, 193, 237; Great Depression, 151; inflation, 117; insurance, 94, Keynes, 168, 189; as political issue, 99
Unemployment compensation, 95, 99, 229-35, 263; payments in 1956, 279
United States, affluence in, 57, 250; agriculture, 95; inequality as economic issue, 72; national output, 104; New Class, 266; poverty, 258;

President of, 147; production, 96; social legislation, 54; taxation, 246; wages, 30, 37, 207-8

United States Chamber of Commerce, 18, 102

United States Department of Commerce, 74 n.

United States Steel Corporation, 21, 77, 147

United States Strategic Bombing Survey, 133 n.

Vanderbilt, Cornelius, 212
Vanderbilt, William H., 78
Vanderbilt, Mrs. William K., 55
Veblen, Thorstein, 48, 50-2
Veld, 37
Versailles, 55
Villard, Henry H., 107 n.
Voltaire, 22

Wage control, 194-7; inflation, 177, 238

Wage-price spiral, 170, 177, 182, 195; and controls, 238

Wages, Carey's view, 47; fiscal policy, 190, 194; inflation, 171-3, 176, 208, 232; marginal productivity, 38, 39; Marshall, 38; minimum, 40; monetary policy, 182; prices, 174, 177-8, 194-5, 231-2; of public worker, 208; in steel industry, 174-5; Taussig, 39; unemployment compensation, 229-32; unions, 175, 177. *See also* Iron law of wages

Wages fund, 38

Waldorf-Astoria, 55

Want creation and monetary policy, 182-3; inflation, 183; social balance, 204-5, 220. *See also* Dependence effect

Washington, 20, 76, 138

Watt, James, 213

Wealth, inequality of, 38, 55; in privately produced goods, 198-202; and social and political prestige, 76-81, 143-4; U. S. foreign policy, 144-5; Veblen, 51. *See also* Affluence

Webb, Beatrice, 23

Webb, Sidney, 23

Weimar, 221

Welfare state, 23

West Virginia, 253

Whitney, John Hay, 80

Wiles, Peter, 134 n.

Wilson, Charles E., 141-2

Work, conditions of, 261-2, 264, 268; enjoyment, 265, 266; leisure, 263

Workers, and inflation, 208; malingering, 97, 107, 230, 232; 19th century England, 107; search for economic security, 87, 88, 90-1, 93; unemployment compensation, 231-4

Work week, 237, 259, 260, 261

World War I, 28, 44, 109, 134, 135 n.

World War II, 28, 72, 95, 109, 131-3, 135, 137-9, 159, 167, 177, 181, 190, 198, 207, 209, 232, 265

Wyllie, Irving G., 226 n.

Yale University, 54

Other MENTOR Books You Will Enjoy

The Folklore of Management by *Clarence Randall*. A provocative study of modern business methods and of the misconceptions which threaten good management.

(#MT744—75¢)

Ideas of the Great Economists by *George Soule*. The views, times, and lives of over fifty great economists from ancient days to the present. (#MT680—75¢)

Men, Wages and Employment in the Modern U.S. Economy by *George Soule*. A noted economist analyzes present trends in wages, employment, labor, and management.

(#MD115—50¢)

The Concept of the Corporation by *Peter F. Drucker*. An updated edition of the classic study of General Motors—the company that has become the model for modern large-scale corporations throughout the world. (#MT569—75¢)

The Managers by *Roy Lewis and Rosemary Stewart*. An examination of English, German, and American executives, comparing and contrasting them on economic and sociological levels. (#MT342—75¢)

Toward the Liberally Educated Executive *edited by R. A. Goldwin and C. A. Nelson*. Top men in the fields of industry and education analyze the type of leadership needed in business. (#MT669—75¢)

Religion and the Rise of Capitalism by *R. H. Tawney*. The influences of religious thought on the social and economic structures of the world. (#MT507—75¢)

The Dynamics of Soviet Society by *W. W. Rostow and others*. An authoritative synthesis and interpretation of the political, economic, and social structure of Soviet Russia. Prepared by a group of M.I.T. experts. (#MP406—60¢)

The Public Philosophy by *Walter Lippman*. A penetrating analysis of the changing state of Western democracies, by one of our most influential political commentators.

(#MT718—75¢)

Ethics in a Business Society *by Marquis W. Childs and Douglass Cater.* A challenging analysis of the nature of moral values in the modern world. (#MT724—75¢)

Human Society in Ethics and in Politics *by Bertrand Russell.* A brilliant and controversial philosopher examines accepted standards of morality, religion, and politics, and urges a new evaluation of their function today. (#MP429—60¢)

Managers For Tomorrow *by the staff of Rohrer, Hibler and Replogle, edited by Charles D. Flory.* A team of highly qualified industrial psychologists and management consultants examine the characteristics of the successful manager in industry's increasingly complex management positions. Foreword by Clarence B. Randall, former president of Inland Steel. (#MQ746—95¢)

Mainsprings of Civilization *by Ellsworth Huntington.* How climate, weather, geography, and heredity determine a nation's character and history. (#MQ248—95¢)

The Complete Estate Planning Guide *by Robert Brosterman.* A comprehensive plan for adopting a lifetime personal financial program. (#MQ690—95¢)

American Skyline *by Christopher Tunnard and Henry Hope Reed.* A panorama of American civilization as shown in the growth and form of our cities and towns, from log cabins to skyscrapers. Profusely illustrated. (#MP175—60¢)

On Population *by Thomas Malthus, Julian Huxley, and Frederick Osborn.* Three timely and important essays that explore a crucial world problem. (#MP446—60¢)